T0350046

# I. HOWARD MARSHALL

# A CONCISE
# NEW TESTAMENT
# THEOLOGY

**IVP Academic**
An imprint of InterVarsity Press
Downers Grove, Illinois

**Inter-Varsity Press**
Nottingham, England

InterVarsity Press, USA
P.O. Box 1400, Downers Grove, IL 60515-1426, USA
World Wide Web: www.ivpress.com
Email: email@ivpress.com

Inter-Varsity Press, England
Norton Street, Nottingham NG7 3HR, England
Website: www.ivpbooks.com
Email: ivp@ivpbooks.com

InterVarsity Press®, USA, is the book-publishing division of InterVarsity Christian Fellowship/USA®, a student movement active on campus at hundreds of universities, colleges and schools of nursing in the United States of America, and a member movement of the International Fellowship of Evangelical Students. For information about local and regional activities, write Public Relations Dept., InterVarsity Christian Fellowship/USA, 6400 Schroeder Rd., P.O. Box 7895, Madison, WI 53707-7895, or visit the IVCF website at <www.intervarsity.org>.

Inter-Varsity Press, England, is closely linked with the Universities and Colleges Christian Fellowship, a student movement connecting Christian Unions in universities and colleges throughout Great Britain, and a member movement of the International Fellowship of Evangelical Students. Website: www.uccf.org.uk.

All Scripture quotations, unless otherwise indicated, are taken from the Holy Bible, Today's New International Version™ Copyright © 2001 by International Bible Society. All rights reserved.

Typeset by The Livingstone Corporation (www.LivingstoneCorp.com).

Design: Cindy Kiple
Images: Erich Lessing/Art Resource, NY

USA ISBN 978-0-8308-2878-7
UK ISBN 978-1-84474-289-9

Printed in the UK by 4edge Limited

 InterVarsity Press is committed to protecting the environment and to the responsible use of natural resources. As a member of Green Press Initiative we use recycled paper whenever possible. To learn more about the Green Press Initiative, visit <www.greenpressinitiative.org>.

Library of Congress Cataloging-in-Publication Data

Marshall, I. Howard.
A concise New Testament theology/ I. Howard Marshall.
    p cm.
    Includes bibliographical references and index.
    ISBN 978-0-8308-2878-4 (pbk.: alk. paper)
    1. Bible, N.T.—Theology.  I. Title.
    BS2397.M37 2008
    230'.0415—dc22

                              2008017360

British Library Cataloguing in Publication Data
A catalogue record for this book is available from the British Library.

P   20   19   18   17   16   15   14   13   12   11   10   9   8   7   6   5   4   3   2   1

Y   24   23   22   21   20   19   18   17   16   15   14   13   12   11   10   09   08

*To my grandchildren:*

*Michael, Rebecca, Isobel, Ben,*

*Naomi, Jonathan, Katie, Callum and Isla*

# CONTENTS

# PREFACE

This book is intended to provide a reasonably succinct account of the theology that comes to expression in the individual books of the New Testament and in the New Testament itself as a whole. It arises out of the work that I did in producing a much larger volume—*New Testament Theology: Many Witnesses, One Gospel* (Downers Grove, Ill.: InterVarsity Press; Leicester, U.K.: Inter-Varsity Press, 2004); literary detectives will recognize this as essentially an abridgment and simplification of my *New Testament Theology* for a wider audience. I have tried to give as much space as possible to what the New Testament writers themselves say. To make the book widely accessible, I have deliberately omitted references to scholarly debates and the accompanying documentation; consequently, statements are often made without any indication of the many problems of interpretation that surround them and discussion of the relative merits of the different solutions that are offered to them. This may give a somewhat oversimplified and dogmatic tone to the book, with statements being made more bluntly and with an appearance of greater confidence than in the longer work, where there was more room for discussing alternative interpretations and recognizing the existence of difficulties that are here passed over in silence. Readers who want a larger-scale treatment with fuller evidence and a more nuanced presentation of what is said here will, I hope, find what they need by turning to the longer volume. Historical questions regarding the composition and circumstances of the various New Testament books are left on one side, and readers are referred to other books for such matters.

There are many English translations of the Bible in current use. I have generally used Today's New International Version (TNIV); occasionally I refer to the English Standard Version (ESV) and the New Revised Standard Version (NRSV). Other versions rarely cited are noted as they appear.

Having dedicated the book which is parent to this one to the spouses of my three daughters and my son, I am delighted to dedicate it to their children, my grandchildren; most of them are presently too young to make much of it, but I pray that in the future it may play some part in helping to nurture faith in them and their generation.

*I. Howard Marshall*

# 1

# INTRODUCTION

## THEOLOGIES AND THEOLOGY

This book offers an outline of the theology of the twenty-seven documents that comprise the New Testament. In the course of the first four centuries of the church, these documents were collected, set apart from other Christian writings, and recognized as the authoritative foundation of Christian doctrine and practice. Along with the books contained in what now came to be called the Old Testament, these books of the New Testament were listed as the canon of Holy Scripture. They were the work of the earliest followers of Jesus, and they constitute virtually the whole of the surviving Christian literature of the first century. There is a manifest unity of theme about them, even if there is considerable diversity in the way in which the theme is presented. It therefore makes good sense to ask what they severally and distinctively teach and whether they bear witness to a common, basic theology.

None of them was written specifically as a textbook of theology. Most were written on specific occasions to particular groups of people for particular purposes, and they give us what the authors thought was relevant to their audiences. Our goal is to discover what theological outlook that finds expression in them, just as one might piece together a modern politician's basic thinking from the evidence of speeches delivered in different places. Moreover, the New Testament documents were written over a wide geographical and cultural area and over a period of time, possibly as much as seventy years, during which the thinking of the first followers of Jesus was developing and deepening. It follows that they cannot all be treated on the flat but must be seen as documenting a gradual process of fuller understanding of Jesus' significance.

In this book we are exploring the writings as they have been handed down to us. We are not primarily concerned here with the history of the process of composition, although some knowledge of that history helps us to understand the final products. Nor are we primarily concerned with them as literary endeavors, although again an examination of the rhetorical tools that are used will shed light on the meaning conveyed. Nor are we trying to describe the religious experience of the early Christians. Our concern is rather with the written texts that are both the expression of this religious movement and also one of the major factors that shaped it.

Basically, then, we are trying to expound their theological thinking. Such a description must go beyond merely summarizing what was said and must attempt to ascertain whether there is a coherent, unified "theology" expressed in and underlying the documents. In so doing, we need to be aware of the dangers of over-systematization of what was said and of reading back anachronistically the developed thinking and insights of later periods of Christian thought.

Some other discussions of our topic do little more than present the individual theologies of the different New Testament writers side by side, but our concern is also with the question of whether it makes sense to talk of a common theology and to discover whether there was a body of beliefs that were substantially shared by the different writers, even if they express them in different ways and show different stages of development. Some scholars have concluded that the degree of difference between the writers (or between different stages in development) is such that, rather than our speaking in terms of diversity in the expression of a common theology, we cannot avoid seeing contradictory positions that cannot be easily harmonized.

Although as Christian believers, we may be predisposed to think that the New Testament writings were canonized because they were rightly perceived to be united in theology, we cannot start by simply using material from anywhere in the New Testament to create a common theology; to do so runs the risk of assuming (for example) that the writers use the same terms with precisely the same meanings. Rather, we must begin with each individual document (or writer) and understand it on its own terms so that we may see where it is distinctive and then see how it may witness to a common faith. A mathematical analogy is that of the greatest common factor (GCF) and least common multiple (LCM) of a set of numbers. We can look for the elements that are common to our documents (or to a majority of them) or for the totality of the contributions that they make. For the purposes of this book, we shall do no more than endeavor to show the distinctive theology of each document and inquire whether there is a basic theological understanding indicating that each document fits into a unified development. The task of writing a synthetic account, including all that the New Testament writers severally say theologically, is not being attempted; doing so would in any case produce an artificial, summative account corresponding to the beliefs of no early Christian thinker.

## THE SHAPE OF THE DISCUSSION

In looking at each document or group of documents, we shall generally carry out a four-stage process that attempts to do justice to the literary shape and distinctive features of the material. First, then, we trace the theological "story" or "argument" in each document, to see what its author is thematizing and how the themes are developed. Then, second, we shall analyze the material more systematically in terms of the emerging theological concepts that are important for the author. Third, we shall briefly summarize the basic points that have emerged, so that the main characteristics and distinctives stand out clearly. And, fourth, at appropriate points (e.g., after considering all the Pauline letters one by one rather than at the end of each one individually) we shall carry out some comparisons between the various documents and authors that will enable us to see whether they are essentially expressing a common basic theology that can rightly be called "New Testament theology".

It will be important to bear in mind the several contexts of the writers. Most important, the early Christians were the heirs of the Jewish religion and took over the Jewish Bible as their Scriptures. An essential inquiry, therefore, is to ask how the Scriptures affected their thought and, conversely, how their Christian beliefs affected their understanding of these Scriptures. Naturally they understood the Scriptures in the manner of contemporary Judaism, but what difference did their Christianity make to that understanding?

We shall also need to bear in mind the influence of the surrounding world upon them, both Jewish and Greco-Roman. For example, references to Jesus as "Lord" would arouse echoes of a Roman emperor who was venerated politically and religiously as lord in a manner that might not occur to those of us living in secular democracies.

And we should not ignore the way in which slightly later Christians practiced their Christianity and understood the New Testament documents, since their understanding may also throw light on them; no doubt later Christians sometimes misunderstood the Scriptures, but in other cases they were in a better position to grasp the original meaning than we are many centuries later.

## MISSION AND THEOLOGY

The focus of the New Testament writings is to be found in their presentation of Jesus as the Savior and Lord sent by God, through whom he is acting to bring salvation to the world. More specifically, they are the documents of a mission. The subject matter is not Jesus in himself (or God in himself), but Jesus in his role as Savior and Lord. New Testament theology is essentially missionary theology. The documents came into being as the result of a two-part mission: first, the mission of Jesus, sent by God to inaugurate his kingdom; then, the mission of Jesus' followers, called to continue his work by proclaiming him as Lord and Savior and calling people to faith and ongoing commitment to him, as a result of which his church grows. The theology springs out of this movement and is shaped by it, and in turn the theology shapes the continuing mission of the church. The primary function of the documents is thus to testify to the gospel that is proclaimed by Jesus and his followers. Their teaching can be

seen as the fuller exposition of that gospel. They are also concerned with
the spiritual growth of those who are converted to the Christian faith.
They show how the church should be shaped for its mission, and they deal
with the problems that form obstacles to the advancement of the mission.
In short, people who are called by God to be missionaries are carrying out
their calling by the writing of Gospels, Letters and related material. They
are concerned to make converts and then to provide for their nurture, to
bring new believers to birth and to nourish them to maturity.

Recognition of this missionary character of the documents will help us
to see them in true perspective and to interpret them in the light of their
intention. The theology of the New Testament is not primarily ecclesiastical or ecclesiological, with a central interest in the church and its life and
its structures. Nor is it an exercise in intellectual understanding for its own
sake. Recognition of the missionary orientation of the New Testament
will lead us to a more dynamic view of the church as the agent of mission
instead of the static view that we sometimes have; it will also ward off the
danger of seeing New Testament study as a purely academic exercise.

There is a quite helpful classification saying that actions in the New
Testament have three aspects: doxological (glorifying God), antagonistic
(opposing and overcoming evil) and soteriological (saving the lost). There
is a natural tendency to give primacy to the doxological on the grounds
that the highest activity of human beings is to glorify God and even what
God does is intended to increase his glory. That is correct, but since the
glorification of God should be the ultimate aim of all our activity, a focus
on glorification may fail to express what is especially characteristic of
the New Testament: *the specific way in which God is glorified is through
mission.* The New Testament is primarily about God's mission and the
message associated with it. Similarly, the antagonistic motif is clearly of
great importance, in that the powers of evil and death must be overcome
if humanity is to be rescued, but this victory is not an end in itself: the
triumph of the crucified must be proclaimed to humankind and become a
reality for them—through mission. Again, soteriology is understood in a
one-sided manner if attention is centered purely on the work of Christ as
if it were an end in itself. It is significant that in Paul the *fact* of reconciliation achieved by the death of Christ and the *proclamation* of reconciliation

by his messengers (leading to the human acceptance of reconciliation) belong together as the two essential and integral parts of God's saving action (2 Cor 5:18-21).

## THE HISTORICAL JESUS AND NEW TESTAMENT THEOLOGY

Historically the beginnings of New Testament theology lie in the mission and teaching of Jesus. Nevertheless, this book does not have a section dealing directly with the teaching (and underlying thought) of Jesus himself. This is not just because he did not write a New Testament book! We have access to his deeds and teaching only through the medium of the Gospels. Clearly he was not a Christian theologian since Christian theology is largely concerned with his significance, particularly with an understanding of him that his followers could grasp only after his death and resurrection. But the question of the relationship between his earthly life and teaching and his followers' theology is important, inasmuch as the latter was certainly based in part on the former. His life and teaching form part of the New Testament in that the four Evangelists recount them in different ways. We shall therefore consider Jesus as he was seen by the writers of the Gospels.

Here, however, we encounter the serious problem that a strong body of scholarly opinion considers the accounts in the Gospels to be largely unhistorical, reflecting the lack of reliable information available to their authors, the lapse of time between the events and the written records, and the conscious and unconscious tendencies of the Evangelists (and their sources) to distort the story, not least by imaginative confabulation and ideological constraints. This case has been contested by other, equally competent scholars, who have shown that such skepticism is unwarranted. This is not the place to discuss the issue in detail, and all that I can do here is to record my belief that the picture in the Gospels is so close to the history that to offer a separate reconstruction of the historical Jesus alongside what the Evangelists have given us would be tediously repetitious and unnecessary. I shall therefore proceed on the well-founded basis that their presentations of Jesus are sufficiently close to historical reality to enable us to use them to understand his mission and message. Likewise,

I stand alongside those who argue that the account of the early church in Acts is essentially based on reliable evidence and is not the product of a fertile imagination.

Like any biographies the Gospels give us the individual, distinctive accounts of their authors. Three of them (Matthew, Mark and Luke) give quite similar accounts of Jesus, with a common core of accounts of the same incidents and teaching, each Evangelist using much the same wording as the others, especially when recording what Jesus said. Collectively they are often called "the Synoptic Gospels". This term derives from the possibility of printing them in parallel columns and thus seeing them together in a "synopsis" for ease of comparison, whereas there is much less material in common between them and the Gospel of John, which gives us its own distinctive collection of narratives and sayings of Jesus. This similarity is due to the Synoptic Gospels' use of shared sources and other individual sources that were of the same general kind. Specifically, it is reasonably certain that both Matthew and Luke used the Gospel of Mark as their main source; most probably they each also had access to the same collection (or collections) of other materials, consisting mostly of reported teaching of Jesus that had not found its way into Mark. All of this source material was likely originally handed down by word of mouth (though written records of some of it may have existed right from the earliest days).

The question then arises as to how this material was handed down. Clearly a word-for-word transmission is unlikely; Jesus certainly taught for the most part in Aramaic, but the Gospels contain translations into Greek. What he said must have been abbreviated and summarized (e.g., the Sermon on the Plain in Luke 6:20-49 is a mere 600 words or so, compared with a typical sermon of my own running to ca. 2,500 words). This inevitably led to changes of wording. Storytellers would naturally vary the wording to emphasize one point or clarify another or extend an application, and so on. This sort of thing could have happened during the process of oral memory and also at the stage of written composition (as a detailed comparison of the same stories and sayings in the different Gospels will quickly demonstrate). All this, however, is a different matter from the creation of completely fresh material or the tendentious manipulation of the text, for which some scholars have argued. We have good grounds for defending the historical reliability of the first three Gospels.

In the Gospel of John the general style and content of the teaching ascribed to Jesus is markedly different from that of the material in the other Gospels (and their putative sources). For whatever reason, John has taken the historical traditions accessible to him regarding Jesus and expressed them in a way that makes it difficult to work back to the actual words of Jesus. It therefore makes best sense to look at the first three Gospels together, treating them as being more like three photographs of Jesus from different angles, while seeing the Fourth Gospel as more like an artist's portrait that incorporates more of the artist's skill in giving a fresh presentation of Jesus for his particular audience.

# 2

# The Gospel of Mark

## MARK'S THEOLOGICAL STORY

*The preliminaries (Mk 1:1-13).* Mark's opening words "The beginning of the good news about Jesus the Messiah" define what follows as "good news" (or "gospel"). It comes from God and is concerned with salvation, human well-being in the truest and fullest sense (cf. Is 52:7). It is about a person called "Jesus" (i.e., "Yahweh saves"). His title, "the Messiah" (lit., "anointed", for which the New Testament writers use the corresponding Greek word "Christ"), indicates a person appointed by God to a specific role: to be the regent in God's kingdom. The further phrase "the Son of God" (Mk 1:1 TNIV note) indicates his identity in an even more exalted manner. Such terms were used by early Christians to express who Jesus was and what he came to do. Mark tells us the story of how his first followers came to believe this about him.

The story is regarded as "beginning from John's baptism" (Acts 1:22; 10:37). John's activity is seen to fulfill prophecies of how God's coming will be preceded by that of his messenger in the wilderness (Mal 3:1; Is 40:3). Nicknamed "the baptizer", he calls people to repent of their sins and receive forgiveness, symbolized by a religious rite of washing with water;

he will shortly be followed by another person who will carry out a similar, inward washing with the Holy Spirit.

Among John's subjects for baptism is Jesus, apparently present as an ordinary member of the crowd, but one to whom something remarkable happens. After his water baptism the Spirit comes down upon him, and he hears a voice identifying him as "my Son ...; with you I am well pleased". This presumably is the baptism of the Spirit happening to the One who himself will baptize others with the Spirit. From now on, Jesus acts under the guidance and power of the Spirit (Mk 1:12; cf. Mk 3:29). The heavenly message repeats what God said to the anointed king (Ps 2:7) and to his servant (Is 42:1-4). Jesus is thus initiated into the office of God's coming king; he immediately enters into conflict with Satan, God's archopponent (Mk 1:12-13).

*A summary of Jesus' message (Mk 1:14-15).* The readers of the Gospel now know of Jesus' appointment to carry out his mission for God, but not so the people of Galilee, who are confronted by a man who acts like a prophet. Earlier prophets announced what God would do in the future, conditional upon the actions of the people; typically they pronounced prophecies of doom upon them because of their rebellion and idolatry, unless they repented, in which case there would be salvation instead of judgment. Jesus' teaching, however, is about immediate fulfillment. It is summed up in a single verse that constitutes the "secret" (Mk 4:11) revealed by Jesus to those who will listen to him: "The time has come. The kingdom of God has come near. Repent and believe the good news" (Mk 1:15).

"Kingdom" refers to a geographical area and/or a people living in it under an all-powerful monarch or to the actual exercise of rule by the king. God's kingdom is the transcendent realm into which people may *enter* (Mk 9:47; 10:23-25; cf. Mk 14:25), apparently in a future state beyond death. It is also understood as something that is to *come* in the future (Mk 9:1; 11:10; 15:43). The future realm will become a reality here in this world, so that the kingdom as transcendent and the kingdom as future merge into each other. One might think of the heavenly "realm" of God, into which people may enter through death, becoming a reality by extending itself to take in this world.

The period of waiting is over. God's promised heavenly rule has already

arrived or is about to arrive. It can be said to *belong* already to certain people in that they are destined to become part of it (Mk 10:14) and enjoy its
benefits. The present world has become the realm of Satan, where people
are under his control (Mk 3:24-25). To say that the kingdom of God is
near implies an invasion, with the recovery of territory and people from
the enemy who controls them. But to some extent the captives are willing captives, who need to shake themselves free of what binds them, and
therefore the proclamation of Jesus includes the call to repentance.

Finally, there is the summons to belief in this good news. What is about
to happen is something ambiguous, something other than what is expected
by people hoping for a military leader to liberate Judea from its enemies.
Believing in the good news means believing that God is acting in what
Jesus says and does.

*The mission in Galilee (Mk 1:16—8:26).* Jesus' activity is presented in a
series of brief episodes, many of which climax in something he says with
great authority. Often he performs unusual healings of various human
disorders simply by uttering a saying that has an instantaneous effect. He
cures people who appear to be (as we would say) mentally deranged, suffering from delusions or feeling possessed by alien powers. Such mala-
dies are attributed to a demonic power controlling the person; the cure is
exorcism (a command by a more powerful being to the demon to depart
elsewhere). The person cured, or rather the demonic spirit, attests that
Jesus is God's authoritative agent (Mk 3:11).

The overwhelming impression is of a positive impact by Jesus. He
arouses great popular interest but simultaneously falls afoul of people who
evidently do not see in him an authoritative agent of God. In a series of
incidents whatever Jesus does raises opposition. He tells a paralyzed man
that his sins are forgiven, thereby laying himself open to an accusation
of usurping God's authority without any authorization to do so. Most
peculiarly, he comments that this authority to forgive sins is attributed to
"the Son of Man", an enigmatic phrase that is evidently a way of referring
to himself (Mk 2:10, 28).

Jesus also shows friendship to people marginalized by the respect-
able religious society of the time. He does not follow the strict religious
practices of some Jews, which involve abstention from food on certain

days and from all kinds of work (including healing) on the seventh day of the week.

The unfolding story thus has three strands. First, Jesus speaks to the people and heals the sick in large numbers, and the people generally receive him positively. Second, developing opposition comes from upholders of a religion characterized by keeping many detailed commandments. And third, Jesus gathers a small group of people to be his companions and to share in the work that he is doing.

*Jesus and the people.* Jesus' activity among the people can be categorized in terms of his teaching and his action. In his first parable, about the sower whose seed produces varying amounts of growth in different soils (Mk 4:1-9), the seed is the message of the kingdom; it produces different results in different people, depending on whether external factors hinder its growth, but in some cases it grows as it should. Perhaps surprisingly, even Jesus' closest associates did not understand the point of it and asked for an explanation. He makes the general comment that an understanding of the "mystery" of the kingdom is given to some people, but others hear nothing more than the stories, so that they are in the position of people who (e.g.) see a set of words in a foreign language that they can read but do not understand (Mk 4:10-12 NRSV note).

Jesus' recorded actions are principally mighty works, culminating in raising to life a child who died before Jesus could reach her (Mk 5). Some of the stories contain echoes of Old Testament material, implying that Jesus is the prophet expected to come in the end time, through whom God would exercise his transforming power to bring about well-being (peace). One or two incidents take place in territory inhabited mainly by non-Jews: the coming of Jesus is not solely for the benefit of the Jews.

*Jesus in conflict.* Simultaneously there is growing conflict with the religious establishment (teachers of the law and Pharisees). The superhuman powers of Jesus are attributed to black magic, empowered by the ruler of the demons himself. Jesus himself regards his mighty works as being done by the power of God's Spirit and warns his opponents about the danger of scorning God's power (Mk 3:22-30). The religious leaders observe that Jesus ignores the ritual washings before meals, which are supposed to wash away the spiritual defilement believed to inhere in articles touched by sinners (especially Gentiles). Jesus argues that these regulations were human inventions and go beyond what Scripture requires. He accuses his hearers of keeping these trivial rules while neglecting more important commands that are in Scripture. And he attacks the belief that what people eat can make them religiously unclean; real uncleanness springs from immoral desires in a person's mind. Mark recognizes that Jesus subverts the concept of ritually unclean foods (Mk 7:1-23).

The story of how King Herod Antipas executes John (Mk 6:14-29) casts a shadow over the story of Jesus: he will finish up in the same way if he too gets on the wrong side of the political establishment.

*Jesus and his disciples.* Jesus gathers twelve companions and helpers. His public teaching is followed by private explanation to them (Mk 4). Remarkable incidents happen when only they are present. When Jesus quells a storm as they are crossing the Lake of Galilee, the Twelve can only ask in wonder, "Who is this"? (Mk 4:35-41). In another sea scene, Jesus contravenes nature by walking on the sea as if on dry land, and they do not know what to make of it (Mk 6:45-52). The Twelve are sent off on their own for a time to carry his message and do mighty works just as he did (Mk 6:6b-13).

*Recognition of Jesus as the Messiah (Mk 8:27—9:13).* The story thus far culminates at literally the center point in the Gospel. The Twelve, who have been admitted to the secret of the kingdom, now face the fundamental question: Who do we think that Jesus is? Peter succinctly answers that Jesus is the Christ (the agent through whom God establishes the kingdom on earth). The attainment of this insight fulfills the first part of what Mark sees as the aim of Jesus. But it now needs to be followed by a second part. The Gospel goes on to narrate the crucifixion of Jesus. Even though he later comes to life again, this is not what people have expected of the Messiah. So Jesus tries to get the Twelve to realize that the Son of Man has to suffer, be killed, and then come to life again. The recognition that he is the Messiah is immediately followed by the correction: "Yes, that is right, but the Messiah must suffer".

As if that is not startling enough, the disciples and the crowds are told that followers of Jesus must be prepared for the same kind of fate. Just as Jesus has given up the possibility of a life lived for his own enjoyment and faces rejection by those opposed to his mission, so too his followers must be prepared for self-sacrifice for his cause; only so will they attain to a life that is really worth having.

Enigmatically Jesus promises that some of his hearers will live to see the kingdom of God come with power (Mk 9:1). Although the saying appears to promise a future event that will be recognizable as the coming of the kingdom, Mark goes on to describe a private vision of Jesus in heavenly glory along with Moses and Elijah (as his forerunners or models for his role) and a heavenly voice affirming that Jesus is the Son of God (Mk 9:2-8). This is a divine reaffirmation of Jesus despite the fact that he is going to suffer. What lies ahead forms part of a divine plan that has already been announced in Scripture and dictates what "must" happen.

*From Galilee to Jerusalem—prophecies of suffering (Mk 9:14—10:52).* The ensuing story is much like that in the first half of the Gospel, but the focus shifts from action among the people at large to instruction for the disciples, yet always in the context of growing opposition (Mk 9:14-29). Jesus repeats his statement about what is going to happen to him; the reaction is one of incomprehension (Mk 9:30-32). He further teaches that one aspect of following him is giving up claims to superiority over one another.

Now in full cognizance of what is in store for him, Jesus chooses to leave Galilee and go toward Jerusalem and his fate there. On the way he encounters more controversy, this time concerning the grounds for divorce (Mk 10:2-12). Jesus uses the account in Genesis 1 to relativize the permission given later by Moses for divorce and to prioritize the principle that marriage should be unbreakable. He adds the fresh point that men who divorce their wives to remarry are guilty of adultery. In another conversation self-denial is made very concrete and practical. It is not easy for a person captivated by wealth to enter the kingdom and so gain eternal life. Indeed, nobody can enter without God having a hand in it (Mk 10:17-31).

Again Jesus foretells his suffering in even greater detail. The incomprehension of the disciples climaxes with the request of James and John for a share in the dominion that (they assume) he will enjoy in the future. All that Jesus can offer is a share in his suffering, which he characterizes as a cup and a baptism. The poisonous cup of wine that causes total intoxication is an acknowledged metaphor for an experience of suffering, specifically of wrath from God. "Baptism" here reflects the metaphor of being engulfed in a flood or drowned in the sea. Talk of greatness is incompatible with accepting the divine call to service that Jesus exemplifies with his willingness to give his life as a ransom for other people (Mk 10:32-45).

*Confrontations in Jerusalem (Mk 11:1—13:37).* To ride into a city, as Jesus now does, is the mark of a king or a conqueror; his companions recognize this and proclaim the coming kingdom of David (Mk 11:1-11). The immediate sequel is a series of confrontations with the various religious authorities. Jesus criticizes the existing religion for not honoring God and his kingly requirements (Mk 11:12-25), although one friendly teacher of the law does agree with him on the primacy of love for God and one's neighbor (Mk 12:28-34). Taking the offensive, Jesus tells the parable about the wicked tenants of God's vineyard: people who behave like that will be brought to account (Is 5). Finally, he challenges the authorities: how can the Messiah be at one and the same time both the descendant (son) of David, and therefore inferior to him, and yet his lord (since in Ps 110 David refers to him as "my lord")? His hearers do not know that, although the Messiah is a human being, descended from David, he is also God's Son, who will be exalted by God and so is superior to David (Mk 12:35-37).

Jesus has already accused the temple authorities of misusing its facilities. Now to his disciples he prophesies that the temple will be destroyed (Mk 13). This leads to a significantly long statement on what is going to happen in the future. Its style and subject matter—making detailed forecasts of unprecedented evil uprisings, persecution, wars and divine judgments on a cosmic scale, leading to God's final triumph, all described with vivid imagery—has much in common with the type of Jewish literature exemplified in the book of Daniel and known as "apocalyptic". Jesus warns about various cataclysmic events that are not necessarily signs that the end has come. His followers can expect suffering like their Master. Events will come to a climax with the appearance of "the abomination that causes desolation" (the desecration of the temple; Mk 13:14), when unprecedented suffering will take place in and around Jerusalem. False claimants to be deliverers will appear, but they are not to be trusted. Only after all this happens will the Son of Man appear to gather God's people together. All of this is near: the signs of the end happening will occur

before this generation passes away. But since people do not know when it
will happen, they must always be on the alert.

*Passover meal, arrest, crucifixion and burial (Mk 14:1—16:8).* At his
Passover meal with the Twelve, Jesus again announces that he will go (to
death), as has been foretold (Mk 14:12-31). He shares bread and a cup
with his disciples and uses them as symbols of his body and his blood. The
language again suggests death (cf. Mk 10:45), with Jesus being compared
to the sacrificial animal whose blood was sprinkled on the people to initi-
ate the covenant that God made with Israel at Sinai (Ex 24). He will die
alone, for his followers will be scattered. "But," he prophesies, "after I have
risen, I will go ahead of you into Galilee" (Mk 14:28).

Arrest and examination follow rapidly (Mk 14:43-72). No convincing
grounds for condemnation can be found; even the accusation of threatening to destroy the temple cannot be made to stick. The high priest resorts
to a direct question "Are you the Christ?" (ESV). Jesus replies, "I am", and
he proceeds to elaborate that they will "see the Son of Man sitting at the
right hand of the Mighty One and coming on the clouds of heaven" (Mk
14:62). This is interpreted as a blasphemous statement, and Jesus is condemned to death. The convicted man is handed over to the Roman gov-
ernor to carry out the sentence (Mk 15:1-20). The charge now is treason
in that Jesus is said to be claiming to be "the king of the Jews"; this is the
political significance of being "the Christ".

The execution is related with allusions to the Old Testament so that
Jesus is depicted as the kind of innocent sufferer typified in Psalms 22 and
69. The climax is his dying cry, reflecting the sense of dereliction felt by
the author of Psalm 22:1: God has apparently forsaken him, and he dies
without vindication. Yet his tragic end is immediately followed by the exe-
cutioner's comment that he was in reality the Son of God (Mk 15:21-39).

Three women friends go to the tomb to complete the task of burial and
find inside it a young man (an angel), who tells them that Jesus has risen
and is not there: they are to go and tell his companions that he is going
before them to Galilee, and there they will see him. Utterly shaken by
this experience, they came out of the tomb and say nothing to anybody
(Mk 16:1-8). Is this Mark's intended conclusion? Or is the story meant to
continue with an account of the appearances of Jesus to his friends but is

either left unfinished or accidentally cut short (Mk 16:9-20 is not in the earliest manuscripts)? We simply do not know for certain.

## THEOLOGICAL THEMES

The dominant theme of Mark is Jesus as the Messiah and Son of God, who proclaims the kingdom and acts it out in ways that express who he is. In the first part of the narrative, the identity of Jesus as the Messiah is gradually recognized; in the second part, it is intimated that the Son of Man must suffer and be raised from the dead, and this intimation is fulfilled. In many ways it is a mysterious story, with the enigmatic use of different terms to refer to Jesus, principally *Christ (Messiah), Son of God* and *Son of Man;* the puzzling manner in which Jesus says things incomprehensible to the crowds and even to the disciples; the remarkable teaching about events leading up to the coming of the Son of Man; and the way in which the story leads one to expect the appearances of Jesus in Galilee and yet leaves the reader with a sense of frustration and mystique.

*The background in Scripture.* What takes place in Mark's story right from the beginning (Mk 1:2) is the fulfillment of Scripture and specifically of its prophecies of future redemption through the coming of a messianic figure. Scripture explains the course of the Son of Man (Mk 9:12; 14:21, 27, 49) and the rebelliousness and lack of spiritual comprehension of the people (Mk 4:10-12; 7:6; 11:17).

*The kingdom of God.* The kingdom of God is the main theme in Jesus' teaching. It is a realm into which people can enter rather than being cast into Gehenna. It is also something that "comes", as if the end of the present age is succeeded at some not-too-distant point by the new age replacing it. For Jesus, the waiting time is over, and he can announce that it has come near (Mk 1:15). If the present time is one of growth, as the parables clearly indicate, there must be a sense in which the kingdom has already come and is present.

The coming of the kingdom is closely linked with the Messiah; if he is here, the kingdom is already being established. For Mark, Jesus is acting as Messiah (or king) but is scarcely recognized and is rather rejected and crucified. The association of the kingdom with his entry to Jerusalem indicates that his suffering and death are crucially related to its coming. His death is not simply an expression of sinners rejecting the Son of Man, an obstacle to the working of God; it is also part of the same divine purpose that has led to his being equipped with the Spirit and announcing that the time of fulfillment has come. Jesus' giving up his life in death functions to give a ransom for many (Mk 10:45), whereby people are delivered from sin and its dire consequences (Mk 9:42-50). Within the same context, Jesus refers to drinking the cup of divine wrath, and he uses the same metaphor in Gethsemane (Mk 10:38; 14:36). At the Last Supper he speaks about his blood being poured out, like the sacrifice that inaugurated the old covenant at Sinai (Ex 24).

Those who respond to Jesus' call to discipleship are given the secret of the kingdom. The parables in which this secret is revealed alternate between those in which the principal actor is a sower (Mk 4:3-8) and those in which the principal object is the seed (Mk 4:26-32). The work of the Messiah effects the coming of the kingdom. The kingdom consists of those who respond to the message in repentance and faith and thereby come into the sphere of God's salvation.

*Who Jesus is.* Jesus tries to keep his identity as *Messiah* quiet by silencing both people and demons who confess who he is, but to his disciples he gives fuller teaching, which he withholds from the crowds and his opponents. His predictions of suffering are made only to the disciples. He uses the word "mystery" (or "secret"; Mk 4:11) to refer to something that God has kept secret in the past but is now revealing to the disciples, who have committed themselves (however imperfectly at this stage) to him. Full understanding of Jesus is gained by personal encounter and willingness to share his way in self-denial. There is no indication that the disciples totally fail to understand what Jesus explains to them. Their story is one of gradual, fuller recognition of Jesus and his message. To be a disciple means recognizing Jesus as who he really is and acknowledging that the kingdom really is present in him.

Jesus announces the coming of the kingdom rather than his own coming as Messiah, but he speaks and acts with authority in such a way as to raise the question of his role in relation to the kingdom. *Christ* (i.e., *Messiah*) appears in the opening words of the Gospel (Mk 1:1) and in Peter's confession (Mk 8:29). Then it figures in the trial scene and in the irony of the cross, where *Messiah* is synonymous with *King of Israel* (Mk 14:61; 15:32). Elsewhere related language is used. In the baptismal scene Jesus is understood to be *anointed* by the Spirit. He is addressed as "Son of David" (Mk 10:47; 12:35), a term that equals *Messiah* and is associated with the mighty work of healing the blind.

Alongside *Christ* we have *Son of God* (Mk 1:11). It brings out more deeply who Jesus is. His identity is acknowledged by demons, who are forbidden to make him known (Mk 3:11-12); it is confirmed by God to the inner group of disciples (Mk 9:7). Jesus refers to himself by this title in the patent allusions in Mark 12:6; 13:32. "Son of the Blessed [God]" is used in apposition to *Christ* in a way that strongly suggests that the two terms are closely related (Mk 14:61). The manner of his death leads to the centurion's confession (Mk 15:39). This phrase suggests that Jesus as the divine agent is close to God himself.

The enigmatic phrase "Son of Man" is first used as a self-reference by Jesus in statements about his present authority to forgive sins and to control the sabbath (Mk 2:10, 28) and then especially in statements about his suffering, death and resurrection (Mk 8:31; 9:12, 31; 10:33, 45; 14:21, 41). It is also the preferred term for use about his future functions: coming in judgment, sitting at the right hand of God, and coming to gather the people of God. Twice there is a clear use of the language of Daniel 7:13, where the Son of Man comes with the clouds of heaven (Mk 13:26; 14:62). The element of judgment in his role (Mk 8:38) fits in with the references to a judgment scene in Daniel 7:10, 26. The earlier sayings do not have obvious allusions to Daniel, and at first people can hear them simply as self-designations; only later do the "future" references show that this self-designation contains an allusion to Daniel 7. *Son of Man* can apparently function both as a self-reference and as a messianic designation. Maybe one constituent for perceiving the messianic secret lies in recognizing that when Jesus speaks about the Son of Man, he is identifying himself as the figure prophesied in Daniel 7.

Jesus' mighty works are essentially concerned with his authority and identity rather than being simply signs of the presence of God's kingdom. These two functions naturally merge with each other, since the Messiah and the kingdom of God are correlates, but the emphasis is on how the

signs relate to the Messiah, whether to demonstrate who Jesus is or to af-
ford grounds for opposition to him. In a world where mighty works were
accepted more easily than they are today, the problem was not so much
whether they actually happened, but rather by what power they were done:
is the inspiration from the Holy Spirit or Beelzebul?

*The future of the kingdom and the Messiah.* Mark 13 discusses the
relationship between the future destruction of the temple and the coming of the Messiah. Its purpose is partly to reassure the readers that
these things were foretold and therefore not out of God's control. Such
sufferings would be the birth pains of the new age (Mk 13:8). There
are also promises that the disciples will have divine help to withstand
the temptations and suffering of this period. The coming of the Son
of Man is not necessarily closely tied in time to the destruction of the
temple. It could happen at any time, and therefore constant vigilance
is required.

*Response to Jesus.* Like John, Jesus calls people to repentance in view of
the imminence of the kingdom of God, but he goes further in announcing
the good news of its arrival. Belief in this good news proclaimed by Jesus
is closely tied to belief in the messenger. Discipleship and following Jesus
express faith in him. While *follow* can simply mean being with Jesus, he
himself uses the term to indicate a close personal attachment to himself
that demands total commitment (Mk 8:34; cf. 10:28). Much the most
common term to express this commitment is *disciples*, even though the
group could contain an uncommitted Judas. Mark usually uses the term
for the twelve traveling companions of Jesus (Mk 3:13-19). However, the
group of people committed to Jesus is wider than the Twelve, as is shown
by the call to a wider group to become followers of Jesus (Mk 8:34) and
the example of Bartimaeus (Mk 10:52).

The disciples are the privileged recipients of Jesus' fuller revelation
concerning the kingdom of God, and yet they persistently misunderstand
what Jesus is saying to them. They ought to understand the parables (Mk
4:13), but they fail to do so. They behave ignorantly (like Peter in Mk
9:5-6) and weakly (Mk 9:18). At his arrest they all flee from the scene
(Mk 14:50). The picture is that of people learning what discipleship
involves, and it fits with the imperfections and need for growth found in

the converts; only after the cross and resurrection does full understanding become possible.

A further element in the people's reaction to Jesus that should not be overlooked is wonder and amazement coupled with fear. Mark has a deeper sense of the numinous quality of the actions of Jesus than the other writers and brings out more fully this element of mystery. He does not want his readers to think that everything can be easily grasped and simply explained.

## CONCLUSION

The main theme of the Gospel is the identity of Jesus in his relationship to the kingdom of God. Mark spells this out in two stages: Recognition of him as Messiah and Son of God, through whose presence, proclamation and mighty works the kingdom is manifested; this must be followed by the realization that Jesus must suffer and be raised from the dead. The kingdom will not fully come without suffering on the part of the Messiah and those who share in his task. Throughout the Gospel is a sense of mystery: the Messiah is no ordinary, human person, and the Gospel is a secret revelation of who he is to those who are willing to accept the revelation and become his disciples, even though they are puzzled and even inclined to reject it. Significant points are:

1. Jesus addresses people with needs: physical, social and spiritual. He criticizes Pharisaic religion for its insistence on obedience to the minutiae of the law, its concentration on outward observance regardless of the attitude of the heart, and its lack of concern for those who do not live up to its standards.

2. Jesus' basic teaching is about the rule of God, understood as God's sovereign, gracious power operating through himself to create a sphere of blessing for humankind and to overcome the power of Satan and destroy evil; it will be fully manifested in the near future but is already at work. He brings good news to the poor and needy and demonstrates the power of God at work in acts of healing and compassion. He tries to bring sinners to a consciousness of their real condition in the sight of God.

3. His own role in this is like that of a teacher and prophet sent from God, but the way in which he speaks and acts with the sovereign authority of God raises the question whether he is be seen in the framework of Jewish expectations about the coming of the Messiah. He regards God as his Father and prays to him accordingly.

4. Jesus closely identifies himself with his cause, so that response to his message is expressed in terms of following him as disciples. Although he does not organize a new society of his followers, he does call some people to share closely in his mission.

5. His task is the renewal of the people of Israel who have fallen away from a true relationship with God. Despite restricting his activity almost exclusively to the Jews, Jesus shows a particular concern for the marginalized and did not exclude Gentiles from his concern.

6. Jesus approves the summary of Jewish religion as wholehearted love for God and one's neighbor.

7. He carries his principles to the utmost limit by dying for them. His suffering is not something accidental but is part of his divinely destined vocation, and he regards it as being in some way on behalf of other people and sacrificial and redemptive in effect.

8. Jesus awaits the imminent consummation of God's rule, when humankind will be upheld or judged at God's bar in accordance with their response to himself.

# 3

# THE GOSPEL OF MATTHEW

## MATTHEW'S THEOLOGICAL STORY

Matthew includes most of the individual story items in Mark in much the same order and with much of his wording, yet the plentiful additional material, mostly sayings of Jesus, makes us see the story in a fresh light. He has the same basic two-part *theological* structure as Mark, marked by his use of the phrase "From that time on Jesus began to . . ." (Mt 4:17; 16:21). Upon this is superimposed a *narrative* structure that gives an alternation of actions and discourses.

*The birth, baptism and temptation of Jesus (Mt 1—4).* A lengthy preface tells the story of the birth of Jesus (Mt 1—2). His genealogical tree roots him in the Jewish people (starting from Abraham) and in its royal line (through David). The four women mentioned had irregular unions and/or were non-Jews. This foreshadows Jesus' own unusual birth and the inclusion of Gentiles in the people of God. Joseph's acceptance of Jesus as if he were his own son legally entitles him to belong to this genealogy as a descendant of David, thus literally fulfilling one qualification for messiahship.

When Mary becomes pregnant, it is revealed to Joseph that this has come about by the Holy Spirit without human intervention. Her child is to be named "Jesus" ("the Lord saves"), and his birth will fulfill the prophecy of a virgin's child to be called "Immanuel" ("God [is] with us"; Mt 1:21-23; Is 7:14). He will be the future king of the Jews, the "Christ" (Mt 2:2, 4). His identity as the Son of God emerges incidentally (Mt 2:15, citing Hos 11:1).

The story of Jesus' mission begins, as in Mark, with John's activity and Jesus' baptism by him (Mt 3). John's preaching (Mt 3:7-10) stresses the judgment awaiting those who do not repent of their sins. Mark's brief note of Jesus' temptation is replaced by a lengthier account of three attempts by the devil to tempt him to disobey and distrust God (Mt 4:1-11).

*The manifesto of the teacher (Mt 4:12—7:29).* Jesus' mission fulfills Isaiah 9:1-2 (Mt 4:15-16). Frequent citations show that significant events in his life correspond with Old Testament prophecies and types. His message is briefly summarized as "Repent, for the kingdom of heaven has come near" (Mt 4:17). This is almost immediately followed by the first of five lengthy accounts of his teaching, thereby emphasizing that Jesus is a teacher who is also a healer rather than vice versa.

The Sermon on the Mount (Mt 5—7) is addressed both to those as yet uncommitted to Jesus and his message and also, primarily, to those with some kind of commitment. It begins with promises to those who follow Jesus but majors on the kind of conduct required of them. Although Matthew is not lacking in material about the gracious, saving action of God, this sermon is about the new way of life associated with repentance.

1. The *kingdom of heaven* (Matthew's phrase for *kingdom of God*) belongs now to those who are poor in spirit and are persecuted for the sake of righteousness (Mt 5:3, 10). Other blessings spelling out the promises in detail are in the future tense (Mt 5:4-9, 11-12). Although the promises are not yet completely fulfilled but will be in the future, the kingdom is in some sense already present, and its blessings are already real (Mt 12:28).

2. The law remains in force for Jesus' Jewish audience (Mt 5:17-20), but it is the law as reinterpreted by him that is now to be kept. Various commandments, all taken from the law, are lifted up to a higher level; if

some of them are made redundant (e.g., Mt 5:38-39), they still remain in force as a kind of safety net.

3. Teaching about God's goodness and his providential care as the heavenly Father encourages the disciples to trust in him (Mt 6:8, 25-34). Jesus consistently teaches that God is related as Father only to disciples and not to people in general. The relationship is spiritual rather than being based on creation.

4. God's goodness is seen in his answers to prayer and good gifts to his children (Mt 7:11).

5. It is essential to obey the words of Jesus, here equated with the will of God (Mt 7:21-27). Discipleship is a matter of obedience and not just of faith.

The Sermon juxtaposes total faith in the goodness of God, who answers prayer, and total obedience to his will. It does not relax God's commandments but raises them to a higher plane of fulfillment, which goes beyond simply obeying the letter of the law.

*The mission of Jesus—and his disciples (Mt 8—10).* Matthew now relates the stories of Jesus' activity that we find in the early chapters of Mark (Mk 1—5). Where Mark focuses on the build-up of opposition to Jesus, Matthew stresses more the remarkable character of Jesus as healer, in accordance with prophecy (Mt 8:17), his calls to discipleship and his growing reputation. The work becomes too great for one person, so Jesus sends twelve disciples out to extend his own mission. The second main teaching section (Mt 10:5—11:1) provides instructions, warnings and encouragements for these missionaries. Alongside material directly relevant to the mission of the Twelve (Mt 10:5-15) is instruction for the post-Easter situation (Mt 10:16-42).

The disciples are instructed not to go the Gentiles or to the Samaritans but to the lost sheep of Israel (Mt 10:5-6). The priority is Israel and specifically the needy people in it (the marginalized and the poor; cf. Mt 15:21-28). Yet there is some openness to Gentiles, indicating that this limitation is confined to the lifetime of Jesus and is not to be binding on the early church.

*The growth of opposition and division (Mt 11:1—13:52).* The narrator now calls Jesus the "Christ" (Mt 11:2 NRSV note), thereby implicitly answering John's question: "Are you the one who was to come?" Jesus' mighty works fulfill what was prophesied concerning the future era when God comes (Is 35). He contrasts the previous era of the Prophets and the Law with the new era in which the kingdom of heaven is active (Mt 11:12-13). Now God as Father reveals himself to those to whom his Son chooses to reveal him, and there is a general invitation to all who are burdened to come to him (Mt 11:25-30). Jesus as God's Son mediates knowledge of God (and his will). The wise people of this world, typified by the Pharisees, have failed to know God (Mt 12:2, 24, 38), but God reveals himself to the "little children" who are prepared to be taught. Scripture (Is 42:1-4) reveals the meek and quiet mission of the Lord's Servant in the power of the Spirit (cf. Mt 11:28-30; 12:28) and shows that the mission of Jesus is ultimately not confined to the Jewish people (cf. 12:39-42).

The third discourse (Mt 13) is an extended set of parables (cf. Mk 4) commenting on the way in which people respond, or fail to respond, to God's message. They show what "the kingdom of heaven is like" and invite the readers to stretch beyond the story to the reality presented by it. Matthew stresses the need for understanding the message (Mt 13:13, 15, 23). As in Mark, there may be the implication that it is only after many people have begun to reject his message that Jesus begins to speak in parables that are not understood by everybody. Matthew contrasts the remorse and fury of the unrighteous who suffer eternal destruction with the joy of those who find the kingdom for themselves, like finding a hidden treasure or a valuable pearl.

*The revelation of Jesus as the Messiah (Mt 13:53—17:27).* Here Matthew follows Mark rather more closely but with some significant additions. The story of Jesus walking on the sea now includes the incident of Peter trying to emulate Jesus and failing. And where the disciples in Mark are filled with amazement and do not understand what is going on, in Matthew they worship Jesus as the Son of God.

Most important, when Jesus asks his disciples who they think he is, Peter confesses him as "the Son of the living God" (Mt 16:16). Jesus comments that God has revealed this to him (cf. Mt 11:25-27) and adds that Peter is the rock on which he will build his church. Only here (Mt 16:18) and in Matthew 18:17 does the term "church" *(ekklēsia)* occur in the Gospels; the disciples form a new ongoing community that will be invincible against all opposition. The "gates of Hades" (Mt 16:18 NRSV) symbolize the powers of the underworld, which will attack the church. Jesus' authority to open the kingdom of heaven to all believers is extended to his disciples (cf. Mt 18:18). With this teaching authority Peter stands over against the Pharisees, whose teaching is rejected. For the future, Jesus thus hands on his own authority to his disciples. The church is accordingly the new Israel, established by Jesus.

*The community of disciples (Mt 18).* Conduct in this new community figures in the fourth teaching section (Mt 18). Jesus stresses the importance of the "little ones" (humble believers rather than just children). The parable of the lost sheep is oriented to the duty of disciples to care for erring believers rather than, as in Luke 15, to the justification of Jesus' own evangelistic mission. A procedure is established to deal with faults and disputes. Readiness to forgive one another, as God forgives us, is crucial. The congregation is given the same authority as Peter has received. A gathering of even two believers is assured that their prayers will be answered because if they come together in the name of Jesus, he is with them and his prayers reinforce theirs (Mt 18:19-20; cf. Jn 16:23-24). Here we see the pastoral aspects of Matthew's theology and his insight into the sheer grace of God toward sinners.

*Jesus teaches in Jerusalem (Mt 19:1—25:46).* Matthew 19:1 marks the shift from Galilee to Judea and Jerusalem; Matthew again follows and supplements Mark. The promise that in the age to come the disciples will receive recompense for their self-denial in this age is supplemented by the saying that when the Son of Man comes, those who have followed Jesus will sit on twelve thrones, judging the twelve tribes of Israel (Mt 19:28-29). The mission of Jesus is thus concerned with the renewal of Israel in the new age.

Meanwhile, the shadow of the impending cross becomes more pronounced. There will be no crowns or thrones for disciples without their first drinking the cup of suffering with Jesus. Yet in a sense Jesus enters Jerusalem as already its king (cf. the citation of Zech 9:9). Although the crowds recognize him only as a prophet (Mt 21:11), the children in the temple (cf. Mt 11:25!) recognize him as the "Son of David" (Mt 21:15).

The response of the hearers to the parable of the tenants lays them open to the prophecy that the kingdom of God will be taken away from them and given to a people who will produce the fruit (Mt 21:40-46). This is primarily a judgment upon the Jewish leaders, who will be replaced by the church (or its leaders) as the overseers of the people of God. Those who are originally invited into the kingdom of heaven make light of the invitation, whereas a very mixed bag of people, both good and bad, are brought in (Mt 22:1-14).

The final discourse begins with a lengthy series of accusations against the scribes and Pharisees (Mt 23; cf. Mk 12:38-40). Although the concern is largely with their inconsistent punctilious observance of certain pious customs alongside a basic impiety, there is also a clear call to Jesus' followers to be consistent in their way of life. The scribes are to give way to one teacher, the Christ, and human teachers should not seek the title of "father". There is an insistence on the brotherhood of all believers and a call to all to act as servants of one another.

Some among the disciples may be tempted to fall away and so should live in such a way that they will not be caught unawares and be liable to judgment instead of salvation (Mt 24). Three parables warn against the danger of not being ready at the time and stress the need to occupy the intervening period in conduct that wins the Lord's approval (Mt 25). The final "parable" is surely not a parable but a pictorial description of the final judgment, carried out by the Son of Man as "the king". Although it is commonly interpreted to teach that people can serve God or Christ unawares, the point would rather seem to be simply that the service of God or Christ takes place when the command to love one another (and one's enemies) is fulfilled.

*The death and resurrection of Jesus (Mt 26—28).* There are no particularly notable theological additions to Mark's story of the passion except that the blood of Jesus is now explicitly said to be poured out "for the forgiveness of sins" (Mt 26:28).

After the death of Jesus, there is an earthquake, and the bodies of dead holy people are raised to life and appear after Jesus' own resurrection to many people (Mt 27:52-53): the death and resurrection of Jesus have decisive consequences for the fate of the dead. Matthew records the meeting of Jesus with the women who have visited the tomb (Mt 28:8-10). The promise that his followers will see him is thus fulfilled, and indeed more than fulfilled. For the prophecy referred only to the disciples seeing the risen Jesus in Galilee, but here there is already a fulfillment to the women in Jerusalem itself.

At their meeting in Galilee, the disciples are moved to worship (Mt 28:16-20). Jesus' final words to them demonstrate tremendous authority. Now they must go to all the nations and make disciples. They are assured of the presence of Jesus everywhere and for all time. Nothing could bring out more forcibly the supreme position of Jesus alongside God the Father, and at the same time the fulfillment of the Immanuel prophecy at his birth.

## THEOLOGICAL THEMES

*Matthew's understanding of Jesus.* Jesus is a genuine human being, a feature that is simply taken for granted and therefore in danger of being overlooked. Matthew uses the same names and titles as Mark, such as *Jesus, Christ* and *Son of God,* but in the birth narrative their significance emerges more clearly. The name *Jesus* is associated with salvation. Jesus' role as Messiah is brought out by the quest of the Magi for the king of the Jews (Mt 2:2, 4). *King* is also used at the entry of Jesus into Jerusalem and with reference to his future judgmental role. The motif of the king or messiah as a shepherd of the people appears in the motif of compassion for the shepherdless sheep (Mt 9:36) and in the last judgment scene (Mt 25:32-33).

Jesus is also given the messianic title *Son of David* (Mt 1:1), especially in his role as compassionate healer (Mt 9:27; 12:23; 15:22; 20:30-31). He is frequently addressed as *Lord (Kyrie)* by sympathetic, committed people. Although sometimes this is no more than a formal title of respect, there is often a rather greater degree of reverence expressed by it. Showing reverence to Jesus is the appropriate attitude toward a king (Mt 2:2; cf. Mt 14:33; 28:9, 17).

Matthew has more *Son of Man* sayings than Mark, bringing out more strongly Jesus' identity as the coming king and yet as a figure who is rejected on earth. *Son of God* is also more prominent (Mt 14:33; 16:16). Matthew includes the explicit statement of Jesus about the relationship of the Father and the Son and the latter's role in revelation of the Father (Mt 11:25-27). Yet this exalted figure is the Servant of the Lord, who works quietly and gently rather than by raising his voice (Mt 12:18-21, citing Is 42:1-4), and this is confirmed by his claim to be gentle and humble (Mt 11:29; cf. 21:5).

Sometimes Jesus speaks in the manner of a wise teacher (Mt 8:8; 11:28-30; 23:34-39; cf. Lk 11:49-51). Matthew may have identified Jesus with Wisdom, but there is no clear use of the term as a title, and one cannot claim it as playing a major role in the Gospel. More probably Jesus is to be seen as a counterpart to Moses, yet with a greater authority than his.

*The Gospel and Judaism.* One reason for Matthew's particular focus on Jesus' coming as a fulfillment of prophecy may simply be apologetic, to prove that Jesus is indeed the expected deliverer, since his role corresponds with the job description provided by the prophets. Another reason is to develop an understanding of the nature of Jesus' activity as the fulfillment of the scriptural prophecies of the Messiah and the coming era of divine blessing. There is a distinction between the time up to John, when the Prophets and the Law were foretelling what would happen, and the period from John onward, during which the kingdom of heaven is active (Mt 11:12-13). During the period of promise *Israel* is the people of God; during the period of fulfillment the *followers of Jesus* (the church) believe that the promises are being fulfilled in them. How, then, are the Jews in the time of Jesus and the church related to the people of God? And what is the place of Gentiles in the church?

The Jews were the descendants of the people to whom the scriptural promises had been made. They had inherited the law of Moses. But the church included both Jewish and Gentile Christians. Judaism certainly allowed for the entry of proselytes (Mt 23:15), but on nothing like the scale on which Gentiles flooded into the early church and only if the converts would accept the law of Moses in full. The dominant Pharisaic party encouraged minute observance of the law by all the people, not just by the priests. The Jewish-Christian author of the Gospel could not avoid the resulting questions.

In Matthew, Jesus' teaching is given mostly to a practicing Jewish audience (Mt 5:23-24; 6:1-17). He tells them to obey what the scribes and the Pharisees teach them to do (Mt 23:2-3, 23). This stands in some tension with other teaching in which Jesus contrasts the tradition of the elders with God's command (Mt 15:1-11), and with Jesus' characterization of the scribes' teaching as "heavy loads" (Mt 23:4). Jesus is probably affirming the stress on the law of Moses by the scribes and Pharisees yet critiquing the way in which they interpret and practice it.

Jesus himself goes beyond the law in demanding obedience from the heart. The law limits revenge to "an eye for an eye"; Jesus leaves that limit standing but insists that people should not take revenge at all, and in that situation the law would be superfluous. Where the law commands love to neighbors, Jesus extends it to enemies. Thus the law is both internalized and radicalized. It is to be seen as an embodiment of the two commandments to love God and one's neighbor; these involve people's motives as well as their outward behavior and prioritize moral behavior over against ritual and ceremonial (cf. Mt 9:13; 12:7, citing Hos 6:6). At the end of the Gospel, the disciples are to teach people "to obey everything *I* have commanded you"—with no mention of the law. What Jesus says is more concerned with attitudes of the heart, and instruction about these is not "law" in the normal sense of the term.

An important element in Matthew's vocabulary is *righteousness* and *righteous*. The adjective describes godly people, both past (Mt 13:17; 23:35) and present (Mt 13:43, 49; 25:37, 46), who live according to the will of God as expressed in his commandments and are closely associated with the kingdom of heaven (Mt 6:33), even if they incur persecution for doing so (Mt 5:10). In Matthew 5:20 Jesus is probably emphasizing the importance of keeping the law as a whole and rhetorically using hyperbolical language to do so.

The Gospels do not explicitly promise divine help in living in the kingdom, such as we find in Paul's teaching about the function of the Holy Spirit. Certainly for Matthew the life and activity of Jesus himself are closely related to the Spirit. The Spirit is active in his conception and baptism (Mt 1:18, 20; 3:16). He casts out demons by the power of God's Spirit (Mt 12:28). But apart from the promises of baptism with the Holy

Spirit and fire (Mt 3:11) and of help in times of persecution (Mt 10:20), there is nothing about any kind of life in the Spirit's power. However, we do have the promise of Jesus to be with his disciples (Mt 18:20; 28:20; cf. Mt 1:23), implicit in which may be the ability to live life according to the commands of Jesus.

*The God of the kingdom.* Within the new relationship of disciples to Jesus, God is experienced as Father, who cares for their needs (Mt 6:25-34). This depiction of God is by no means unknown in the Old Testament and Judaism, but only with the teaching of Jesus does it become dominant to such an extent that the New Testament writers (such as Paul) can simply assume it as the normal way of understanding God. It is more prominent in Matthew's Gospel than in Mark or Luke.

None of this diminishes God's greatness (Mt 5:34-35) and his activity as judge. Strong metaphors are used to express the results of the latter: the wicked are cast into darkness (Mt 8:12; 22:13; 25:30) or into the eternal fire of Gehenna (Mt 5:22; 18:8-9; 25:41; cf. the imagery in Mt 3:10-12; 7:19; 13:40, 42, 50; cf. Mk 9:43, 47-48; Lk 3:9, 16-17).

*Israel, the Gentiles and the church.* The leaders of the Jews are the agents of God, and the kingdom belongs to them in the sense that they have jurisdiction over it (Mt 21:43). But Jesus threatens that this will be taken from them and given to another group of people. If they would have responded positively to the Messiah, it is conceivable that things might have been otherwise. It is the attitude to Jesus and his teaching that is decisive; as Luke's version states, he is the stone over which people stumble and fall, and equally he is the stone that falls on people and destroys them (Lk 20:18).

The new people of the kingdom are the disciples of Jesus. Despite the fact that Jesus has come for the lost sheep of the house of Israel and forbids his disciples to go to non-Jews (Mt 10:5-6; cf. Mt 15:24), there are plenty of signs that Matthew envisaged this new people as including the Gentiles (Mt 24:14; 28:19). Matthew records the visit of the Magi (Mt 2); the prophecy of many coming from east and west into the kingdom (Mt 8:11); the mission of the Servant (Mt 12:18-21, esp. vv. 18 and 21); Jesus' eventual response to the Canaanite woman (Mt 15:21-28); and the judgment on the sheep and the goats, which deals with people from "all the nations"

(Mt 25:31-46). Consequently, the restriction of Jesus' own mission to the Jews can be understood only as a case of priorities. Jesus is concerned with the renewal of God's people, who are to fulfill the biblical picture of the Servant as a light to the nations.

Matthew twice uses the term *ekklēsia*, a word that can be translated as church (the totality of believers) or as congregation (a particular group of believers who meet together). Once it evidently has the latter sense of a limited, local group of people (Mt 18:17). In a Jewish context this could simply be a synagogue community, but to Christian readers the word would undoubtedly signify a Christian congregation. This is particularly so in the light of the earlier reference where the language is of a different kind (Mt 16:18). Here Jesus himself founds an *ekklēsia* that has a cosmic role in that it has the powers of death arrayed against it, and it (or its leaders) has the key that controls entry to the kingdom of heaven. This community is initially small and insignificant by human standards, but as the parables of the mustard seed and the leaven show, it is set for stupendous growth. Jesus is particularly concerned about how people relate to one another and care for one another within this community.

For Matthew, Israel finds its future in the church, the people who recognize that the Messiah has come. The church is the sole entity that continues into the future; there cannot be any place for another church that will withstand the onslaught of Hades. The position of the Twelve on their thrones as the judges of Israel indicates that the present leaders of Judaism have their rule over the God's people taken away from them. This emphatically does not mean that there is no future for Jews in the kingdom or that the church's mission goes solely to the Gentiles. The church or the new Israel consists of believing Jews and Gentiles; the disciples' mission is to *all* nations, which includes the Jewish nation.

## CONCLUSION

Matthew's main theme is Jesus' teaching as the announcement of the coming of the kingdom of heaven; it requires a new way of life from its members, involving a rejection of inadequate religion and its replacement by a radical obedience to God's law, as expressed in love and compassion. The mission and teaching of Jesus provide a foundation for a church composed of Jews and Gentiles, conscious of itself as inheriting the gracious promises of God to his people in the Scriptures and called to a mission to all nations (including Jews). We list the following significant elements:

1. Jesus sees the people in their needy condition and attacks their religious leaders for their failure to carry out the religion that they teach.

2. Jesus demonstrates the presence of God's rule by powerful acts of healing and compassion. He understands God's character in terms of fatherhood toward those who respond to the good news of the kingdom of heaven.

3. By virtue of his birth, Jesus' own role combines being Messiah and being Son of God, but he also functions as a new Moses, who authoritatively teaches God's law, and as the humble yet powerful Servant of the Lord. He mediates God's presence to people, and he himself is present spiritually with his followers.

4. The law given by Moses is still valid but only as it is taken up by Jesus and re-expressed in his new teaching.

5. Jesus gathers followers and intends to raise up an *ekklēsia* on the foundation of his first followers. He anticipates the development of community life among them.

6. Although Jesus tends to restrict his activity to the Jewish population, the Gospel looks forward to the ongoing mission to bring in Gentiles as followers of Jesus. Despite the transfer of the leadership of God's people to the disciples, believing Jews have their place in the new people of God.

7. The understanding of God's will as love is intensified by including enemies as proper objects of love. There is also a stress on the need for true righteousness as opposed to empty piety.

8. The death of Jesus is seen as sacrificial and redemptive, leading to forgiveness of sins by God.

9. God's final judgment will be carried out by the Son of Man; it issues in eternal bliss or condemnation.

# 4

# LUKE-ACTS
## The Former Treatise

## LUKE'S THEOLOGICAL STORY: PART 1

In many ways Luke shares Mark and Matthew's understandings of the story of Jesus, but there is a fresh accent, created in part by the Gospel being placed in the context created by its sequel.

*The overture (Lk 1—2).* Luke interlinks the stories of the births of Jesus and John. The aged Zechariah and his wife learn that their son will have the spirit and power of Elijah to prepare people for the Lord (cf. Mk 9:11-13). Mary's child Jesus will be the Son of the Most High God and rule eternally over God's people. This reflects the Old Testament description of the Messiah as having the relationship of a son to God (e.g., 2 Sam 7:14); twelve years later the young boy displays his self-understanding as he refers to God as his Father (Lk 2:49).

Mary understands the announcement in terms of God acting to bring down evil people, to satisfy the needy, and to show concern and care for the Jews. Zechariah brings out the nature of salvation as the gift of forgiveness and light. At his birth the significance of Jesus as a Savior is explained to shepherds, a despised group of people. Simeon adds a further element: this salvation is not just for the people of Israel (Lk 2:38) but is for all peoples (Lk 2:29-32).

God's new order for society is coming through his Son and royal agent, the Messiah. Just as in the Old Testament the Spirit will rest on the Messiah (Is 11:1-3; 61:1-2; cf. Lk 4:18), so here the Spirit acts in bringing the Messiah to birth. The outcome includes salvation, deliverance from enemies, forgiveness, peace, judgment upon the proud and the mighty (who owe their position to sinful behavior), and satisfaction for the empty and deprived.

*Jesus in Galilee (Lk 3:1—9:50).* The beginning of the story proper (cf. Acts 1:22; 10:37) is carefully dated in world history. The account of Jesus' baptism highlights that this is the occasion for the Spirit descending upon him while he is praying and the heavenly confirmation that he is God's Son.

Jesus' mission begins with a typical synagogue scene at Nazareth. He appears as the prophesied spokesman anointed by God to announce good news of deliverance and divine favor (Is 61:1-2). Mark's good news of the kingdom of God is thus expanded in terms of the benefits that it brings. The proclamation brings into being what is announced, as when a powerful conqueror announces the overturning of the oppressive regime that previously existed. Yet by the end of the story, when Jesus has observed that prophets tend not to be accepted as such by their own people, his words are immediately and dramatically fulfilled in an act of mass violence against him (Lk 4:16-30).

Now the story follows Mark with the same motifs of proclaiming the kingdom of God in word and deed, the calling of disciples and the rise of opposition. In place of Matthew's lengthy discourse (Mt 5—7) Luke has a shorter one, largely concerned with the behavior of disciples and the divine rewards (and judgments) that are promised to them. It presents a picture of a new society in which the oppressed are delivered and the well-off are deprived (Lk 6:20-49).

A rich variety of mighty works, including the resuscitation of a dead man, provide evidence that Jesus really is the person promised in Jewish prophecy who brings about the new exodus (cf. Is 35). In the story of the transfiguration, the discussion between Jesus and the heavenly visitors is about his "departure [*exodos*] . . . at Jerusalem" (Lk 9:31). Jesus is on a journey that will take him via Jerusalem and death to his goal. There he will be "taken up", which probably includes the idea of his ascension to heaven (Lk 9:51).

*Teaching on the way to Jerusalem (Lk 9:51—19:27).* The success of Jesus' followers as they themselves go out on mission is interpreted as the defeat of Satan (Lk 10:18). Jesus teaches the importance of treating enemies as neighbors (Lk 10:25-37) and of praying to God as the Father, who will answer prayer by bestowing the gift of the Spirit (Lk 11:1-13). By contrast, some unbelieving Pharisees attribute his mighty works to Beelzebul rather than to the finger of God (cf. Ex 8:19) and do not recognize them as signs that his kingdom has arrived (Lk 11:14-54).

The present time is one of crisis, which calls for repentance (Lk 12:54—13:21). Even disciples need to be warned against hypocrisy and failure to confess the Son of Man (Lk 12:1-12). They are encouraged by God's care for them and his provision of the Holy Spirit. If they seek his kingdom, they will be supplied with whatever they need for daily living without having to worry over it.

But many refuse to accept the message, and this leads to Jesus' lament over Jerusalem's refusal to respond to him. If Jews individually fail to respond to God's invitation, Gentiles will take their places (Lk 13:22—14:35).

Jesus distinguishes between the coming of God's kingdom, which does not come in a way that can be observed but is already present and "among you" (Lk 17:21 NRSV), and the coming of the Son of Man, which will be dazzlingly obvious when it happens and will spell judgment for those who are not ready and waiting for him (Lk 17:20-37). The immediately following parable of the unjust judge (Lk 18:1-8) envisages the situation of the disciples longing for "one of the days of the Son of Man" (Lk 17:22) and encourages them to persevere in faith and prayer, even if it seems that God is never going to intervene in their difficult situation.

Another parable about prayer depicts a tax collector who recognizes his sinfulness and casts himself on the mercy of God rather than depending upon self-righteousness. Children typify the proper attitude of humility and trust in God (Lk 18:14-17). The blind beggar and Zacchaeus are paradigms of response to Jesus, whose mission is summed up as that of the shepherd who goes out to look for and to rescue those who are lost (Lk 18:35—19:10).

*The passion and resurrection (Lk 19:28—24:53).* Jesus' arrival outside Jerusalem occasions a parable teaching that this is not the point at which God's kingdom will finally appear; first, there will be a time of service for the disciples (cf. Lk 12:35-48). He laments over the fate that awaits a Jerusalem that did not recognize the King's coming (Lk 19:41-44; cf. 23:27-31). Disciples will inevitably be caught up in the catastrophe; the hard time ahead for them could lead them to abandon faith, and therefore again Jesus appeals for perseverance in watchfulness and prayer.

Luke's account of the Last Supper has a double saying before the sharing of the bread and the cup, in which Jesus states that he will not eat or drink again until the kingdom of God comes. In some sense the kingdom is not yet present. (Note, however, that some of the wording in this part of the Gospel is textually uncertain: Luke's record of the words of Jesus [Lk 22:19b-20] and the account of Jesus being strengthened by an angel and sweating what looked like drops of blood while he was praying [Lk 22:43-44] are omitted in some manuscripts; see also below on Lk 23:34).

Then, after the meal Jesus teaches the disciples not to seek greatness but to be content with humble service, and yet he promises that in his kingdom they will sit at his table and judge the tribes of Israel. Their perseverance as believers is made dependent (in part at least) on the prayer of Jesus (Lk 22:21-38).

At his trial Jesus affirms that from that point onward the Son of Man would be seated at the right hand of God: this stresses the element of exaltation associated with the resurrection (Lk 22:69). During the crucifixion itself there is the incident of the dying criminal who acknowledges the innocence of Jesus and is promised a place with Jesus in paradise (Lk 23:39-43). There is also the textually insecure prayer of Jesus for the forgiveness of his executioners (Lk 23:34). Luke omits the cry of dereliction in Matthew and Mark, and Jesus dies with an expression of trust in God on his lips (Lk 23:46). The general effect is to depict Jesus more as a righteous man (Lk 23:47), a martyr and a savior.

Like Matthew, Luke records appearances of Jesus after the discovery of the empty tomb. But there is no mention of Galilee; Jesus appears near and in Jerusalem itself. The walk to Emmaus provides an occasion to explain his career as a fulfillment of what was written in the Scriptures and reaches its climax when his identity becomes apparent to the travelers as they sit at table for an evening meal. At the later appearance to a wider group of disciples, he commissions them to continue his work; both events—the career of the Christ and the ongoing task of his witnesses—are again seen to be a fulfillment of Scripture.

## THEOLOGICAL THEMES IN THE GOSPEL

*History and the gospel.* Luke provides a historical backing to the Christian message that will strengthen existing faith and also lead to new faith (Lk 1:1-4). He sees himself as more than the writer of a story that may or may not be historical. The story has force only if it recounts salvation history (the historical events in which God is active to bring about salvation) that really happened. Luke may be most self-consciously the historian, but the other Evangelists share his outlook.

*God and his purpose.* God is active in this history and takes the initiative through his various agents and other means. A divine plan is being put into effect, prophesied in the Scriptures (cf. Lk 1:69-70, 73-75) and involving Jesus in obedience to a destiny that he must fulfill. Yet people respond freely to God, as when they pray to him not only in praise and thanksgiving but also in petition, asking him to do things with the expectation that he will respond by answering them. Nevertheless, what has been prophesied will be fulfilled because the ultimate author of the prophecies has the ability to fulfill them. Consequently, various events take place "as it is written" (Lk 3:4; 7:27; 18:31; 22:37; 24:46-47). God's plan constrains Jesus to obedience that involves suffering (Lk 2:49; 4:43; 13:16; 17:25; 22:37; 24:7, 26, 44).

*A people in need of salvation.* Luke's story is concerned with the renewal of the people of Israel, many of whom have fallen away from their God and turned themselves into sinners (Lk 1:16). Some are devout and keep God's commandments. But Luke shares the view of other early Christians and of various sectarian Jewish groups that the people as a whole, and especially their leaders, have fallen away from God. Failure to recognize and respond to God's message through Jesus and to Jesus himself becomes the most characteristic expression of sin (Lk 9:26; 10:8-15; 11:29-32; 12:8-10, 54-59; 13:34; 16:30-31).

*God's Spirit-empowered agents.* The coming of both John and Jesus takes place by a divine intervention that bursts the bounds of ordinary human events. Messages can be conveyed by an angel (Lk 1:11, 19, 26), but also the Holy Spirit can fill human agents so that they can convey God's messages (Lk 1:15, 67). The Holy Spirit reveals a divine message to Simeon (Lk 2:25-27). John is filled with the Spirit from his birth (Lk 1:41), and the birth of Jesus takes place because the Holy Spirit came upon Mary (Lk 1:35). The Spirit comes upon Jesus himself at his baptism, and his subsequent activity is empowered by the Spirit (Lk 3:22; 4:1, 14, 18; 10:21; cf. Lk 11:20). The Spirit is promised to all who ask God for this gift (Lk 11:13; cf. Mt 7:11).

*Salvation.* God the Savior brings a Savior, Christ the Lord, to his people (Lk 1:47; 2:11). The coming of John is the first step in raising up "a horn [powerful source] of salvation" (Lk 1:69). The redemption or deliverance of Israel could be taken literally to refer to the coming of a Messiah who would cast out the foreign power that ruled the Jews, but the rest of the story hardly encourages such an interpretation. The language of warfare and victory is used metaphorically to celebrate the redemptive activity of God.

Similarly, the Nazareth manifesto of Jesus could be taken in literal terms of release of the oppressed and recovery of sight for the blind, and good news for the poor could refer to economic alleviation (Lk 4:18-19). Yet, despite the signs and wonders that bring sight and healing, the deliverance brought by Jesus is basically spiritual, with wider effects.

*Mercy and judgment.* The theme of reversal is more prominent in Luke than elsewhere. Jesus brings into the open the division in society (Lk 12:51-53). The offer of salvation is very much for the poor and weak (Lk 4:18; 7:22). These are the neediest people; literal poverty and other wants go hand in hand. Luke describes Jesus' concern for the sinners and for women and other marginalized groups, including Samaritans and foreigners. These people are also most open to the message of Jesus and find salvation (Lk 10:21), whereas those who are wealthy and strong face judgment. Nevertheless, not all the rich people reject the message (Zacchaeus!), and not all the needy accept it (the impenitent criminal!).

God, then, shows his mercy to the needy, who have not been treated with compassion by their fellow human beings, although this comes out more in the way the story is told than in the use of words like *mercy* and *grace* (Lk 15:20). His judgment upon sin is also prominent, although not as strongly stated as in Matthew (Lk 11:50-51; 12:20, 45-48, 57-59; 13:1-9, 22-30; 16:19-31; 17:26-37).

*Promise and fulfillment.* Luke uses the temporal structure of the two periods of promises and fulfillment, the latter being the time of Jesus and that of the church. Jesus contrasts the former period of the Law and the Prophets with the present time, in which the good news of the kingdom is being proclaimed (Lk 16:16). This proclamation continues after the death and resurrection of Jesus, as the followers of Jesus also make the kingdom the object of their preaching. However, Luke makes more use than Mark and Matthew of the vocabulary of salvation to indicate its significance.

*Jesus the Savior.* The opening announcement of the birth of Jesus brings together the name "Jesus", divine sonship and Davidic descent in much the same way as we saw in Matthew 1—2. Messiahship is a thread running through the Gospel. Although the anointing in Luke 4:18 is apparently a prophetic anointing, the job description here assigned to the prophet strongly suggests that the roles of the prophet and the anointed king are amalgamated. The strong Elijah-Elisha typology confirms that Jesus is a counterpart to these two prophets. Jesus also describes his own activity as fulfilling prophecies of divine blessing in the coming age (Lk 7:22; Is 35), and this raises the possibility that he is to be seen as the end-time prophet like Moses, who again is a messianic type of figure (Deut 18:15-19).

Jesus acts prophetically as a proclaimer of God's word, announcing the good news that the kingdom is present in power (Lk 24:19). It is a mission of compassion toward the needy but is also accompanied by expressions of deep sorrow for the impenitent because of the impending judgment. In this respect, Jesus is not unlike Jeremiah.

The disciples are forced to go further than defining Jesus in prophetic terms when they see him able to command the winds and the water (Lk 8:25). Peter confesses that Jesus is the Messiah. As in Mark, Jesus teaches that the Son of Man must suffer (Lk 9:22). Jesus has already used this designation with reference to himself, apparently as a human figure who is said to have, or is implied to have, authority, but who is also the object of some scorn and opposition (Lk 5:24; 6:5, 22; 7:34; cf. Lk 9:58). From Luke 12:8 onward, the term is used with increasing frequency to refer to a specific figure who has a role at the last judgment and who will come to the earth or will be revealed. This Gospel does not have the "ransom" saying about the Son of Man (Mk 10:45); Luke 19:10 is effectively a replacement for it, using the idiom of the shepherd who saves the lost sheep.

Luke has a distinctive use of the term *Lord (kyrios)*. Matthew frequently records its use in the vocative form *(kyrie)* as a respectful form of address (cf. Mk 7:28), sometimes with a deeper sense. But Luke also uses it (from Lk 7:13 onward) as a narrator's way of referring to his main character. After Easter it was usual for Christians to refer to Jesus as their Lord. Luke appears to be anticipating the later church usage by recognizing that Jesus had God's authority both as a teacher and as the doer of mighty works. But the motif may well go deeper. There is some ambiguity right through Luke-Acts with respect to the use of *kyrios* for God and Jesus, so that there is an implied identity between the bearers of the title.

The concept of Jesus as the Servant of Yahweh is seen in the formal quotation from Isaiah 53:12 in Luke 22:37; the citation of Isaiah 61:1-2 in Luke 4:18-19 was probably understood likewise. The motif of humble service is commended by Jesus (Lk 22:26-27).

*Mission to Israel and the Gentiles.* As in the other Gospels, Jesus' work is best summed up as mission. The task of John is preaching good news (Lk 3:18), and the words of Isaiah 61:1 make the same point for Jesus (Lk 4:18; cf. 4:43; 8:1; 16:16; 20:1). Similarly, when the disciples go out on mission, they preach the good news of the kingdom of God and heal everywhere (Lk 9:6). Luke records the two missions, of the Twelve and of the seventy-two; the numerical symbolism indicates that mission to both Jews and Gentiles is foreshadowed in these accounts.

The mission is primarily to Israel, where not only those generally recognized as sinners but all alike are seen to be in need. The proclamation of the kingdom of God demands a response by all people. It thus has the effect of compelling people to renew their commitment to God. This involves accepting Jesus as the agent of God, authorized to demand allegiance on his behalf.

Although the Gospel has a strongly Jewish flavor, there are repeated indications that the ultimate scope of salvation includes the Gentiles. This is already apparent in Luke 2:32 and 3:6, yet also in the occasional contacts between Jesus and those outside Israel (Lk 7:1-10; 17:11-19), and becomes explicit in Lk 24:47. The mission of the seventy-two is symbolic of the mission to all the nations, even though in context it is directed to Israel.

*The saved people.* The mission of John (and Jesus) is to bring back the people of Israel to the Lord (Lk 1:16-17). The appropriate response to the message is repentance, a concept that figures more prominently in Luke than in the other Gospels; the term is significantly added in Luke 5:32 and expresses the fundamental response to God in Luke 13:1-9 (cf. Lk 10:13; 15:7). Such repentance must be wholehearted and lifelong; it is dangerous to turn back (Lk 8:13-15; 9:57-62; 14:25-35).

In the birth narratives the leading characters keep the commandments of God as prescribed by the law (Lk 1:6, 59; 2:21-24, 27, 39, 41). A question about inheriting eternal life is answered in terms of what is written in the law (Lk 10:25-29); but more is needed: following Jesus and self-denial are also integral to the answer (Lk 18:18-30). It is impossible for the least stroke of a pen to drop out of the law (Lk 16:16-17; cf. Lk 11:42; Mt 5:17-20; 11:12-13). Yet Jesus can also forbid what the law allowed and made provision for, such as divorce. Although it is not said explicitly, what continues to be valid is probably the law as newly understood by Jesus.

*The everlasting kingdom.* The reign of the Messiah is "forever" (Lk 1:33). Teaching about his future coming is found in two main passages (Lk 17:20-37; 21:5-38). They are worded more openly about the forthcoming destruction of Jerusalem and its remaining desolate until the times of the Gentiles are fulfilled. Jesus makes it quite clear that people must at all times live in readiness for the end and not be taken unawares by it (Lk 21:34-36). Luke also powerfully stresses how the followers of Jesus have the task laid upon them of being witnesses to Jesus in the intervening period.

## CONCLUSION

The theological emphases in this Gospel arrange themselves naturally around the broad theme of God's purpose to bring salvation to Jews and Gentiles alike through the activity of his missionary agent, Jesus, who functions as prophet and Messiah. If Jesus is a prophet in Luke, he is more of a teacher in Matthew. Where Mark and Matthew present Jesus' message more in terms of the kingdom of God/heaven, Luke has a more salvific thrust.

1. Jesus assumes the need and sinfulness of human beings in much the same way as Mark and Matthew.

2. Luke reports the teaching of Jesus about the rule of God, but stresses how this action offers salvation to people and calls them to repentance. The continuity between what Jesus offers in his lifetime and what the church preaches after his resurrection is made more obvious.

3. There is more stress on Jesus' authoritative position as Lord, even before his resurrection and exaltation.

4. Jesus calls disciples and sends them out to share his mission.

5. His mission is primarily to Israel, but it foreshadows the wider mission to the Gentiles.

6. There is perhaps more overt stress on Jesus' compassion for the poor and needy, and this reinforces the command to love that Jesus gives his disciples.

7. Jesus' death is to be seen as sacrificial and redemptive.

8. His view of the future is much the same as in Mark and Matthew.

# 5

# LUKE-ACTS
## The Sequel

Luke's two-part work is intended to provide his readers with an account of Christian origins that will confirm the reliability of the message being preached and taught to them. According to the divine program laid down in prophecy, the life, suffering, resurrection and glorification of the Messiah are to be followed by the preaching of repentance and forgiveness of sins to all nations (Lk 24:47). So, after telling the story of Jesus in the Gospel, it is necessary to show how this second, equally crucial, part of God's plan is fulfilled. In particular, Acts shows the fulfillment of God's plan to create "a people for his name", including both believing Jews and Gentiles (Acts 15:14). So Acts is the second part of a work composed of two parts that belong closely together.

This approach goes beyond that of the other Evangelists, who apparently wrote only Gospels. Luke is demonstrating that the purpose of God included both the Messiah's coming and establishing the Christian mission of witness to the gospel. To that extent his theology can be regarded as more consciously ecclesiastical than that of the other Evangelists.

## LUKE'S THEOLOGICAL STORY: PART II

*The story lines.* The theology of Acts is essentially a theology of mission, describing the mission of the early church and powerfully implying that this must continue to be the nature of the church, even if there is opposition and persecution. The story acquaints us with the theological content of the gospel and the theology on which the mission to Jews and Gentiles rests. It is the story of how the Word of God grows *territorially* as witness to Jesus commences in Jerusalem and spreads out to Judea and Samaria and the wider world, until at last it reaches Rome (Acts 1:8). It is also a story of *cultural* spread: the gospel first reaches Aramaic-speaking Jews, then Greek-speaking Jews in Jerusalem, then the Samaritans and the Ethiopian traveler, and finally Gentiles. Alongside the growth of the church is the development of Christian *theology*, especially as the church responds to problems raised by the negative response of Jewish leaders and the admission of uncircumcised Gentiles into the people of God.

*Transition and preparation.* The closing event in the Gospel now becomes the basis for a new beginning. For the time being, the task of disciples is worldwide witness to Jesus, commencing with the Jewish people (Acts 1:6-8). The number of witnesses to the resurrection of Jesus has to be restored to the original symbolical number of twelve apostles (cf. Lk 22:30).

For their task they need divine power, just as Jesus did. This comes with the Spirit's descent, probably upon the entire group of disciples rather than just upon the Twelve (cf. Acts 2:16-18). The story shows some correspondences to the giving of the Law at Sinai, although these are not emphasized. It is more important that the event fulfills Joel's prophecy concerning the last days, in which God's saving action is extended to cover all kinds of people and salvation is available to all who call on the Lord's name. For the moment, however, the audience is international but Jewish. Only the variety of languages spoken perhaps hints at a symbolism of the nations of the world.

*Witness to the resurrection.* Through Peter as their spokesperson, the apostles testify to the resurrection of Jesus. The essence of his message is that despite his divine accreditation, Jesus has been put to death by the Jewish leaders, but God has raised him to life and exalted him to heaven as a clear token of confirming his position as Lord and Christ. Although his crucifixion has happened in fulfillment of God's purpose,

Peter accuses his hearers of responsibility for it through tacit acceptance of what their leaders have done. Yet they can be pardoned for their sins through repenting and submitting to baptism, and they will receive not only forgiveness but also the gift of the Spirit. Forgiveness comes "in the name of Jesus Christ", the Lord who now has the authority to save (Joel 2:32) and to confer the Spirit. Luke has previously recorded Jesus' own use of Psalm 110:1 to refer to his exercise of lordship. The gift of the Spirit to him may reflect Psalm 68:18 (cf. Eph 4:8), taken to mean "you have received gifts for humankind".

Although Jesus is not physically present, he is still active. Baptism is efficaciously performed in his name. Healings are also performed in his name as his agents operate by his authority and not by their own (Acts 3:6). Statements about actions "in the name of Jesus" must be heard against the background of Old Testament texts where the name of Yahweh functions in this way (Acts 4:12).

The apostles continue the work of Jesus: the signs of God's kingdom are seen, and salvation is made effective in people's lives. The content of the message, however, has shifted: though Jesus has proclaimed the rule of God and called people to be disciples, his followers tell people about Jesus and the need for faith in him (cf. Acts 3:16; 4:9-10).

Peter describes Jesus as being a prophet and leader of the people like Moses (Deut 18:15-19; Acts 3:21-23). The description applies to Jesus in his earthly life yet also to his future activity, when he returns to restore everything. Anybody, including any Jew, who does not listen to this prophet will be cut off from the people of God.

The other principal divine agent, the Holy Spirit, fills the apostles. They receive courage to stand up amid threatening audiences and receive wisdom to frame their message aptly.

The activity of Jesus and the Spirit as God's agents does not mean that God himself is not directly involved in what goes on. It is his plan that is being carried out. God has allowed Jesus to be crucified, and God raised Jesus from the dead. God gave the Spirit to Jesus to pour out on believers. God's calling to salvation is expressed in the preaching (Acts 2:39). Prayer is addressed to God and only rarely to Jesus himself. Christians have confidence that his purposes will be fulfilled. Even a leading Pharisee recognizes that, if the apostles' activity is of God, then the Sanhedrin cannot thwart it (Acts 5:38-39). Acts is the story of this ongoing activity of God.

*The spreading mission—to the uncircumcised.* Quite soon Christians testify about Jesus to non-Jews. Philip goes to Samaria and then is guided to meet an Ethiopian official. Saul is commissioned to go to Gentiles as well as to the people of Israel. Peter contacts a Gentile centurion after a series of visions. Cypriots and Cyrenians speak spontaneously to Greeks about Jesus. At God's direction, the church of Jews and Gentiles in Antioch sends out two missionaries, who discover an audience of Gentiles eager to hear their message (Acts 13:7). The mission to both Jews and Gentiles is carried on in response to varied stimuli, but above all is due to God's direction of events.

But do Gentile converts to this Jewish-Christian faith need to fulfill all the other requirements of the Jewish religion as ordinary Jewish proselytes have to do? What about the practical problems for Jews associated with meeting and eating with Gentiles? Peter is assured in a dream that God no longer requires his people to abstain from so-called unclean foods, and by implication, from association with so-called unclean people. The Holy Spirit comes upon the uncircumcised Cornelius and his family, and they are baptized then and there. Clearly circumcision is not required. At Antioch, Gentiles become Christian believers without having been circumcised, and this becomes the pattern on Paul's first missionary campaign.

But, if Gentiles become believers in Israel's Messiah, why should they not be required to be circumcised and keep the rest of the law, as proselytes do? The experiential answer is that many Gentiles have already become believers and received the Spirit from God without being required to be circumcised. Peter argues theologically that the law is an unbearable yoke and cannot save people anyhow; Christ saves from all sins, from none of which the law of Moses could save (Acts 15:10; cf. 13:39). If so, there is no need for Gentiles to keep it. Rather, "through the grace of the Lord Jesus Christ we believe [in order] to be saved", whether Jews or Gentiles (Acts 15:11 Gk.). Here grace and faith stand over against performance of the law.

The conclusion is that circumcision is not required of Gentiles; they are not to be burdened with it. Nevertheless, certain requirements are laid upon them so that the Gentiles will not be forcing Jewish Christians to eat food prepared in unacceptable ways, nor will they be living in sexual immorality. Jewish Christians can maintain their traditional ways, including circumcision.

*The divine plan.* The expansion of God's people raises the question of the place of the Jews in God's plan. Stephen's speech gives a reply in the form of a historical survey of God's dealings with Israel, from the call of Abraham onward through to their entry into the promised land (Acts 7). Despite having the mobile tabernacle of God and then the temple built by Solomon, the people continually worshiped idols, rebelled against Moses and the prophets, and eventually killed Jesus. Stephen claims that God is not tied to a temple built in a single place, but moves with his people wherever they go. He does not explicitly state that God now dwells in a new building not made with hands, in the church composed of believing people, but this is implied. He is cut short before saying anything about the Messiah, although the depiction of Moses as ruler and deliverer ("redeemer"; Acts 7:35 ESV) implicitly points forward to Jesus (cf. Acts 3:22-23).

In Acts 13 Paul speaks about God's past provision of leaders for the people and then moves rapidly to David's descendant Jesus, who was put to death by the rulers. His resurrection is seen as the fulfillment of God's promises to the Jews in Scripture.

These two speeches sum up the Jews' past history as one rejecting leadership provided by God, leading up to their rejection of Jesus and his vindication by God. Yet, despite the past rejection, Jesus is sent first of all as the Savior for the Jews (Acts 3:26), and it is only after the Jews reject Jesus that the apostles turn to the Gentiles (cf. Acts 13:46).

*Mission in an ever-wider field.* The rest of the story explores further what happens when Paul comes into contact with Gentiles who have no connections with Judaism (cf. Acts 13:6-12; 14:8-20). The evangelistic preaching now has to begin with the reality of the one God who does not need human worship, but who has appointed the life of the nations in such a way that people should be able to find him without falling into idolatry.

The guilt of a world that has failed to appreciate the signals of God's reality stands revealed, and judgment confronts all. History has moved to its climax with the revelation of the One through whom God will exercise this judgment (Acts 17:16-33). The narrative provides further evidence of divine approval for Paul's mission to the Gentiles.

By the end of Acts 20, Paul's mission has reached its preliminary conclusion, to be followed by his arrest and imprisonment. At Miletus, Paul addresses the church leaders and offers his missionary work as a model for local congregational leaders. As the gospel of God's grace, Paul's message is directed to both Jews and Greeks and culminates in an appeal for repentance and faith in the Lord Jesus. The foundation for that appeal is God's purchasing the church with his own blood (meaning Christ's blood; Acts 20:28). Henceforth the church is the new people of God, in continuity with the old but now composed of believers in the Messiah. Language appropriate to God's people in the previous age can be applied to it, such as the flock of God (Acts 20:28) or the holy ones ("those who are sanctified"; Acts 20:32).

*Paul as a prisoner—but still a missionary.* The remaining quarter of Acts is concerned with Paul as a prisoner and his justification for his missionary work. Even under arrest and in prison, Paul continues his mission and is effective in Christian witness. Luke portrays the harsh realities under which Christians may be called to live out their lives and bear witness to Christ (Acts 14:22). God can use their suffering and testimony before judges to forward the gospel. The story of Paul's journey to Rome is told partly for its own vivid interest but also because the ship's deliverance from disaster and Paul's protection from being bitten by a snake are indications that God looks upon him with favor (cf. Acts 27:24; 28:6).

The main accusations against Paul are that he has been teaching everywhere against the Jewish people, their law and the temple (Acts 21:28). Paul therefore emphasizes that his beliefs are those of Judaism, specifically of the Pharisees, in that he believes in the hope of the resurrection; his way of life is in line with Jewish piety, in both ritual observance of the law and works of love (almsgiving). He has done nothing contrary to Judaism.

Nevertheless, to the end of the book Paul remains a prisoner awaiting the outcome of a trial in Rome. He continues to proclaim the gospel, to which the Jewish Scriptures bear testimony. Some Jews believe, and others reject the message. In the case of the latter, the prophecy in Isaiah 6:9-10 is fulfilled. Although God's salvation is open to any Jews who will repent and believe the good news, Paul focuses on the Gentiles, with better hope of acceptance.

## THEOLOGICAL THEMES IN ACTS

*God and his purpose.* God initiates salvation history, having foretold what is to happen in broad terms in Scripture and then acting through his agents, heavenly and human. Luke does not recount a totally predetermined course of action; there are times in Acts when people do things by their own initiative and other times when they act under a divine guidance that can sometimes amount to compulsion (Acts 20:22). Nevertheless, the motif of God's plan being carried out remains dominant and assures the readers that God's purpose will succeed, despite whatever opposition and suffering there may be.

*According to Scripture.* The establishment of the church and its mission is the object of prophecy, just like the coming of the Messiah. There is considerable use of Scripture in Acts, particularly in the speeches. Often it is used in an apologetic manner to demonstrate from Scripture what the Messiah would be and do, and then to argue that (only) Jesus fits both the personal profile and the job description (Acts 17:2-3, 11). But God's creating the church of Jews and Gentiles is also seen to be prophesied in Scripture (Acts 13:47; 15:16-18). The outpouring of the Spirit, which initiates the formation of the church, is clearly foretold in Scripture in a passage that also anticipates people calling upon the Lord for salvation (Acts 2:17-21).

*Salvation history.* These two factors, God's plan and the laying out of it in Scripture, entail that Luke envisages a "history of salvation". God's salvation issues from events in history that are to be understood as divine actions, such as freeing the Israelites from Egyptian (and later Babylonian) captivity and supremely in the coming, death and resurrection of Jesus; people are not saved through an act of preaching that rests on little or nothing in the way of divine action and simply demands an existential decision by the hearers.

Salvation history includes the ongoing activity of God stretching throughout the story told in the Old Testament, so that the coming of Jesus is the appropriate climax to what has gone before by way of anticipation and foretelling. Scripture contains the vital heritage of a church whose roots lie firmly in God's past activity in raising up a people for himself. God's activity continues in the unfinished history of Christian mission, of which Luke has reported only the first stage. History falls into two eras, that of Israel (characterized by partial realization and by promise) and that of Christ and the church (characterized by fulfillment and continuing promise).

*The Christ-event.* Within this broad period of fulfillment are three major events: the Christ-event, the coming of the Spirit, and the mission of the church.

First, there is the coming of "the Lord's/God's Messiah" (Lk 2:26; 9:20; Acts 4:26) or the "Servant of the Lord" (Acts 3:13, 26; 4:27, 30). His resurrection, ascension and glorification are of particular significance. Luke distinguishes the ascension as a separate, significant event from the resurrection. The resurrection is God's triumph over death and gives a firm basis for the hope of resurrection. The ascension establishes the position of Jesus as Lord and Messiah (Acts 2:33-36). As the Messiah or authoritative ruler in the kingdom of God, Jesus is entitled *Lord*, but the alternation between Jesus and God as *Lord* and the use of God-language (such as "name") establish a functional equivalence between Jesus and God. This is tied in with the fact that Jesus is also recognized as the Son of God (Acts 9:20; 13:33).

Jesus is known as the Son of God right from his birth (Lk 1:32). Luke refers to Jesus as Lord when narrating the story in the Gospel; the earthly Jesus is the Lord appearing in the humble guise of the servant. The resurrection of Jesus is, therefore, not simply the result of God's decision to raise up a good man; rather, Jesus is the Holy One whom death could not hold (cf. Acts 2:24, 27). The final judgment will take place through a *man* whom God has appointed and set apart by raising him from the dead rather than by a heavenly agent (Acts 17:31).

Occasional references in Acts to the life of Jesus show that God was working salvation through him and that he was not recognized but rather opposed by those who put him to death. But an explanation of why God allowed his death and what purpose it serves is surprisingly absent from the apostolic preaching, although in Acts 20:28 the church is "bought" by God with "blood" and so made his own special possession. The resurrection and ascension of Jesus establish his position as the author of salvation, who dispenses repentance and forgiveness of sins (Acts 5:30-31).

The human situation thereby implied is one of sinfulness and guilt. In the case of the Jewish authorities, this is summed up in their rejection of Jesus; the people share in that guilt unless they repudiate what was done to Jesus and accept him as Messiah and Lord. The Gentiles live in ignorance of God, and their salvation lies in turning to God and repenting of their idolatry.

*Salvation and the Holy Spirit.* Salvation consists in forgiveness of sins (or justification; Acts 13:38-39) with its positive counterpart, eternal life (Acts 13:46). People are brought out of darkness into light (Acts 26:18) and enter the kingdom of God. God has authority to forgive sin, and this authority has been shared with Jesus.

Alongside forgiveness, the gift of the Holy Spirit is an essential component of salvation, and the natural inference is that the converts at Pentecost received the Spirit there and then (Acts 2:38). But the order of events can vary. The Spirit comes only later upon the Samaritan believers who have received Christian baptism and the disciples at Ephesus who have received John's baptism (Acts 8:14-17; 19:1-7); but contrariwise, the gift of the Spirit precedes the Christian baptism of Cornelius and his family (Acts 10:44-48). In both of the former cases, laying on of hands was applied to the converts, but there is no mention of it elsewhere in relation to other converts.

The gift of the Spirit is part of the promise of salvation (Acts 2:38) and creates assurance of salvation. These early Christians experience phenomena understood to indicate the presence of the Spirit, including on occasion the gift of tongues or of prophecy or simply the sense of joy. The Spirit is particularly associated with guidance and empowerment for Christian mission and proclamation. Individual believers are filled with the Spirit when they are about to speak in the name of Christ. A person who is already filled with the Spirit can receive a further filling (Acts 6:5; 7:55). Luke is so taken up with mission that he is almost completely silent about the effects of the Spirit in Christian growth, but he does associate the Spirit with joy (Acts 13:52).

*The church, Jews and Gentiles.* The fundamental theological question in Acts concerns the relationship of the church to Israel and the Gentiles. Luke calls Christian believers "disciples", thereby indicating that there is a basic continuity between the followers of Jesus before Easter and the believers thereafter. The use of the term "Israel" to refer to the church as the "new Israel" develops only gradually. The general practice is to use "Israel" as a term for the existing Jewish people (Acts 2:22; 4:10; 5:21; et al.). God had sent the Messiah to them, and salvation lies in accepting the Messiah. Failure to do so equals apostasy from Israel. Gentiles become members of God's people through believing in the Messiah, and thus a new situation arises in which the people of God consist of both (circumcised) Jews and uncircumcised Gentiles. Believing Jews continue to follow the law of Moses with regard to circumcision and other matters (including the making of vows and the offering of sacrifices). Any suggestion that Paul has been advocating a non-Jewish way of life for Jews is repudiated (Acts 21:24). At the same time there is a weakening of Jewish attitudes so far as the question of foods and association with Gentiles is concerned. For their part, Gentiles are required to avoid practices that would make it difficult for Jewish believers to have fellowship with them.

*Leaders and missionaries.* Luke is unconcerned about the structure of the church. It is important that the early church have a full complement of twelve apostles as symbolical figures, whose mission is essentially to bear witness to Israel concerning the Messiah. The leadership of the church in Jerusalem is initially in the hands of the Twelve together with a group called "elders" (Acts 11:30). From chapter 13 onward, the interest shifts to the Gentile mission and to its most significant missionary, Paul. Paul and Barnabas are termed "apostles" only in Acts 14:4, 14; elsewhere Luke reserves the designation for the Twelve.

What matters for Luke is the function of the apostles as witnesses to Christ and the saving events. It is arguable that only the apostles actually function as witnesses in the strict sense of the term, and that the task of other and later believers is to repeat the apostolic witness rather than to be witnesses themselves.

## CONCLUSION

Luke's main theme is that God has raised and exalted the crucified Jesus to be the Messiah and Lord, through whom forgiveness and the Holy Spirit are offered to all who call on the Lord. A people of God is being formed of believing Jews and Gentiles, a people standing in continuity with Israel but now being reconstituted around the Messiah. The followers of Jesus are committed to carrying out God's plan for them to preach God's salvation to the whole world.

1. All people are sinners and commanded to call upon the Lord (Jesus) to be saved. This applies to Jews, who are otherwise reckoned to be guilty (by association with their leaders) of the death of Jesus, and also to Gentiles.

2. The Gospel of Luke is about what Jesus began to do and to teach. In Acts Jesus continues to be active as the Lord, who has the power to save and to bestow the gift of the Spirit to all people. Repentance and faith, expressed in submission to baptism, are the appropriate responses to the proclamation.

3. The exaltation of Jesus shows him to be the Messiah and Lord, commissioned by God to pour out the Spirit, and sharing functions with God to such an extent that it is not always clear whether the term *Lord* refers to God the Father or to Jesus.

4. Continuity with the earthly mission of Jesus is seen in preserving the term *disciples* for converts, but a church consciousness develops, and Acts traces the development of congregations with leadership. The mission is primarily in the hands of the twelve apostles, but this group is augmented in numerous ways, such as by the Seven and by Paul and his associates.

5. The mission begins with Jews but soon spreads to Gentiles; they form one people of God, but the Gentiles are not required to be circumcised.

6. Jewish believers continue to practice their own law and customs, but Gentile believers are not required to do more than would be expected of Gentiles living alongside Jews.

7. Little is said about the function of Jesus' death in achieving salvation, and more stress is placed on his authoritative position as the exalted Lord.

8. The hope of Jesus' second coming is not abandoned, but all the stress in Acts lies on the missionary responsibility of the church in the present age.

# 6

# THE THEOLOGY OF THE FIRST
# THREE GOSPELS AND ACTS

Most of this book expounds the individual theologies of the various New
Testament books so that we may be able to appreciate their distinctive
contributions to the total picture. But how do they stand in relation to
one another? Do the three Synoptic Gospels reflect the same basic theology? How is the theology expressed in the mission and teaching of Jesus
related to that of his followers after his death? We shall deal with these
two questions in turn.

## THE THEOLOGY OF THE GOSPELS

The first three Gospels naturally show a complex web of likenesses and
differences. A comparison of the individual Gospels shows a considerable
amount of general agreement between them in their theological presentations. They all tell the story of Jesus in similar ways: they have a large number of stories about Jesus in common, and their transcriptions of many of
the sayings of Jesus show a high degree of verbal agreement. Our concern
here is to ask whether their varied pictures have an essential unity despite

their considerable diversity. A comparison of the closing summaries in each of the three chapters on the Gospels should be sufficient to show that this is the case, but it may be helpful to draw the evidence together.

*The identity of Jesus.* The beginning of each Gospel is particularly important in setting the expectations of the readers. Mark begins with Jesus coming from Nazareth to be baptized, whereas Matthew and Luke each have a birth story indicating his divine origin in clear terms and leading readers to see Jesus as the Son of God and the Messiah right from the outset. Mark achieves the same end briefly with his opening words: "The beginning of the gospel about Jesus the Messiah" (Mk 1:1 NIV), who is then identified by God as "my Son, whom I love" (Mk 1:11). Mark invites his readers to accompany Jesus' original contemporaries in their journey of discovery, to ascertain who the carpenter from Nazareth really is. Matthew and Luke are more inclined to take the status of Jesus for granted and to concentrate on what he says and does.

Toward the end of the story all three Gospels contain the same forward-looking announcements that the Son of Man must die and be raised from the dead. In the case of Mark we cannot be certain whether he deliberately concluded with the discovery of the empty tomb, leaving his readers to ponder its significance, or whether he also included some account of resurrection appearances. Matthew portrays a figure who is now glorified and majestic and is the object of worship; Jesus claims omnipotence and issues his lordly command, which is cosmic in its scope. In Luke, Jesus appears as another human being (admittedly unrecognized at first) who is prepared to discuss crucifixion, resurrection and messiahship with his disciples and who then reappears in another meal scene where he gives instruction rather than commands. Yet the element of worship is not absent from Luke, and the lordly figure in Matthew calls his disciples "my brothers". The paradoxical motifs of lordship and brotherhood are common to these two Gospels. And all three Gospels have the same stupendous discovery of an open tomb with an angelic presence.

The picture of Jesus that develops between these two poles shows the same mixture of constants and varied emphases. There is no need to show that Jesus is a human being: that is taken for granted. In the story's main thread, Mark is concerned to show Jesus as the Messiah and then specifically as the suffering one. But divine sonship is at least as important a category; though in some cases sonship may simply be an alternative to messiahship, some passages show that it does refer to a particular relationship with God that is peculiar to Jesus. For the most part Mark avoids directly naming Jesus as *Messiah* and stresses his unwillingness to be made known, whether by demons or other people. Much more frequent is the term *Son of Man*, which, as the Gospel stands, is open to understanding in the light of Daniel 7 (cf. *4 Ezra* [= 2 Esdras]; *1 Enoch*), although at times it may simply be a self-designation of the user as a human being like other human beings. In the former sense, the phrase identifies Jesus as a figure who is presently humble and humiliated but whose authority will one day be openly revealed and exercised. Other people address Jesus with the respect appropriate to a teacher but sometimes go beyond it (Mk 10:47-48; but cf. Mk 10:51).

In the other two Synoptic Gospels, the identity of Jesus is presented less ambiguously to the reader. Matthew uses "Son of David" as an address by people who see him as Messiah and able to perform mighty works. There are frequent references to people showing reverence to him. Both Matthew and Luke have *kyrie* as an address to Jesus that on occasion suggests a deeper reverence than simply that due to a teacher. Matthew also has the important name "Immanuel" for Jesus, signifying that in him "God is with us" (Mt 1:23; cf. 18:20; 28:20).

Various other ways in which Jesus is understood are significant. The concept of Jesus as a new Moses is found in Matthew but is not explicit in the other Gospels (see, however, Acts 3:22-23). In Matthew, Jesus speaks on occasion in the manner of wisdom, but an identification of him with the figure of Wisdom is only weakly present, if at all. Identification with the Servant of Yahweh (Is 40—55) is implicit in Mark 10:45 (Mt 20:28) and is explicit in the scriptural citations in Matthew 8:17; 12:17-21; Luke 22:37; it brings out the status and mission of Jesus as Yahweh's appointed agent but also his humiliation and suffering as the rejected messenger.

*The place of Scripture.* For all the Evangelists, the Jewish Scriptures throw light on who Jesus is; they look for prophecies and patterns that would be fulfilled by the coming One and observe elements in his words and deeds indicating that he does in fact correspond to the scriptural descriptions. Matthew contains numerous formal quotations: what was happening took place in order that the Scripture might be fulfilled. Luke cites texts that are taken to refer to the coming Messiah and specifically to his death and resurrection; then he argues that they are fulfilled by Jesus. There are also prophecies of the mission of the church. This procedure is ascribed to the early preachers in Acts (typically, Acts 17:3) and also to Jesus (Lk 24:25-27, 44-48). There is also a rich use of Scripture, making use of allusions and biblical language rather than formal citations, in the birth stories of John and Jesus and in the passion narrative. Both Matthew and Luke are carrying further what we already find in Mark's Gospel, where Jesus and the narrator both cite and allude to Scripture.

*The understanding of God.* The most significant feature in the theology (in the narrow sense) of all the Gospels is the central and distinctive understanding of God as Father. For disciples, as for Jesus himself, God is experienced as a loving Father who cares for his children and with whom they have an intimate personal relationship expressed in prayer. This relationship is not stressed in Mark (Mk 8:38; 11:25; 13:32; 14:36), but is prominent in Luke and above all in Matthew, where Jesus frequently refers to God as "my Father" or as "your Father".

The coming of Jesus takes place according to God's will as Scripture already reveals it. His advent, his mission, his rejection and crucifixion, and his resurrection are all events that *must* take place because God has planned them and laid down in Scripture the pattern that Jesus must follow. Scripture is also determinative in establishing the way of life that God expects from Jesus' followers.

Prayer to this God is integral to the life of Jesus and his followers. Jesus himself both prays and expects his disciples to pray, as is indeed only natural in the context of Jewish religion. Prayer includes joyful thanksgiving (Mt 11:25-26; Lk 10:21) and appeals to God to do mighty works, requests for guidance and strength, intercession for opponents, confession of sin and petition—all based on the assurance that God is a loving Father to the disciples and will answer their prayers, even if the desired answer is not immediately forthcoming.

*Human sin and need.* The mission of Jesus as the Messiah is to proclaim in word and deed the coming of God's kingdom. The establishment of

God's rule is seen as the overcoming and defeat of Satan, resulting in the deliverance of those he has held captive, whether through demon possession, illness or sin, or through social marginalization resulting from the misuse of power. It thrusts Jesus into opposition against those whose activities contribute to an unjust and noncompassionate society. He speaks out strongly in condemning the leaders in Jewish society for failing to care for the people.

*The message of Jesus and discipleship.* In Mark, the proclamation of the kingdom of God is characterized as gospel or good news. It brings healing to the ill and the disabled, delivers people from Satan and the demons, and offers forgiveness to sinners. It also leads to a fresh statement on how life should be lived. Response to it is understood in terms of repentance and faith, but most weight is placed on discipleship as personal, active, self-denying commitment to Jesus and the gospel. The terms "eternal life" and "being saved" are also employed to signify the benefits that come to those who are disciples.

Essentially the same picture is presented in Matthew, but the nature of the new life is spelled out in greater detail, and there is fuller recognition that a new community life will develop among the followers of Jesus. In Luke, there is more emphasis on salvation and the benefits of discipleship, sufficiently so to justify the view that this is a major motif for him. Luke has put a name to what is actually going on in Mark.

*Discipleship and community.* There is a group of close associates of Jesus, both male and female, who itinerate with him, but we hear nothing about the other people who respond to his message forming themselves into distinctive communities in their own towns and villages. The word *church* is not used, except in Matthew 16:18; 18:17. The latter of these references might suggest that the formation of such groups was in Jesus' mind. Disciples no doubt continue to live according to Jewish religion and custom (cf. Mt 5:23-24), but nothing is made of this point. The Evangelists do not anachronistically read back the life of the church into the pre-Easter period.

*The death of Jesus.* The rejection and death of Jesus are seen as the expression of opposition to God's plan. Nevertheless, the whole process, including his resurrection, takes place because it must happen as part of

God's plan as prophesied in Scripture. What, then, is this divine purpose? At the Last Supper Jesus symbolically interprets his impending death as a sacrificial action related to establishing the covenant; Luke clarifies that this is the new covenant. The death is understood to be for the benefit of many people, including the disciples of Jesus. Matthew adds that it is for the forgiveness of sins, echoing the opening scene where John's baptism is for the forgiveness of sins and the still-earlier statement that Jesus "will save his people from their sins" (Mt 1:21; cf. Lk 1:77). The theme recurs at the end of Luke, as Jesus instructs the disciples concerning the future proclamation (Lk 24:47). The Jewish ethos with its sacrificially based worship takes it for granted that offering sacrifice is necessary for removing sin and inaugurating a covenant. Hence Jesus' interpretation of his death as a sacrifice on behalf of the people is appropriate. Here is the ultimate necessity for his death, tying in with the statement of purpose in Mark 10:45 (Mt 20:28). Although Luke does not record the scene containing this statement, he has an equivalent statement in Acts 20:28, and his citation about Jesus being numbered with the transgressors (Is 53:12, cited in Lk 22:37) may also be relevant.

*The Holy Spirit.* The role of the Spirit in inspiring scriptural authors (Mk 12:36 and parallels) continues in the activity of contemporary persons who give Spirit-inspired commentary on events (Lk 1—2). Since the Spirit's resting on the Messiah is promised in the Old Testament, it is appropriate that at his baptism Jesus receives the Spirit at the outset of his work, so that he is guided by the Spirit and his mighty works are empowered by the Spirit (and are not the result of satanic or demonic influence). Mark gives us the bare essentials. Matthew and Luke both cite scriptural backing (Mt 12:18; Lk 4:18). Expressions about the power of God have the same force (cf. Mt 12:28; Lk 11:20). Both Matthew and Luke associate the conception of Jesus with the Spirit's activity. Luke has a distinctive vocabulary of being filled with the Spirit (Lk 1:15, 41, 67; 4:1). The Evangelists are aware of the Old Testament picture of the Messiah and Servant of the Lord, on whom the Spirit rests, and see no incongruity in the Son of God receiving the Spirit of God.

All the Gospels record the prophecy by John that the Stronger One will baptize with the Spirit (and with fire, according to Mt and Lk), but only

Luke is in a position to show that this prophecy is fulfilled in the early church (Acts 11:16). Jesus briefly mentions the Spirit's enabling disciples to say the right things when they are persecuted and put on trial. The Spirit is apparently not bestowed on the disciples during the time of Jesus except for the actors in Luke 1—2, who function like Old Testament prophets in announcing the birth of the Messiah, and possibly the disciples who receive "power" from Jesus for their mission (Lk 9:1). Jesus promises that the Father will give the Spirit to those who pray to him (Lk 11:13).

*Jesus, Israel and the Gentiles.* Mark's Gospel presents Jesus' mission among the Jews. He enters non-Jewish territory from time to time and has contacts with non-Jews, but little is made of this. In his teaching he criticizes the practice of the teachers of the law, but the criticism is directed against the traditions of the elders and not against the law itself. When Mark comments that by his teaching he declares all foods clean, this looks like a criticism of current practice. The implications of the condemnation uttered in the parable of the vineyard are not followed through explicitly. A mission to Gentiles throughout the world is anticipated at a later stage.

Matthew's Gospel thematizes the issue. The law as interpreted by Jesus is understood to be binding on disciples; Jesus has not come to abolish the law. The main thrust of the Sermon on the Mount is to give teaching that deepens the law by dealing with attitudes and motives in a way calling for a radical lifestyle governed by love. It is assumed that people continue to live by the Jewish religion, offering sacrifices in the temple. Nevertheless, there is a strong criticism of the Jewish leaders for their failure to obey God and to recognize the coming of the Messiah. The kingdom will be taken from them and given to others. The Jews are compared unfavorably with the Gentiles who will believe, and the mission to Gentiles is anticipated over and over again, even though the mission of Jesus and his disciples is essentially limited to Jews during his lifetime. The Gospel concludes with a tremendous emphasis on making disciples of the nations.

Luke likewise respects the fact that Jesus goes primarily to the Jews but in various ways points forward to the mission to the Gentiles; the symbolism of the seventy-two witnesses is unmistakable. Like Matthew, he assumes that Jesus' audience continues to keep the law.

*Jesus and the future.* Teaching about the final events in God's plan for the world features fairly prominently in the Gospels. The kingdom of God is thought of as the final intervention of God into human history, to establish his rule and bring to naught the opposition to it. It is also understood as the eternal state, so that to talk of the kingdom is to talk of the transcendent sphere where God reigns eternally. Jesus announces that the kingdom of God is near or has arrived, thus signaling the initiation of the end-time events. His teaching also contains sufficient information about the final judgment and the preceding times of stress to make people feel that the end is near. In fact, the immediate future is one of increasing breakdown of society in Judea and further afield, culminating in the horrific events of the war with Rome, which must inevitably have seemed to people like the onset of final doom.

Yet at the same time it seems to have been possible to think of "business as usual". Right up to Mark 8, the impression given by Mark is much more that Jesus is announcing a new state of affairs in this-worldly terms, in which he is bringing healing to individuals and to society through mighty works indicating that God is at work in an unusual way. The teaching of Jesus about human life is a combination of rules and norms for ordinary human life and of calls to wholehearted commitment to the Messiah, whatever the cost in self-denial and readiness for loyalty to death in the face of opposition.

Alongside this is also the promise of some kind of vindication. On the one hand, Jesus prophesies that he himself will somehow survive being put to death. On the other hand, there is a prophecy of the Son of Man's coming with language suggesting final judgment. James and John proceed to ask for seats beside Jesus when he enters his glory. Do they think that they will be martyred, pass straight to heaven, and join Jesus there? Or do they think that he will be resurrected, and then the new world will begin on earth? Jesus' arrival in Jerusalem is heralded as being associated with the coming messianic kingdom. Is the messianic kingdom thought of as a temporary stage before the final reign of God? Then comes Mark 13, in which Jesus speaks of the destruction of the temple and a period in which they will be without him, since people will come claiming to be "he".

*Conclusion.* Without any straining of the evidence, it is clear that there is a common basic theology expressed in all three Synoptic Gospels. Their varied emphases cohere with one another.

## THE THEOLOGY OF ACTS

Compared with their later understanding, the disciples' apprehension of Jesus and his teaching before his death and resurrection was inevitably undeveloped and incomplete. What Jesus taught them would naturally be limited to what they could understand at that point. But was it significantly different, so that the teaching of Jesus and the teaching of early Christians must be seen as separate entities? Or was there an organic relationship between them? At this point we shall simply consider the picture given by Acts in relation to the Gospels and especially to the Gospel of Luke.

*The identity of Jesus.* In Acts, Jesus is presented in the way that one would expect in a sequel to the Gospel of Luke. The Gospel has prepared the way for Acts by presenting Jesus as the Messiah and Son of God, whose identity is jeopardized by his death on the cross. The story ends with his resurrection and entry into glory. The task of mission, begun by Jesus, goes on, now aiming at bringing people to acknowledge Jesus as the messianic King. The proclamation of the kingdom, already shared by the disciples, naturally continues through them, and it is inevitable that the accent moves from the kingdom to the Messiah. This is a very significant shift in emphasis, but the message is still essentially the same: it is about the new way in which God is acting to establish his rule. Therefore, it can still be presented as in effect a call to discipleship, seen in the continued use of this term for those who respond to the message. Luke uses the verb "to make disciples" to clarify what evangelism is (Acts 14:21). Naturally, the character of discipleship shifts from adhering to an earthly leader to recognizing that the earthly person, Jesus, was actually the Messiah and that his rule continues, even though he is translated to heaven and is no longer physically present.

In the Gospels the evidence that Jesus is the Messiah is threefold. First, there is the activity of Jesus in his authoritative teaching and proclamation of the kingdom in word and deed: he acts as the Messiah. Second, there is the appeal to Scripture to confirm that he corresponds to the picture presented there. And, third, there is the confirmation supplied by the resurrection. Essentially the testimony of the resurrection is to three things: the fact of Jesus being alive; the fact that this corresponds with his own prophecies and with Scripture; and the fact that only God could have brought it about, thereby implicitly declaring Jesus to be the Messiah. In the Gospels this testimony is largely confined to the resurrection narratives. It is hardly prominent in Mark, where the emphasis is on the reunion of the disciples with Jesus in Galilee (Mk 16:7; cf. Mk 14:28). In Matthew, there is more emphasis on overcoming the doubts of the disciples as to whether Jesus has really been resurrected, but there is also the vision of the omnipotent Lord. In Luke, there is much more stress on the argument from the correspondence between the scriptural picture of the Messiah and the role of Jesus.

The same elements are present in Acts, but there is a new one, the witness of those who have seen the resurrected Jesus. There is also considerably more exploration of the scriptural evidence for the role of the Messiah. There is little about the earthly life of Jesus, except in the sermon to Cornelius (Acts 10:37-39); after telling the story in the Gospel, Luke probably sees no need to repeat it in Acts. The fact that Jesus was a human being emerges naturally. He is identified as the prophet like Moses and also as the Servant of God in a manner paralleling this term's use for the king (Acts 4:25, 27) in the Old Testament but specifically echoing the usage in Isaiah 40—55. The self-designation *Son of Man* drops out of use (except in Acts 7:56).

Luke majors on the scriptural evidence for the death and resurrection of Jesus. The extraordinary character of the resurrection and the need to overcome the scandal of the cross inevitably overshadow the story of what Jesus said and did. The sermons offer the needed confirmation that Jesus is the Messiah, but the Lord's status is specifically added to this. This is a clarification of the Messiah's role, but at the same time it moves beyond purely Jewish terms. Jesus is now the exalted and glorified Lord (Acts 2:33; 3:13; 5:31), envisaged as seated beside God in heaven (Acts 2:34; 7:55-56), with a future role as judge of the world (Acts 17:31). He is now in a position of authority that he did not exercise (or did not exercise in the same way) in his earthly life. Prayer can be made to him (Acts 7:59), and mighty works are done in his name (Acts 3:6; 4:10, 30; 16:18; cf. Luke

9:49; 10:17). Inevitably it is this exalted Lord who occupies center stage.

As we turn from the Gospels to Acts, we thus see a natural development in their understanding of Jesus once his followers believe that God raised Jesus from the dead and exalted him.

*God as Sovereign and Father.* This motif of God as the sovereign initiator of all that is done in and through Jesus is central in Acts. Luke's teaching in both the Gospel and Acts further indicates how the mission of the disciples to preach the gospel to both Jews and Gentiles is part of this same plan and foretold in Scripture. He is the normal addressee of prayer, but prayer is also addressed to Jesus.

In Acts the understanding of God as Father is not as prominent as in the Gospels, where Jesus regularly uses the term in speaking to his disciples. The locution is confined to statements by the risen Jesus (Acts 1:4, 7) and Peter (Acts 2:33). The omission is understandable because Acts lacks statements addressed directly to believers about their spiritual relationship with God.

*Sin and salvation.* The understanding of sin in Acts centers, so far as the Jews are concerned, on their rejection of Jesus as the Messiah. Granted that God's vindication of Jesus as Messiah is central in early Christians' proclamation, this is exactly what one would expect.

There is clearly also a shift in emphasis from declaring the kingdom of God in the sense of affirming his kingly rule to announcing salvation in the form of blessings from God for those who respond to the message (Acts 13:26; 16:17). "Being saved" is the characteristic expression for the benefit that comes to believers. A term that has a specific application to deliverance from final judgment takes on a much broader meaning, now signifying the wholeness of deliverance and the positive conferring of God's blessings. Yet kingdom language is still used in what is understood more and more as teaching about the King (Acts 17:7; cf. Acts 1:3; 28:31).

From the beginning there is a community of Jesus' disciples that quickly expands in Jerusalem and is characterized by communal activities. Wherever Christians travel in Acts, they form such communities that meet together; it can be safely presumed that the activities ascribed to the Jerusalem Christians are typical of the new communities being formed. Consequently, there is a new association called "the church", consisting of individual communities within it that are known as "churches [*or congregations*]".

*The death and exaltation of Jesus.* The rejection and death of Jesus is a theme in the sermons, where it is argued that, although it was the deed of wicked people, nevertheless it occurred in accordance with God's set purpose, and that it was followed by God's own act in raising Jesus from the dead. The sermons aim to overcome the obstacle to recognizing Jesus as the Messiah, an obstacle created by his rejection and death: it is argued that God overcame the death by raising and exalting Jesus, thus vindicating him, and that in any case the death itself, though carried out by sinners acting sinfully, nevertheless took place by God's purpose. In only one place (Acts 20:28) is reference made to the church being bought with the blood of Jesus. Since the sermons are concerned primarily with the basic point of overcoming the scandal of the cross, it is less important to develop the thought of redemptive suffering. What does happen is that the sermons declare God's exaltation of Jesus to be a Savior for Israel (Acts 5:31): the authority that God himself has to forgive and to save is transferred to Jesus.

The earliest preaching about Jesus is an appropriate development from the way in which the story of Jesus is told in the Gospels. The identity of Jesus as the Messiah, now exalted by God, continues to be the basic point in debate and evangelism with the Jews.

*The Holy Spirit.* In Acts a prominent place is given to the powerful descent of the Spirit at Pentecost, which is clearly identified as the fulfillment of the prophecy of baptism with the Spirit (Acts 1:5). Since the coming of the Spirit upon the household of Cornelius is also identified as baptism with the Spirit, it is clear that the Pentecostal gift is given to all believers and not just to the original recipients. The citation from Joel favors this understanding, and it is confirmed by Peter's words to the crowd in Acts 2:38. This is the new element in Acts as compared with the Gospels.

In the Gospels the Spirit is primarily concerned with equipping individuals for the messianic mission. This role persists in Acts, where the majority of references are to the work of mission. Individuals are filled with the Spirit before they speak and bear witness, so that rejection of their testimony can be said to be resistance to the Spirit (Acts 7:51). Guidance is given by the Spirit (and by other heavenly agents). At the same time reception of the Spirit is evidently the sine qua non of being a Christian and is the clear mark that God has accepted such recipients into his people (Acts 15:8). It inescapably follows that the Spirit is not only the agent of mission but also the mark of belonging to Christ. There is a tension in that some individuals are said to be full of the Spirit (Acts 6:3, 5, 8; 7:55; 11:24) in a way that might suggest degrees of possession (the Seven appear to be more "spiritual" than the rank and file of believers out of whom they are chosen), and there is the phenomenon of "filling" people who already have the Spirit for specific tasks (Acts 2:4; 4:8; 9:17; 13:9). Evidently the baptism of the Spirit is a permanent endowment of believers, a mark of belonging to the new covenant, and is common to them all. It equips them all for the mission, but this is entirely compatible with specific endowments for particular occasions. Like the Gospels, Acts says little about the functions of the Spirit in relation to what we might call the spiritual life of the individual and the community, but this motif is not entirely absent, and a one-sided insistence that the Spirit is *purely* the Spirit of prophecy and mission in Acts is unjustified. Nor is the baptism with the Spirit a later experience detached from the initial act of belief in Christ. The onus lies on those who would argue that the promise in Acts 2:38 is not fulfilled there and then.

*The Jewish law.* In Acts Luke traces the story of a church that in many ways found it hard to adjust for mission to the Gentiles: opposition continues on the part of some. There is one new people of God. Believers debate, To what extent is this new people required to keep the law? The decisive point that Gentiles are not required to be circumcised stands firm; this is an issue never raised one way or the other in the Synoptic Gospels (where the only circumcision ever mentioned is that of Jesus himself), simply because it was not an issue at that historical point.

*Jesus and the future.* When the disciples ask a question about when the kingdom will be restored to Israel, they are in effect told that this is none of their business. Their task is to be witnesses to Jesus "to the ends of the earth", a saying that implies a considerable period of time, initiating a task that has not been completed by the end of the book (Acts 1:6-8). The promise of the return of Jesus stands firm, but it does give the impression of being less imminent or at least not immediate (Acts 3:20). Yet the last days have begun, in that the Spirit has been poured out. Heaven is near: Stephen has a vision that takes him into sight of it (Acts 7:55-56). But thereafter the interest is centered on the mission, particularly to the Gentiles. The message includes Jesus' warning about the day of judgment (Acts 10:42; 17:31). Thus Acts does not deal to any extent with the issue. Whatever its chronological relationship to the war with Rome and the fall of Jerusalem, it is silent on the matter, in stark contrast to Luke 21, where the fall of Jerusalem is unambiguously thematized (contrast the more opaque language in Mark and Matthew). Luke, then, respects the way in which apocalyptic prophecy is a known part of Jesus' teaching, but in Acts he presents a picture in which it is of marginal importance for a church primarily engaged with mission and facing human opposition.

## CONCLUSION

The presentation of the early Christians' theology in Acts can be understood as a straightforward development from that in the Gospel, although there are some vital new understandings as well. This theology is what we expect from a group of the earthly Jesus' followers who believe that he is risen from the dead and still active among them. The differences between Acts and the Synoptic Gospels demonstrate clearly enough that the teaching of Jesus has not been assimilated to that of the early church. The vital distinction between Jesus' proclamation of the kingdom and the early church's proclamation of Jesus is carefully preserved. This is all the more noteworthy, granted that the temptation to assimilate the teaching of Jesus to that of the early church must have been quite strong.

The two theologies, that of Jesus and that of his followers, express the same underlying structure and content in different idioms. On the one hand, we have the message of Jesus announcing the kingdom of God as something coming to pass in the here and now, a message to the oppressed and to sinners, offering deliverance from the powers of evil, bringing entry into a new relationship with God as Father, and promising eternal life. Jesus is more than simply a proclaimer of what God is doing; he is also the agent through whom God acts by the power of the Spirit. His position as Son of Man, Messiah and Son of God emerges as the story is told by the Evangelists. Jesus' message requires hearers to respond by committing themselves in discipleship to Jesus himself and entering a new way of living that goes beyond the requirements of the Mosaic law. Jesus is God's missionary, bringing this message to the Jews so that Israel might be restored to being truly and not just nominally God's people; yet there is an openness to Gentiles even if this is not fully exploited at this stage. His mission runs foul of opposition from the Jewish leaders, which sets in train a series of events purposed by God, events through which Jesus is rejected, crucified, and then vindicated by God raising him from the dead. This is how the Evangelists see Jesus, and their presentation rests firmly on reliable traditions of his life and teaching.

On the other hand, we have the theology of the early Christians. The resurrection of Jesus and their experience of the Spirit confirm for them that the message of Jesus is true and that God has now confirmed him as Messiah and Lord. He is therefore now active from heaven through a variety of agencies. Their discipleship continues, and they are aware of a continuing obligation to mission, to bring Israel to recognize the Messiah. So their proclamation shifts in emphasis from the kingdom to the Messiah, and consequently it is not so much a repetition of what he has proclaimed; instead, they proclaim Jesus himself. They carry out their mission by the power of the same Holy Spirit who is now a vital part of the experience of all the followers of Jesus. With the shift away from the emphasis on the kingdom of God, there comes an increased emphasis on the experience of salvation and eternal life, including the forgiveness of sins and the reception of the Spirit. A combination of events, in which divine guidance is perceived, leads them to a rapidly expanding mission among the Gentiles, which takes the missionaries all over the Roman world and creates problems regarding the place of the Jewish law and practices for the converts. Opposition to the new movement leads to martyrdom, imprisonment and threats of death; hence, it is recognized that the path taken by Jesus must also be the path for his followers.

# 7

# THE LETTER TO THE GALATIANS

We shall survey the thirteen letters ascribed to Paul in something like their chronological order of composition (the general lines of which are clear, though the details are open to discussion), leaving aside questions as to whether other early Christians may have had some involvement in their composition. Galatians may not be the earliest surviving letter (1 and 2 Thessalonians could be earlier), but its theological content makes it a good starting place.

## THE CONTROVERSY BEHIND GALATIANS

Paul's addressees in Galatia included Gentile believers, some of whom may have been adherents of Judaism without being circumcised. A group of Jewish Christians (often nicknamed "Judaizers"; cf. Gal 2:14; 4:10) were pressing them to be circumcised and observe various Jewish festivals. They opposed Paul because he taught that all the Gentiles needed to do to become members of God's people was to believe in Jesus; circumcision and other requirements of the law were not necessary.

At that time Jews generally practiced a rigid separation from non-Jews; they would not eat with Gentiles or eat food prepared by them, which they considered "unclean" (cf. Acts 10). Jewish Christians were now expected to eat with uncircumcised Gentiles who were unclean. Surely Gentiles who became Christians should be circumcised and keep the law, and then everything would be all right?

If the Judaizers were correct, then Paul was mistaken in the views that he was preaching, or he was even deliberately distorting the gospel. Was he really a true Jew himself, faithful to his ancestral heritage? And if he claimed apostolic authority, from where had he derived it?

And, if people did not keep the law, how could they live consistently with the moral quality of behavior demanded by it? Surely Gentiles who rejected the law would also reject its moral demands and persist in their sinful ways (cf. 1 Cor 5:11; 6:9-11)?

Earlier scholars argued that the purpose of keeping the law was to acquire "merit" by piling up a record of good deeds done and wrong deeds avoided, on the basis of which God would accept sinners despite their sinful past. Many recent interpreters argue that this view misunderstands Judaism. They hold that individual Israelites were situated within God's covenant people on the basis of his electing grace; they were not required to keep the law in order to *get in*, although once in, they kept the law in order to *stay in*. Keeping the law was the response to grace rather than the precondition of it. The required "works of the law" were the marks of belonging to God's people and set a boundary round them.

Either way, Paul objects to the creation of this boundary that requires Gentiles to keep the law in order to enter the people of God. So he warns against yielding to this pressure to keep the law by reminding them of the true nature of the gospel and its benefits. Gentiles do not need to "follow Jewish customs" (Gal 2:14) in order to get right and stay right with God; instead, they simply need to believe in Jesus.

## THE THEOLOGICAL STORY

*Paul's authority and the "other gospel" (Gal 1:1—2:13).* Paul's apostolic authority derives from Jesus Christ and God and is therefore superior to any merely human authority (Gal 1:1). His message for the Gentiles comes directly from Jesus Christ. Salvation rests on what Christ has done—he gave himself for us (Gal 1:4; 2:20; 3:13), redeems us (Gal 4:5), and sets us free (Gal 5:1); through faith in him we are "justified" (Gal 2:17). The apostles at Jerusalem laid down no additional requirements for Paul's Gentile converts but rather encouraged him in his mission (Gal 2:1-10).

*Paul's exposition of the gospel (Gal 2:14—6:18).* When Peter came to Antioch, he was persuaded to withdraw from eating with Gentiles. Paul repeats and develops what he said to Peter to change his mind for the benefit of his readers. Jewish Christians, like Peter and Paul himself, know that as Jews they are "justified" or "made righteous" *by faith in Christ and not by observing the law* (Gal 2:14-16). But justification is also by faith in Jesus Christ for Gentiles; therefore, they do not need to observe the law. If it is objected that people who abandon the law will then drop its moral requirements, the reply is that believers have actually died with Christ, and his righteous life is lived out in them (Gal 2:17-21).

Next, Paul appeals to *experience*. Receiving the Spirit is indispensable for being a Christian and is the fundamental evidence of faith. His readers know that they have received the Spirit without being circumcised and keeping the law. Believers do not need to add the "flesh" to the Spirit. Here "flesh" refers to things done by human beings in their own strength in contrast to what God does for them (Gal 3:1-5).

Paul also appeals to *Scripture*. Abraham was justified by his faith before he was circumcised and before the law had been given, and he was told that God's promise was for him and his descendants. If Abraham was justified by faith, the promise to all nations through him must be on the same principle (Gal 3:6-14). Trying to get right with God by dependence on keeping the law means coming under the curse, which rests on people who try to keep the law but do not keep all its requirements (Deut 27:26).

Further, Scripture upholds the principle of justification by faith (Hab 2:4). Justification by the law is based not upon faith but upon works. Yet the law was never intended to be a means of justification or to give life (Gal 3:21); instead, it had some other function. In any case, nobody is able to keep the law, and therefore everybody who depends on works of the law is under its curse (Gal 3:10). The law cannot deliver people from its own curse, but Christ has delivered those who believe by taking this curse on himself. By believing in Christ, Christians receive the blessing promised to and experienced by Abraham, the blessing identified as the experience of the Spirit. Faith is the means by which we obtain a benefit that has been secured for us by somebody else: Christ.

The later promulgation of the law of Moses could not alter the covenant made with Abraham (Gal 3:15-18). God's promises, once made, cannot be set aside. The law was not intended to cancel the promise (Gal 3:15-25). It had a temporary function as a kind of guardian for the Jews, like a slave who looks after children. It was there to lead people to Christ by making them realize that they were sinners. With the coming of Christ, its function has ceased (Gal 3:25-29). Believers in Christ, whether Jews or Greeks, are adopted as God's children, instead of being like slaves under bondage to keeping the law. With sonship come such privileges as the gift of the Spirit now and the status of being heirs to what God will give them in the future (Gal 4:1-7).

Paul sees an analogy between the pressured Gentile believers in their pre-Christian state and the Jews under the law. They have experienced being slaves to their false gods (Gal 4:8-11). They do not want to return to another kind of slavery to the Jewish law (Gal 4:12-20). Accepting circumcision means ceasing to trust in Christ and moving back into bondage to the law, which requires total obedience and threatens death for those who fail to keep it. God's children live in freedom, not freedom to sin but deliverance from the power of sin, in order to keep the fundamental commandment of love (Gal 5:2-6, 13-15). The flesh is human nature in its weakness against temptation, and the Spirit is the power that enables people to demonstrate the qualities of godly character. Believers need not yield to the pull of this old nature and can experience a new life in which they are led by the Spirit (Gal 5:16-26).

## THEOLOGICAL THEMES

*Salvation history and the gospel.* Paul thinks in terms of salvation history in two periods. In the old era God was active in making promises and partially fulfilling them. But now in the new era the death of Jesus is the means of redemption from the curse imposed by the law. The gospel is expressed by preaching (Gal 1:11). It is not a story that may or may not have a factual counterpart, but the proclamation of what really happened

(Gal 3:1): "Christ...gave himself for our sins" (Gal 1:4). The appropriate response is not simply acceptance of the "word" but essentially faith in the person to whom it bears witness, Jesus crucified (Gal 2:19-20). The threat to Paul's understanding is "another gospel" that requires Gentiles' adherence to the Mosaic law as their way of life and as an integral part of their response.

But Paul is also concerned with the tendency of converts to persist in the sins characteristic of humanity in general. He does not believe that proclamation of the Mosaic law and the need to obey it can deal with the impulses that lead to sin. His own gospel thus has two central aspects. One is the announcement of justification based exclusively on Jesus' bearing the curse, a justification received solely by faith and not by keeping the law. The other is the promise to believers of the Spirit, through whose working in their lives they can overcome the power of the flesh and lead a life pleasing to God, thus fulfilling the single commandment of love.

*Justification.* The basic issue is how a person is "justified". This word is a translation of a Greek verb *(dikaioō)*, which is related to the adjective "just" or "righteous" *(dikaios)*. "Justify" and "justification" refer to the process of making a person righteous.

*Justification* can refer to changing the *character* of a person with evil motives and actions so that they think and act in a righteous way. Or it can refer to changing the *verdict* on wrongdoers by declaring that they are righteous despite the wrong they have done. When Paul uses the verb *justify*, he is certainly referring to this latter type of action: God no longer holds the wrong against them and establishes a positive relationship with them. Apart from Christ, nobody has this righteous status with God. Paul does not need to argue this in the case of the Gentiles; his problem is with Jews who assume that the law is their means of obtaining such a status.

*The cross and its effects.* The Son of God became a human being and was born "under the law" to deliver people who were under the law (Gal 4:4-5). His death has the effect of delivering people who believe in him from their existing sinful situation. That result is variously expressed as deliverance from the present evil age (Gal 1:4), redemption from the curse of the law (Gal 3:13), or crediting people who believe with a righteous status (a verdict of not guilty; Gal 3:6). This deliverance is achieved at a cost that frees people from the curse or judgment that they are under because they have not kept the law. In one of the clearest New Testament statements of "substitution", Paul says that people who stand under the curse are delivered from it because Christ has delivered them by himself coming under it (Gal 3:10, 13; cf. the scapegoat in Lev 16:20-22). Paul sees no difficulty in one person identifying closely with a group and then representatively bearing the curse for them (just as when somebody pays a fine owed by somebody else), particularly when this action springs out of love.

Theoretically a wrongdoer may accept what Christ has done without any change of character, as expressed in feelings of remorse and a resolve not to sin again. But Paul safeguards against this objection. First, he is talking about something that becomes effective only when people have faith in God (Gal 3:6) or Christ (Gal 2:16; cf. Gal 2:20; 3:22). Second, Paul says that believers share in being "crucified with Christ" (Gal 2:19). The death of Jesus is not merely the death of another person that God as the lawgiver accepts in place of the death of the sinner. Rather, his death includes the sinner who is crucified with Christ; the "gospel" element is that the sinner is counted as having died, although the believer has not actually suffered death as a penalty with all its pain and yet receives life. And the effect of this death is that they have "crucified" their sinful flesh with its desires (Gal 5:24). Third, believers are said to be "in Christ" or "baptized into Christ" (Gal 3:27-28); this denotes a very close relationship between believers and Christ. Hence, Paul completely refutes the charge that substitution allows a person to avoid judgment on their sin without involving any real change on their part.

*Paul's message and the Jewish Scriptures: Abraham.* Paul appeals to what Scripture teaches about Abraham. He takes up the promise that all the nations would be blessed through Abraham. For him, this means that God will justify the Gentiles in the same way as Abraham: by faith. Abraham's descendants (his "seed") are the people who share his character as believers in God, regardless of whether they are physically his offspring or not; believing Gentiles are included, whereas unbelieving physical descendants are excluded. The promise in Gen 22:18 is *"through your offspring* all nations on earth will be blessed." When Paul says in 3:14 "that the blessing given to Abraham might come to the Gentiles *through Christ Jesus*", he may well be echoing and interpreting this text. He interprets *seed* to refer to one individual (Christ) and with him the Christian community composed of Jews *and* Gentiles, who are "one in Christ" (Gal 3:28; cf. 1 Cor 12:12-13) and are the "body of Christ". The church is understood as the new Israel of God (Gal 6:16), composed as it is of Jews and Gentiles who accept Jesus as the Messiah. They share Abraham's faith by believing in Christ (of which baptism is the outward sign) and by living a life in the Spirit, which issues in "faith working through love" (Gal 5:6 NRSV).

*Paul's message and the Jewish Scriptures: The law.* Nothing more was needed than faith in order to be justified. "A person is not justified by observing the law" (cf. Gal 2:16). The law is not able to give life and was not meant to do so (Gal 3:21). Certainly it appears to promise life to those who keep it (Gal 3:12, citing the promise in Lev 18:5; cf. Rom 10:5). For Paul, only the Spirit can give life (2 Cor 3:6). There is a fundamental difference between the law, which can only demand, and the Spirit, who can empower. True, the law laid down the kind of conduct required by God, and therefore life lay in following it. In that sense it was the doing of the law that led to life. But the law was not able to give life, since there was nothing about it that enabled a person to keep its commandments.

God's election of Israel as a people is worth nothing if it does not issue in faith in Christ on the part of its members (Rom 9:4-5). Like many other Jews of his time, Paul held what we may call a remnant theology, which recognizes that to greater or less extent the people are tainted with sin and apostasy and need to get right with God; for Jewish sects, this was by following the precepts of some particular teacher or group. For Paul, all people, both Jews and Gentiles, lack the blessings of sonship and need to be delivered from "the present evil age" (Gal 1:4). Jews themselves are evidently sinners and breakers of the law (Gal 2:17-18), and as breakers of the law, they are under a curse (Gal 3:10). It is easy to understand that some can think fervent keeping of the law to be necessary for both Jews and Gentiles. Grace and works can thus go together, in that grace is inviting people to do certain things in order for Gentiles to get into God's people and for Jews to stay in. However, Paul insists that the correlate of grace is faith, not works.

But if so, how does Paul understand the purpose of the law? By putting God's commands before people, laws they cannot keep (as their past history has shown), the law is pronouncing a condemnation upon them that should lead them to turn to Christ for justification by faith. Throughout the period before Christ came, the Jews were certainly meant to keep the law, so far as they could. But this was a temporary function; with the coming of Christ, believers are no longer under the supervision of the law. The misuse of the law as a means of justification is the problem, and this misuse is not inherent in the law itself but is due an interpretation put upon it.

Has the law any role in the life of believers? Paul sees the law as brought to completion by Christ in the single command given in the Torah, "You shall love your neighbor as yourself" (Gal 5:14 NRSV; cf. Rom 13:8-10), and he commands his readers to use their freedom from the law to keep that commandment in the Spirit's power. For Paul, the commandment to love retains its validity for believers. One can see the various commands in the law as applying that single command, and therefore it is perfectly possible for Paul to go back to them and cite them approvingly. Consequently, when Paul talks about dying to the law (Gal 2:19), he must mean dying to the Mosaic law as a means of justification: fulfilling the love command in the freedom given by the Spirit is not a means of gaining life and a righteous status; instead, it expresses the fact that one has life and a righteous status.

The matter would be eased if we could find evidence that Paul makes a distinction between the moral and ritual aspects of the law. Certainly it is circumcision, food laws and festivals that he has in mind when he talked of justification by the works of the law. But he does not distinguish very clearly between the moral commandments in the law and those that are concerned with the ritual aspects of the Jews' relationship with God.

*The Holy Spirit.* Paul bases part of his argument on an appeal to the readers' experience of the Spirit, which has taken place before the Judaizers have come on the scene, and they have begun to flirt with keeping the law. They have not been required to keep the law in order for God to give the Spirit's manifestations in the congregations. The reception of the Spirit is understood to be the blessing promised to Abraham, which comes to the Gentiles through the redemption wrought by Christ.

The difference between those under the law and those under grace is that the former are like slaves and the latter are like sons and daughters to God. Their new status is ascribed to two factors. On the one hand, they become children of God through faith in Christ (Gal 3:26). Faith is expressed in the act of baptism. Baptism is "into Christ", which appears to mean that through this act the person is brought into a spiritual relationship with Christ; this can also be expressed in terms of being clothed with Christ. On the other hand, God sends the Spirit of his Son into the hearts of his children. This appears to mean that the Spirit is sent in response to faith and that the Spirit then makes the status of sonship effective by enabling believers to address God as their Father.

The Spirit who has been given to believers is a life-giving principle creating "fruit", specific results identified as the practice of various types of Christian conduct: the demonstration of love, joy, peace and so on (Gal 5:16-25). A contrasting set of sinful activities are ascribed to the "flesh" of believers, to their existing sinful character. These things are contrary to the law and to the Spirit. But the law cannot help people to refrain from them; it can only tell them what not to do. The implication is that the Spirit not only produces in people the positive fruits of character but also enables them to keep the prohibitions. Put otherwise, believers have crucified the flesh and its desires. The crucifixion of the believer with Christ brings about a death to sinful desires; dead people no longer respond to temptations to do wrong actions, provided that they live by the Spirit.

## CONCLUSION

At the heart of Galatians, we find both the cross and the Holy Spirit. It contains Paul's understanding of Jesus as the Son of God, sent into the world to redeem people from the curse of the law. God's Spirit, sent into believers' hearts, makes them children of God, who fulfill the law by keeping the one commandment of love. Hence, salvation is available on the same terms for believing Jews and Gentiles.

# 8

# THE LETTERS TO THE
# THESSALONIANS

## 1 THESSALONIANS—THE THEOLOGICAL STORY

The newly converted, mostly Gentile believers in Thessalonica (cf. Acts 17:1-9) had not been targeted by the Judaizers active in Galatia. But they were suffering outside pressure to abandon their faith, and there were misunderstandings regarding the future coming of the Lord.

*Paul's relationship with the congregation (1 Thess 1:1—3:13).* The opening prayer report (1 Thess 1) is meant to encourage the readers and express Paul's confidence in them as he recollects his mission, which was characterized by Spirit-inspired preaching and response to the message (1 Thess 1:5-6). The hearers had turned from idolatry to serve the living God and now look forward to the future coming of Jesus, who will rescue them from the coming wrath.

Paul compares their subsequent persecution with that of the Judean congregations, where (some of) "the Jews" had killed Jesus and the prophets and driven out the apostles who wished to evangelize the Gentiles (1 Thess 2:12-16). Such suffering is part of the destiny of believers

(1 Thess 3:3), something that God has willed or allowed to happen. In this connection, Paul refers to the activity of Satan, a supernatural being opposed to God.

Paul prays that his readers will stand united in love for one another and firm against their attackers (1 Thess 3:10-13; 5:23-24), and he asks them in turn to pray for him (1 Thess 5:25). They are already "standing firm in the Lord" (1 Thess 3:8), and he urges them to continue to do so.

*Instruction for the congregation (1 Thess 4:1—5:28).* Paul then tells the readers what he would say if he himself were able to visit the church. After teaching on the need to grow in holiness and brotherly love (1 Thess 4:1-12), there is specific instruction on worries the congregation has about what will happen at Christ's return to those who have already died. Paul's reassurance that they will be resurrected to share in meeting with the Lord is followed by further encouragement to the readers so to live that they will be ready for the Lord when he comes (1 Thess 4:13—5:11).

The closing practical instructions for their life together (1 Thess 5:12-28) emphasize the need for harmony and love and give a brief glimpse of a congregation in which the Spirit is active through prophecy and other means (1 Thess 5:19; cf. 1 Cor 12; 14).

## 2 THESSALONIANS—THE THEOLOGICAL STORY

The content of the second letter is similar to that in the first letter, and there are notable echoes in the wording. Three main theological interests dominate the letter and shape its structure.

*The church under persecution (2 Thess 1:1-12).* The readers are presented as making growth in faith, love and steadfastness, despite continuing attacks on them from outside their circle. This circumstance leads Paul straight into a theological discussion of persecution with regard to both the persecuted and those who are attacking them (1 Thess 2:14-16). God will judge those who are hostile to his people and cast them out from his presence on judgment day. Believers will be recompensed for their sufferings by receiving relief from them and by sharing in the risen Christ's glory. Paul prays that they may not be tempted away from their faith but may rather lead lives that will redound to the credit of Christ and also lead to their sharing in his glory (2 Thess 1:5-12).

*The day of the Lord (2 Thess 2:1-17).* Some in the congregation are being led to believe that they are living in the climactic period of history immediately preceding the future coming or advent of Christ *(parousia).* The hopes for an imminent future crisis and climax expressed in 1 Thessalonians could easily have made people feel that they really were living in the last time. Yet, despite all that was said there about the day of the Lord coming unexpectedly and soon, the coming of Christ must be preceded by other events. There will be some kind of "rebellion" and the rise of a powerful opponent to God, who will deceive people into unbelief. This opponent has not yet appeared because of some kind of restraining power. We cannot identify more precisely what Paul is talking about. The course of the struggle between God and his adversaries is mapped out (but not yet fully revealed).

Over against the people deceived by the power of Satan (cf. 2 Cor 4:3-4), Christian believers are assured of God's choice of them to be saved. Their salvation has come about through the work of God's Spirit (cf. 1 Thess 1:5-6) and at the same time through their belief in the "truth", the gospel message (2 Thess 2:13). Therefore they can be encouraged to stand firm in their faith. Once again, the paradox of divine protection and the need for human perseverance is sharply put.

*The place of prayer (2 Thess 3:1-18).* Paul requests prayer for himself and his work. He is confident of the protecting power of God (2 Thess 3:3). Yet he requests prayer for the progress of the mission and for his own safety (2 Thess 3:1-2). Equally he expresses confidence that his readers will remain faithful and still prays that God will enable them to persevere (2 Thess 3:4-5).

## THEOLOGICAL THEMES

The theology of these letters is characterized by its comparative simplicity. Various Pauline features are missing or play little part, such as the vocabulary of *flesh, body, sin, circumcision, law, works, righteousness/ justification,* and the concept of dying and rising with Christ. Much of this vocabulary is associated with Paul's struggle against opposition from so-called Judaizers, who insist on the need for Gentiles to keep the law in order to be truly part of God's people. The essential elements of life in Christ in the here and now are integral to Paul's theology in the letters.

*Mission and apostleship.* In 1 Thessalonians, Paul in large measure bases his appeal on an account of readers' conversion, encouraging them to continue as they have begun, despite the opposition that they are facing and that is destined to become even more fierce (cf. 2 Thess 1). The responsibility for encouraging people to become Christians rests on the apostles; put at its simplest, an apostle is a missionary. Apostles should show commitment to their work and loving concern for their converts. Their task is primarily speaking, but this is accompanied by power (1 Thess 1:5), probably including miraculous signs such as are related in Acts (Gal 3:5; cf. 2 Cor 12:12). Though Paul stresses that the message is expressed in human words, he also emphasizes the Holy Spirit's work, both in proclaiming the message and in receiving it: the converts have welcomed the message with joy given by the Holy Spirit.

*The gospel.* The message is summed up as "the gospel" (1 Thess 1:5; 2:2, 4, 8-9; 3:2). The word never loses its sense of "good news" but tends to be defined more by its specific content as the basic Christian message. The good news is about the death and resurrection of Jesus (1 Thess 4:14), as a result of which people receive salvation instead of experiencing the wrath of God (1 Thess 5:9-10). Throughout the two letters there is a forward look toward the future coming of Jesus. Past and future are closely integrated in that the death and resurrection of Jesus form the basis for this future hope.

*Conversion.* "Turning to God" is natural language to use for erstwhile pagans who had worshiped idols, but less appropriate for Jews who already believed in God. But it is rare compared with the key term *faith*, which signifies a complex of trust, commitment and obedience directed toward both God and his Son, Jesus. Faith is clearly the principal mark of Christians in their relationship toward God, just as it is of God's people in the Old Testament.

Conversion takes place on a human level when apostles and their companions tell people about what God has done to save them and people respond with the commitment of faith. Behind the conversion of the readers lies the initiative of God, expressed in terms of God's "call" to them (1 Thess 2:12; 4:7; 5:24). Paul also uses a term for *election* or *choice* (1 Thess 1:4; 2 Thess 2:13-14) to express the fact that the readers now belong to God as his people. God's choice of the readers is seen in the way in which they have accepted the gospel.

The preaching resulted in the establishment of a church or congregation (1 Thess 1:1), a term that implicitly identifies the readers as standing in continuity with God's people in the Old Testament.

*Steadfastness.* In these letters, Paul is particularly conscious of the activity of Satan ("the tempter"; 1 Thess 2:18; 3:5 NRSV; 2 Thess 2:9). Satan appears to have freedom to tempt people, and yet he can be thwarted by the overriding power of God. Why God does not simply defeat Satan once and for all is never asked; all that Paul knows is that God can defeat his enemies and that one day he will do so completely (cf. 2 Thess 2).

Despite the evil forces at work, there is divine power available to enable believers to resist them. Situations and people are changed through prayer; the rationale obviously is that God responds to what his people ask him to do. The perseverance of believers depends simultaneously on their own steadfastness and on the activity of God. They are to "stand firm in the Lord" (1 Thess 3:8 NRSV), relying on him to keep them. Being "in the Lord" or "in Christ" is distinctive Pauline language. Here it is simply a use of the appropriate construction after a verb to express the basis of the believers' firm stance. Adverbially it characterizes the close relationship between believers and Christ and the way in which their lives must be determined by him as the crucified and risen Lord (cf. 1 Thess 4:1; 5:12, 18). It is also used more adjectivally with the implication that there is some kind of spiritual bond between the readers and Christ (1 Thess 2:14; 4:16).

*Sanctification.* Holiness is the preferred term for the quality that God wishes to bring about in his people. This may be tied up with the preconversion lives of the predominantly Gentile believers at Thessalonica. The Old Testament concept of holiness signifies the position and character that believers already have as God's people and also the actual expression of that character as they grow and develop in their faith. All the soldiers on parade wear the uniform that marks them all out as soldiers, but some are still raw recruits, and others are trained and experienced; the goal is that all become trained soldiers through and through, not simply in appearance. "Holiness" is related to God's gift of the Holy Spirit (1 Thess

4:8); it is linked with blamelessness (1 Thess 3:13; 5:23) and is practically expressed in sexual purity, which entails faithfulness in marriage and the absence of passionate lust (1 Thess 4:3-8).

Alongside holiness stands the traditional triad of faith, love and hope (1 Thess 1:3; 5:8), which sums up the believers' relationships with God, other people and the future. Faith is the acceptance of the reality of God and commitment to him; it is the hallmark of conversion (1 Thess 1:8) and issues in an ongoing attitude of trust and obedience (1 Thess 3:2, 5, 6-7, 10), based on the conviction that Jesus died and rose again (1 Thess 4:14). "Believers" is the characteristic term for referring to Christians (1 Thess 1:7; 2:10, 13). Faith is closely linked with love (1 Thess 3:6; 5:8) as the attitude that believers should have toward one another (1 Thess 4:9-10). It also conveys the sense of "faithfulness", a nuance that expresses God's own utterly reliable character (1 Thess 5:24).

*The resurrection and the future advent of Christ.* These two letters stand out for the way in which they are dominated by the future (1 Thess 1:9-10; 2:19-20; 3:13; 4:13—5:11; 5:23; 2 Thess 1:7-10; 2:8). The Parousia is a significant sanction for Christian living in terms of reward and joy, but also of destruction and judgment.

There was a fear that those of the congregation who died would be at a disadvantage and be excluded from participation in the glorious events surrounding the Lord's second advent. It seems that the readers were familiar with the concept of the advent but had not grasped the concept of the resurrection of believers who had died. Paul insists that those who have died in Christ will be raised from the dead and will meet with the Lord before those still alive are caught up to meet him. If people have "fallen asleep" while being in a relationship with Christ, it surely follows that, just as he has died and has been resurrected, so too will they.

The advent will come as a surprise to unbelievers who are not waiting for it; unwelcomed, it will become judgment for them. But although believers cannot know the time of its arrival, they should always be ready and prepared for it—already, as it were, dressed, with their bags packed, so that they will not be ashamed to meet their Lord.

## CONCLUSION

Both letters have a strong orientation to the future, dealing with misunder-standings but emphasizing the centrality of the hope of Christ's coming. They also discuss the nature of mission and conversion for the Gentiles and develop a theology of the Christian life in terms of holiness.

# 9

# THE FIRST LETTER TO
# THE CORINTHIANS

In his first letter to the church at Corinth, Paul first addresses the disagreements of some of his readers with one another and with him and then takes up various issues raised by them. The letter is deeply theological in its application of the doctrine of the cross to the situation.

## THE THEOLOGICAL STORY

*Greeting and prayer report: The strengths of the congregation (1 Cor 1:1-9).* Paul's readers are called to be holy: they are God's people and must express their standing in their lifestyle. The influence of God's grace in their lives finds expression in spiritual gifts (cf. 1 Cor 12—14). As they look forward to the future revelation of Christ, God will keep them steadfast in their faith and behavior (1 Cor 1:4-9).

*Divisions, the cross and the Spirit (1 Cor 1:10—4:21).* Congregational meetings have become scenes of dissension between partisans of different Christian leaders: Paul himself, Apollos and Cephas (Peter). Others may have responded to the rivalry by countering, "I belong to Christ" (1 Cor

1:12 NRSV). What their distinctive views were is not clear, but there were some fairly serious deviations from Paul.

Paul responds with a theological version of "Grow up and stop bickering!" Putting their human idols on pedestals is not only boasting about human beings but also a subtle way of boasting about themselves. For Paul, the various missionaries are merely servants of God, each doing the specific task assigned to them; none is superior to any other, although Paul expects a loyalty to himself as their father in the gospel, equipped with authority from God.

Christian leaders and specifically apostles should preach the gospel of a crucified Christ—a Christ crucified in weakness and therefore not an object of boasting in a worldly manner. If the Savior was prepared to be so humbled, his servants and followers cannot indulge in pride.

The readers greatly prize wisdom and eloquence, and some despise Paul for lacking them (2 Cor 10:10). But his effectiveness as a preacher comes from the Holy Spirit as he preaches in a manner that befits the theme of a crucified Messiah. God's wise message is recognized as such only by mature people, who possess the Spirit of God and learn from him.

The vital elements in Paul's theology are plain: the weakness of Christ on the cross, which is nevertheless the only means of salvation; the concept of a divine wisdom that is identified with Christ; and the Spirit's work in revealing God's wisdom to believers who possess the Spirit.

*Sexual ethics and litigation (1 Cor 5:1—6:20).* Attention now shifts to three ethical issues. There is a case of incest (1 Cor 5:1-13). Paul insists that the church must discipline the offender and "hand this man over to Satan", which may lead to his ultimate salvation. Toleration of the unrepentant sinner is a blemish that renders the whole church sinful. Blatant sins are incompatible with Christian faith and exclude people from the kingdom of God (1 Cor 6:9-10). But Christian believers are delivered from such sins and their contaminating effects through the act of washing, sanctification and justification.

Second, believers are cheating one another and engaging in litigation before secular courts (1 Cor 6:1-11). They should not take their differences to secular courts. They should remember that one day the saints will share in Christ's judgment on the world.

Third, Paul returns to sexual immorality, but now in more general terms (1 Cor 6:12-20). Some believe that "I have the right to do anything" (1 Cor 6:12). For Paul, the bodies that will be raised from the dead by God must not be used for sinful purposes, such as prostitution. The bodies of believers belong to Christ and therefore should not be united to sinners. Believers are the dwelling places of the Holy Spirit, and they belong to Christ, who has bought them at the high price of his death (1 Cor 6:19-20).

*Problems regarding marriage (1 Cor 7).* Paul upholds marriage as the only divinely authorized setting for sexual activity. Underlying his practical advice on problems such as divorce and remarriage lie such factors as these: the obligation to live a holy life in obedience to divine commands, awareness of the future coming of the Lord, and concern for the work of the Lord. To some extent he relies on his own cognition of God's will in these matters as an apostle entrusted with revelation from God.

*Food and idolatry (1 Cor 8:1—11:1).* May Christians eat food, specifically meat, that has first been offered as a sacrifice to an idol? Certainly worship in a temple, where demonic powers are at work, is incompatible with worshiping God alone. However, since idols do not really exist and there is only one God the Creator (and also, importantly, one Lord Jesus Christ), believers can eat such meat at home without it symbolizing worship of the idol. Yet such eaters must take account of Christian observers who really think that idols exist and that taking such food is a form of worship. The eaters' example may lead these observers to go against their own conscience and commit what is for them a sin. Loving concern for others must override the claims of personal freedom. Paul insists on the rights of the apostles to claim financial and material support from the congregations and then equally firmly insists that he has refused to take his rights, all as part of the surrender of his freedom in order to win people for Christ.

*The conduct of congregational meetings (1 Cor 11:2-34).* At the church meeting with its common meal, some people eat and drink to excess, whereas others go hungry, thus emphasizing social division in the church. For Paul, this was not recognizing the church as church, where there is neither Jew nor Greek, neither free nor slave, and neither rich nor poor. Paul has already mentioned the incompatibility of eating at idolatrous feasts and at the Lord's Supper, since the latter involves both sharing in the body and blood of Christ and uniting the participants with one another as one body (1 Cor 10:16-17). Now, citing the account of the Last Supper held by Jesus, Paul teaches that at this meal, believers partake of bread, which represents the body of Christ for them, and of the cup, which represents the new covenant in his blood, so that they remember Jesus and proclaim his death.

At this sacred occasion people may partake unworthily through failure to recognize the "body". This can refer to recognition that the bread represents the body of Christ who died on the cross or that the church gathered together is his body; lack of love for fellow members has theological significance. Either way, the Lord may act in judgment against those who sin.

*Spiritual gifts and people (1 Cor 12—14).* Spiritual gifts *(pneumatika)*, or "grace gifts" *(charismata)*, are Spirit-inspired qualities or the actions facilitated by them, which function as forms of congregational ministry (including prophesying, healing, teaching) or as spiritual exercises (such as praising God in languages unknown to the speaker or the hearers) benefiting the person exercising them.

Such phenomena do not necessarily originate from the Spirit. Granted that people cannot make the Christian confession "Jesus is Lord" except when led by the Spirit, they might make statements that are clearly not Spirit-inspired and are purely human or possibly even inspired by evil spirits. This seems to have applied in particular to the utterances of prophets (1 Cor 14:29; cf. 1 Jn 4:1-6). It is necessary to "test" the utterances.

Some gifts are thought to express the higher worth of those who exercise them. Paul uses the analogy of the parts of the body to show that gifts may be varied in usefulness, but this does not affect the worth of the gifts and their bearers, all of whom are equally interdependent parts of the same body, inspired and empowered by the same divine source.

Without love as the supremely necessary gift, all other spiritual gifts are valueless; this understanding rules out all thoughts of superiority and rivalry. Faith, hope and love are what matter; they alone will survive into the world to come.

*Affirmation of the resurrection (1 Cor 15).* Some people are apparently denying that physically dead people will be brought back to life. They may think that Christians have been resurrected (spiritually) at their conversion, and that resurrection is nothing more than this.

For Paul, the resurrection of Jesus is an integral part of the apostolic gospel. It was attested by a large group of reliable witnesses and was sufficient to establish the fact that dead people can be raised from the dead. The argument, repeated in various forms, is that if the dead cannot be raised, then Christ as one of them was not raised, but in fact he was raised. On this resurrection depends the possibility of sins being forgiven and Christian hope for those who have died. Christ's resurrection is the first stage in bringing life to the world and conquering the power of death and all that is opposed to God. He will reign until his second coming and the raising of the dead, and then he will, as it were, hand over the spoils of his victory to his Father.

Paul uses the analogy of the way in which apparently dead seeds are sown in the soil, and then they burst into a new and glorious life. A perishable body is "sown", and an incorruptible, eternal one springs from it. All this takes place somehow in and through Christ, who rose from the dead to become a life-giving spirit, conveying eternal life and resurrection to his followers.

*Closing matters (1 Cor 16).* Finally, Paul says that people who do not love the Lord stand under a curse. This is followed by a cry of *Marana tha* (the Aramaic phrase for "Come, Lord"), apparently as a backup warning directed against persistent sinners.

## THEOLOGICAL THEMES

This letter is concerned as much with Christian behavior as with belief. Its framework of thinking is strange to many people, with its acceptance of a world in which the Holy Spirit and Satan and demonic spirits can influence and affect human behavior, in which the ending of the world is taken for granted, and in which dead people can be brought back to life in a new and imperishable manner.

*The center of the gospel.* Paul cites various statements that he has inherited and has passed down because of their authoritative character. Especially important is the summary of the gospel, acceptance of which leads to salvation (1 Cor 15:1-5). His gospel is identical with that of the other apostles. Its center is the affirmation that Christ died for our sins according to the Scriptures and was raised from the dead. Another traditional passage, introduced by a similar rubric, contains the words of the Lord at the Last Supper; the congregational meal was accordingly understood as a proclamation of his death and its significance: his body (given in death) was "for you", and through (the shedding of) his blood a new covenant was inaugurated (1 Cor 11:23-26). The crucifixion and resurrection of Christ has happened "as the Scriptures foretold" (1 Cor 15:3 Phillips), as part of the prophesied purpose of God. The center of the gospel is not the second coming of Jesus (or anything else) but the saving event that has already happened.

*The cross and the divisions in the congregation.* Paul uses this doctrine to deal with the disunity at Corinth. The practice of spiritual gifts has become the most prized characteristic; Christianity is in danger of becoming a religion of spiritual achievement and hence of pride in human position. But the message of the cross utters a decisive "No" to all this. Here Christ's death is an expression of weakness and shame, the last extremity in humiliation, and yet paradoxically it is also the expression of divine power. It is the supreme instance of the way in which God works by doing something that to human eyes is foolish and weak (cf. Phil 2:6-8). The cross is offensive to a world that looks for respectability and even assumes that God will be manifested by showy, miraculous interventions compelling belief.

Yet the cross is both wise and powerful; through it God pulls down the wise and mighty and exalts the foolish and weak. Christ is now powerful; he was crucified in weakness, but "he lives by God's power" (2 Cor 13:4). So God's weakness displayed in the cross is in the end stronger than human strength, and this strength is manifested in the resurrection. In Romans Paul insists that nobody can raise their head in God's presence through works of the law; here he insists that nobody can do so on grounds of power or wisdom.

Paul condemns the merely human wisdom of philosophers and orators, which has failed to find God by its own efforts and stands under his judgment. Preachers of the gospel do not persuade people by means of what seems wise in the eyes of human beings, but by preaching the crucifixion of the Savior. The congregation is meant to live by the paradigm of the cross: it renounces human power and wisdom as qualities in which it can boast and by which other people measure it. Instead, like the apostles, it must value the wisdom and power of God, which are of no value in human eyes and look only for God's rewards (which are real enough).

*Apostles, ministers, servants.* The role of the missionaries (1 Cor 3:5—4:5) is to plant congregations and encourage their growth (the field metaphor) or to lay a foundation and build a congregation on it (the building metaphor). They share in God's work; the foundation is a "given" from God, and the actual growth is produced by God. Although there is to be no human evaluation and assessment of the workers, nevertheless the metaphor of reward and loss is used to indicate that they are responsible to God for the quality of their work as his delegates.

*Jesus Christ, his status and role.* Although crucified in weakness, Jesus now lives in power (2 Cor 13:4), and he is the *Lord* to his followers (1 Cor 12:3). This term refers to the authority of Jesus as teacher (1 Cor 7:10; 9:14) and also to his supreme position alongside God the Father (1 Cor 8:5-6). They are the only divine figures over against the so-called gods and lords of the non-Christian world, beings, whether real (like the emperor) or imaginary (like the numerous deities in the polytheistic world). When Old Testament language is being used, the title *Lord* is appropriately employed and interpreted as a reference to Jesus (1 Cor 10:9). As the Lord he will return in glory (1 Cor 1:7; 4:5).

Paul also uses the term *Christ*. The church is the body, not of the Lord, but of Christ (1 Cor 6:15; 12:12, 27), and it is Christ who was crucified—except in 1 Corinthians 2:8, where the enormity of the outrage is depicted: they crucified *the Lord of glory*. Paul uses *Christ* as a significant name and prefers it to the simple *Jesus*. The identity of Jesus as the Messiah has become so natural that it is easy to use the title as a name; there is no need to reckon with any other possible claimants for the position, since there are and can be none. For Christians, the original Jewish associations of *Christ* are retreating somewhat into the background, and the significance of the name is being defined in terms of the role enacted by Jesus.

*The Holy Spirit.* The Spirit and the Spirit's gifts play a significant role in the theology of this letter. Paul thanks God for the gifts of speaking and knowledge, which are part of a broader range of charismata bestowed on the readers (1 Cor 1:5-7). These gifts, here said to be given "in Christ", are the gifts imparted by the Spirit, who comes into a living relationship with individual believers and bestows different gifts upon them.

The only entity that knows how a person thinks is that person's own "spirit", by which Paul presumably means their own conscious mind (1 Cor 2:11). If the same is true of God, human beings cannot know his mind unaided. God himself must reveal his thoughts to believers. Since they have received the Spirit, they can now understand what God says through his apostles and prophets. Other "natural" people (those "without the Spirit") may hear the same words and either fail to understand what is being said or refuse to accept their truth. To them, what God says—specifically, in the message of the cross—is foolishness.

People are washed, sanctified and justified "in the name of the Lord Jesus Christ and by the Spirit of our God" (1 Cor 6:11). Conversion thus takes place by virtue of what Christ has done, but the Spirit is the agent in applying it to the individual. He is not an outside agent but is said to be "in" believers. The concept of God's presence in the world is familiar in Judaism and has its roots in the Old Testament, where God was present in the temple and his Spirit was envisaged as being in or with individual members of his people (1 Sam 10:10; Ps 51:11; Is 61:1). So here the metaphor of the temple is applied both to individual believers (1 Cor 6:19) and to the congregation as the place in which the Spirit of God is resident (1 Cor 3:16).

In 1 Corinthians 12:13, Paul comments that all members of the congregation have drunk of the one Spirit. The metaphor is not that of people drinking with their mouths but rather that of plants in a field being sprinkled with rain or being watered by the farmer (cf. 1 Cor 3:7-8), and it draws upon the imagery in Isaiah 32:15: just as the plants absorb the moisture, so the members of the congregation receive the Spirit into themselves. They receive the spiritually enabling gifts of God associated with particular functions that they are called upon to perform in the congregation. These charismata can be attributed to the Spirit, the Lord, and God, thereby indicating that no hard and fast line can be drawn between the activities of the different persons to whom Paul assigns divine status.

People said to be lacking in the Spirit are not able to receive and understand his message (1 Cor 3:1). They are still dominated by their non-Christian character and are like mere infants. Evidently, therefore, Paul conceives of progressively developing fuller insight, thanks to the working of the Spirit. People can be more and more enabled by the Spirit to appreciate and understand the mind of God, but this development can be arrested by sub-Christian forms of behavior (specifically, envy and quarrelling); people can return to making spiritual progress through repentance and turning away from these sins.

*The life of the congregation.* The congregation consists of "believers" distinctively characterized by "faith" (1 Cor 2:5; 14:22-23; 15:11, 14, 17; 16:13). The beginning of faith (1 Cor 3:5; 15:2) is marked by baptism (yet more important than being a person who baptizes is being a preacher of the gospel; 1 Cor 1:13-17). Describing Christians as people who have been washed, sanctified and justified (1 Cor 6:11) may allude to the symbolism of baptism. Out of these three terms, the second one *(sanctified)* provides the other characteristic self-description of Christians alongside "believers" (1 Cor 1:2; 6:1-2; 14:33; 16:1, 15). Those who believe can also be described as "the saved" (1 Cor 1:18, 21; 15:2; cf. 3:15).

In no other letter is the Spirit's place in the congregation's communal life discussed so fully as here. Already in 1 Corinthians 1:7 the presence of spiritual gifts in the congregation is applauded. The Spirit is seen to be the agent in conversion and the means whereby God's revelation is received. But in chapter 12 the Spirit is the source of various gifts. *Gifts* are placed in parallelism with *services* and *sources of power:* the three terms refer to essentially the same activities from different aspects. They convey the idea of a divine equipping or empowering to perform acts that would otherwise not be possible. They are related to apprehension of God's words and powers so as to act as his agents. They equip people to act on behalf of God, thus serving him and acting as his agents. Very broadly, the actions are similar to those carried out by Christ in his earthly life with the help of the Spirit. The fact that they can be counterfeited does not call in question the reality of the genuine article. The tests may not be infallible, but there are certain guidelines—denial of Christ and lack of accompanying love are among them.

Congregational meetings accordingly are occasions where God may communicate in word and deed with his people through the agency of any participant, as they are given God's gifts enabling them to function on his behalf with spiritual insight and power. The outsider who comes in rightly concludes that God is among them. Clearly this realization should lead to a sense of awe and worship; praise and prayer are the appropriate responses to the presence and activity of God.

Paul relativizes all the gifts by his insistence on the superiority of love. Still, he cannot avoid a certain ranking in that one should desire to prophesy rather than to speak in tongues, and he recognizes that apostles, prophets and teachers stand at the head of a list in which the gift of tongues comes last. So, though the body metaphor stresses that all are necessary and essential, yet some are more valuable than others.

Although God grants the gifts as he wills, Paul still encourages people to desire the gifts, especially prophecy. The divine apportionment of the gifts is somehow related to the people's prayers. The person on whom God bestows a gift evidently retains control of its use: the spirits of the prophets are subject to the prophets. People with the gift of tongues can and should refrain from exercising it in inappropriate circumstances. The linking of the gifts with service indicates that the possession of a gift carries with it the obligation to use it in serving God as he directs.

*The resurrection of Christ and of believers.* Paul uses the parallelism between God's raising of the Lord and of believers as an argument against sexual intercourse outside of marriage (1 Cor 6:14). The assumption is that raising up is an activity concerned with believers' bodies; a nonbodily resurrection would be irrelevant to the argument here.

In 1 Corinthians 15 Paul's first concern is to establish that dead believers will be raised, a point denied by some of his readers. Christ could not have risen if in principle there can be no resurrection. There would be no hope for those who died believing in Christ. There would also be no forgiveness of sins, since justification is granted to those who believe specifically in the God who raised Jesus from the dead (Rom 4:24-25) and thereby accepted the death of his Son as efficacious.

Christ's resurrection is the pledge of believers' resurrection. The first part of the harvest to be collected is by definition the first part of the larger harvest that is sure to follow. The offering of the firstfruits signifies that the harvest has begun: the general resurrection of God's people has commenced! The resurrection of Jesus is not a onetime event involving only one person, for believers are united with him (cf. esp. Rom 5—6). Alongside the resurrection of believers, Paul also includes the final defeat of the powers of evil arrayed against God and his people. There can be no lasting salvation so long as these powers are still free and active.

Some object to the notion of a *bodily* resurrection. Maybe the objection is that a human body is perishable, so what is the point of resurrecting it? Paul uses the analogy of sowing, where the seed dies and is raised to life in a quite different form as a plant. There are various kinds of flesh and body. So a new sort of body at the resurrection is not surprising. It will be incorruptible and spiritual, like that of the risen Christ.

## CONCLUSION

What stands out particularly in this letter is the place of the cross, or rather, of Christ crucified, as determining Christian behavior. This is a significant counterbalance to any tendencies to depend on human ideas or even to isolate the Spirit as the determining factor in Christian experience. To this letter we also owe the fullest treatment of the resurrection in the New Testament. And nowhere else is the topic of spiritual gifts treated in such depth. These emphases all arise in response to tendencies in the church to prize both human wisdom and spiritual charismata and to deny the future resurrection of believers. First Corinthians is thus a particularly good example of the way in which local problems determine the agenda for Paul. He works from his existing theology to deal with the particular ways in which theological and ethical problems are posed to him.

# 10

# THE SECOND LETTER TO THE CORINTHIANS

Second Corinthians is largely concerned with Paul's own personal circumstances and his relationship with a difficult congregation. He prepares the way for a forthcoming visit by describing how the relationship has been broken and restored (2 Cor 1—9), and then he defends himself against a group who disparages his apostolic mission (2 Cor 10—13).

## THE THEOLOGICAL STORY: 2 CORINTHIANS 1—7

*Paul's experience of suffering (2 Cor 1:1—2:13).* Paul has been near death but gives thanks for his deliverance from it in a manner that he can ascribe only to God himself. Believers know what it is to suffer because of their faith but also to experience divine comfort amid their afflictions and so come to a greater trust in God, as they are united in prayer for one another (2 Cor 1:1-7).

Paul has apparently been accused of selfish inconsistency, saying that he would visit Corinth and then not doing so. But he claims that the faithful God who works in us does not vacillate. What appears to be a change of plans because of self-interest is really because he wants to spare his readers a painful visit from him. Instead he has written a letter promoting reconciliation; consequently, disciplinary action has been taken against a person who has wronged him, and now it is possible to go on to forgive the offender who is sorrowful for what has happened (2 Cor 1:8—2:13).

*The ministry of the new covenant (2 Cor 2:14—7:16).* Paul theologically discusses the implications of all this. Missionaries spread the knowledge of Christ, which may lead to life and salvation or to death and judgment, depending on the reaction of the hearers. They do not need any commendation because the believers themselves are evidence of their carrying out the task of "ministry" *(diakonia),* for which God has equipped them (2 Cor 2:14—3:3).

New covenant service is glorious compared with that of the old covenant. The old brought condemnation by imposing commandments that people were not able to keep, but the new covenant brings the life-giving gift of the Spirit. Mediating the covenants is associated with glory, seen in the physical radiance of Moses' face, which was too bright for the Israelites to bear. The veil that Moses wore signified their inability to understand the old covenant; understanding and salvation come only when people turn to "the Lord", here understood as the Spirit of God, who transforms them into the divine likeness and glory (2 Cor 3:4-18).

The glory of the covenant belongs to its task, not its servants, and thus is not a basis for worldly boasting. Nevertheless, the apostles can be confident even when they face opposition and apparent failure. When people do not respond positively to the gospel, this is due to a satanic blindness to the gospel. When they believe, Christ's glory is revealed to them through the work of the missionaries (2 Cor 4:1-6).

God thus makes his power and glory known through weak human beings. Like the crucified and risen Jesus, the missionaries are always dying in order to bring life. The knowledge that God brings life through their death encourages them to press on in faith. They may face suffering and death, but their vision is focused on the God who bestows life (2 Cor 4:7-18).

Even though their human bodies may perish, they have a heavenly body prepared by God. The future life is not some kind of bodiless existence. The gift of the Spirit already received by believers is a down payment, the first installment of what is to come. A new "spiritual" body is already in process of formation "in" the believer, rather like the development of the butterfly within the chrysalis. With such a hope, believers must now live in a way that will please the God before whom they will one day be judged (2 Cor 5:1-10).

Paul hopes that this exposition of the nature of apostleship, and hence of the character of Christian existence generally, will commend his work to doubters who want some other kind of leadership. Whatever he does springs from God's love, which drives him to urge people to get right with God. Almost in passing, he uses the picture of "a new creation" (2 Cor 5:17; cf. Gal 6:15): a converted person is a new creature, and a new society is formed in which worldly distinctions like circumcised/uncircumcised no longer matter. A more fully developed picture is that of reconciliation, in which a diplomat brings about peace between two estranged parties. Christ is the agent through whom God himself acts in such a way that the sins which have separated people from God no longer count against them, cutting them off from God's friendship. By identifying himself with sinners (literally, with sin) and dying for them, Christ has made it possible for sinners to be regarded as righteous and to have a right standing with God (2 Cor 5:11—6:2).

The missionaries have undergone every kind of hardship; they have undertaken their task in dependence upon God and with utter commitment. Through it all runs the paradox of strength in weakness and weakness in strength (2 Cor 6:3-10). A further appeal to reconciliation (2 Cor 6:11-13) is followed by a call to separation from unbelievers, who would lead them into sin and so separate them from the God who lives in their midst. Being holy is an ongoing process (2 Cor 6:14—7:2).

## THE THEOLOGICAL STORY: 2 CORINTHIANS 8—9

An appeal for practical generosity in aiding the poor believers in Jerusalem forms the basis for a theology of giving. Central is the example of Jesus, who became poor so that others through his poverty might become rich; the metaphorical language refers to the self-emptying of the incarnation (2 Cor 8:9). Poverty is not an ascetic ideal to be cultivated for its own sake but a condition voluntarily endured so that other people who are poor may be enriched (2 Cor 8:13-15). God enriches people so that they may have the resources to help other people generously (2 Cor 9:10). People should not simply give out of their surplus: the people singled out for praise have given despite being comparatively poor themselves (2 Cor 8:1-5). The effect of the giving will be praise to God as the ultimate giver of the generous gift (2 Cor 9:13-15).

## THE THEOLOGICAL STORY: 2 CORINTHIANS 10—13

Despite the reconciliation announced earlier, a group of people still think that Paul has adopted worldly methods rather than (presumably) God's methods in his work. His self-defense is admittedly on a more human level but incorporates statements of theological significance. Mission and pastoral care are aspects of a spiritual conflict whose outcome depends on confuting worldly arguments and preaching Christ as Lord (2 Cor 10:3-6; cf. 2 Cor 4:1-6). Apostles have authority in the congregation (2 Cor 10:8), not only to preach the gospel but also to build up the congregations that they have founded. They may even perform "the signs of a true apostle", including wonders and miracles (2 Cor 12:12 NRSV). Delegates of Christ should put themselves entirely in the hands of God and not commend themselves (2 Cor 10:12-18).

The missionary task can thus be seen metaphorically as the presentation of a chaste virgin to her husband, the congregation to Christ as its Lord (cf. Eph 5:25-32), and this requires an ongoing apostolic task of preserving the congregation from error, sin and disloyalty to Christ (2 Cor 11:2-3). This is not helped by the presence of false missionaries, whom Paul calls emissaries of Satan (2 Cor 11:14-15) because they tolerate sin in the congregation (cf. 2 Cor 12:21) and promote a "different gospel".

Paul responds to these "super-apostles" (2 Cor 11:5; 12:11) in several ways. He picks up on their self-commendation and replies to it by ironically descending to their own level in putting forward his own grounds for boasting (2 Cor 11:21—12:10). Paul claims to have worked harder than they (cf. 1 Cor 15:10) and to have undergone more humiliating experiences. Although he can even boast of having visions of paradise, he has been subjected to some intense weakening experience, from which he can get no respite other than God promising Paul that he will experience God's grace amid his weakness.

Having defended himself, Paul issues a stern warning that action will be taken against sinners. For there is a limit to the weakness of the apostles: Christ, who died in weakness, is now alive by the power of God and exercises his authority through the apostles. Let the readers test themselves to see whether Christ is in them and they are truly believers (2 Cor 13:1-10).

The closing benediction refers to the grace and love coming from Jesus Christ and God and to participation in the Spirit (2 Cor 13:14). This threefold way of referring to Christian experience of divine blessings underlies the development of understanding God as Trinity.

## THEOLOGICAL THEMES

*The God of comfort.* The teaching dominating this letter concerns the mysterious combination of suffering and joy, life and death, which suffuses the life of the Christian believer. Underlying it is the central *theology* in Paul's letters: the Christian God is their focus. Jesus Christ has not replaced the Father but rather has brought a new understanding of God as Father through his own relationship to him as Son. Paul begins with God, as the source of apostleship, the Lord of the church, and the source of grace and peace for his people (2 Cor 1:1-2). God is the source of compassion and comfort in the sufferings that Paul has been enduring (2 Cor 1:3). In a situation that has seemed totally hopeless and utterly depressing, Paul realizes that he can still rely on the God who raises the dead, whether via rescue from a lethal situation or resurrection through physical death to eternal life.

This hope and faith rest on three facts. God has exemplarily raised Jesus from the dead, he is a God of grace and compassion who cares for his people, and he is faithful (2 Cor 1:18; cf. 1 Cor 1:9; 10:13; 1 Thess 5:24; 2 Thess 3:3; 2 Tim 2:13). Present now with his people (who form his living temple, 2 Cor 6:16), God will not abandon them to death and destruction.

*Jesus Christ—suffering and powerful.* Every aspect of God's character is related to Christ. His life-giving power is seen primarily in the resurrection of Christ, and on this basis, Paul affirms the resurrection of believers (2 Cor 4:14). His grace was shown by Christ in becoming poor that others might become rich (2 Cor 8:9); Paul moves to and fro between the grace of God and the grace of Christ (2 Cor 8:1; 9:14; 12:9). The grace of Christ is paired with the love of God. *Grace* brings out more explicitly the way in which God's love contains the elements of spontaneous compassion for the needy and the undeserving. The faithfulness of God is expressed in Christ, who is the proof that God fulfills his promises.

Christ is the archetypical exemplar of the mystery of death and life, suffering and power, humiliation and exaltation. Paul contrasts the "riches" that he originally possessed before the incarnation compared with the "poverty" that he assumed by becoming a mere mortal and taking the role of a slave (cf. Phil 2:7), although some think the reference is to the contrast between his fellowship with God and the nature of his death (2 Cor 8:9). His human life and death were characterized by poverty and weakness, the opposite of what would be expected in the case of a mighty Savior.

*Sin and the work of the missionaries.* Human life is characterized not only by weakness but also by sinfulness. The task of Christian missionaries is to spread the message of Christ, which radiates life or death to the sinners who hear it. To know Christ brings life; to reject him incurs death. Unbelievers are blind to the light given by Christ and are perishing. Controlled by the love of Christ, Paul is engaged in persuasion, based upon what has been achieved by Christ's death.

*The new creation.* All people who join themselves to Jesus by faith are joined to him in his death and resurrection, so that they can be said to have died and risen like him (cf. Gal 2:19-20). This sets them free from the old self-centered life, with sin and rebellion against God, and enables them to live for Christ. In other words, a new creation has begun in Christ, and it takes in everybody who is "in Christ". There is now a new world in which the old categories of circumcised and uncircumcised no longer count for anything, for God has made all things new through Jesus' resurrection.

*Reconciliation.* Paul sees himself as God's ambassador who appeals to people to be reconciled to God. In the first instance, this appeal is directed to those who are sinners and unbelievers, but Paul uses this language here to appeal for harmony and peace within the congregation and with himself. The basis for the appeal is that God was in Christ, reconciling the world to himself, not counting their sins against them. Put otherwise, God made Christ, who had no sin, to be sin for us, so that we might become the righteousness of God (2 Cor 5:11-21).

Here the language of diplomacy provides the imagery. There is a two-sided action. God is said to have reconciled us to himself through Christ and then passed on to his people the agency of reconciliation: it is the church's task to announce an amnesty to sinners. But the message that is passed on does not simply say, "Everything is now all right, because God has reconciled the world to himself"; rather it says, "We urge you on behalf of Christ: be reconciled to God". Without a response to God's initiative, no reconciliation can take place. If the offer is not accepted, people continue to live in alienation from God.

Reconciliation is necessary because people have committed sins against God. These create a barrier because they are acts of rebellion against God and come under his condemnation. The ground of reconciliation is the fact that Christ became sin. Paul cannot say that Christ became a sinner, which would have been seriously misleading. He therefore says that Christ has become one with sin. Thereby a kind of exchange could take place: sinners may become one with him who was sinless and righteous, and thus share in his sinlessness and righteousness.

This transfer depends on the fact that "one died for all, and therefore all died" (2 Cor 5:14). Here it is made clear that his death is equivalent to the death of other people. Since Paul regards the due recompense for sin as death (Rom 6:23; cf. Rom 5:12), he must regard the death of Jesus as his reception of the wage for sin; after its due payment, nothing further stands against the sinner. Christ has displayed full obedience to God in contrast to the disobedience of sinners; his positive act of obedience in dying cancels out their sin. Sinners who identify themselves with him in his death come out from under their condemnation to death.

*The life of believers: Weakness and strength.* The present weakness of believers will be followed by future resurrection, but the power of God is already manifested here and now in the midst of weakness (2 Cor 4; 12:7-10). The weakness is the believers' situation seen from a worldly point of view: a body vulnerable to injury, disease and death; an existence threatened by poverty and deprivation; and their status as "nothing" in the eyes of other people. Their strength is the experience of God's grace, which enables them to cope with this situation and to accept it; the inner communion with God, which imparts a sense of being loved and of consequent joy; and the power to communicate the gospel effectively and thus bring life to other people. This strength does not depend on human position and possessions. The gospel is a divine and not a human power, and there is nothing special about the messengers of the gospel. They are likened to the captives being led in the victorious general's celebratory procession to humiliation and death (2 Cor 2:14a; cf. 1 Cor 4:13). Yet they are messengers of the new covenant; and if the old covenant was accompanied by glory, how much more true must this be of the new covenant? All believers behold the Lord and so reflect his glory as they are transformed into his likeness (2 Cor 3:18; 4:6). The transformation of believers has the effect of making them more Christlike in their character.

*Death, judgment and transformation.* This continuous transformation leads finally to a state of eternal glory; in comparison, the present sufferings are considered light and brief (2 Cor 5:1-10). The destruction of our temporary earthly tent in death will be followed by the acquisition of a permanent, heavenly dwelling. Using the metaphor of receiving new clothing, Paul affirms that the dead will not survive in some bodiless manner. The Holy Spirit is already given to believers as a first installment of the new life, although we who are now in the body are, at least in a relative sense, "absent from the Lord" and walk by faith. The future prospect places a spiritual requirement upon all people to do what pleases the Lord, since all must appear before his judgment.

It is not easy to fit together what Paul says in different letters using varying imagery about the believer's state after death (cf. 1 Cor 15:50-55; Phil 1:20-26). The crucial element is that believers who have died are "at home with the Lord" (2 Cor 5:8).

*Boasting.* Second Corinthians juxtaposes weakness and strength, as exemplified in Christ himself, in Paul's missionary experience and in the lives of ordinary believers. Being conformed to Jesus' death and sharing in his resurrection life are counted not only as a temporal sequence (dying now, resurrection to follow) but also as simultaneous. The life and the corresponding power and glory are entirely God's gift. Consequently there is no place for boasting in the Christian life. If Paul boasts or, better, exults in his converts, it is because of what God is doing in their lives (2 Cor 7:4). Sometimes evaluating oneself and one's work for the Lord seems to require comparisons with other people. Faced by opponents who evidently denigrated him, Paul had to resort to some kind of self-defense in the interests of the gospel. He says that he can express confidence and pride on a human (fleshly) level (2 Cor 11:18), but when he does so, he lists not typical achievements for which others are proud, but rather weaknesses and humiliating situations, such as fleeing ignominiously from Damascus. He refuses to boast of his visions of the Lord, but only of his weaknesses. Instead, he talks about having "a thorn in my flesh", an affliction that persists despite his longing to be rid of it. He had to learn to be strong in weakness. Even then he is not saying that he can be proud of having the spiritual stamina to cope with ongoing weakness; he simply says that in weakness he experiences divine grace (2 Cor 12:7-10).

## CONCLUSION

Above all, this letter offers a theology of suffering from one who is qualified by experience to talk about it. The fragility of the believer's life is always in view. It is a combination of ordinary human weakness as a creature of flesh with the weakness involved in identifying with Christ in his vulnerability and suffering on humankind's behalf. Such a fragile life is sustained by the new life already being imparted by God, which will be fully experienced in the renewal of the body.

# 11

# THE LETTER TO THE ROMANS

Romans prepares the way for Paul's anticipated journey via Rome to evangelize in Spain. He wants to share his understanding of the gospel with a church that he himself has not personally founded. So he has to discuss the place of Jews and Gentiles in God's plan of salvation and their mutual relationship in the church. The main body of the letter lays the doctrinal foundation for Paul's practical teaching in Romans 12—15. On what terms does God accept Gentiles? What is the place of the Jewish law in this matter (Rom 1—8)? And if Gentiles on the whole are responding positively to the gospel but Jews are not, how do we explain the unbelief of so many Jews, since Israel was named by God as his chosen people? Is God dealing justly with humanity, both Jews and Gentiles, in justifying the ungodly Gentiles and apparently no longer being faithful to his promises to the chosen people, the Jews (Rom 9—11)?

## THE THEOLOGICAL STORY: THE GOSPEL ACCORDING TO PAUL (ROM 1:1—8:39)

*Greeting and prayer report (Rom 1:1-17).* Paul introduces himself as a person set apart by God to be a missionary of the gospel. This gospel was promised in the Scriptures, and Scripture will be quoted extensively as an accepted authority in this letter. The content of the gospel is Jesus, the Messiah and Son of God. God's purpose is to call together a people drawn from all the peoples of the world who are committed to him in faith. It is a message that is powerful in conveying salvation to those who believe. All people need to be saved, and they can be saved through faith. The gospel makes possible a right relationship with God, which comes from him and depends entirely on faith (and therefore not on something else), as Scripture itself testifies. Salvation is thus redefined in terms of righteousness for believers.

*Universal sin and guilt (Rom 1:18—3:20).* God's wrath against sinners extends to all people, because they are all sinners. His revelation in nature should have been recognizable by people at large (the non-Jews), but they have rejected it and instead worshiped idols. Therefore God let their lives be taken over by sins that destroy human life and finally lead to eternal death. The Jews are in no better state, despite having God's revelation in history and Scripture. Even those who do not fall into the grosser sins fall short in other ways and are equally culpable. God's patience with them should be seen as a merciful act intended to encourage repentance before it is too late. Mere possession of the law gives the Jews no advantage, since what matters is obedience to what one knows of God's requirements. Observance of circumcision is worthless if it is not accompanied by obedience to the other commandments; Gentiles (not required to be circumcised) who obey the (moral) requirements of the law are in as good a position as Jews or better. Although God's covenant with the Jews as his people is not canceled by their failure, individual sinful Jews stand under judgment. All that the law can do is to make them aware of their sin by labeling their evil conduct as sinful.

*Justification by grace through faith (Rom 3:21-31).* In response to this situation, God has now revealed a righteousness that comes through faith in Jesus Christ. Although *righteousness* can mean the *quality* of treating people fairly, as demonstrated by God (including his provision of salvation; Rom 3:26), here it probably indicates the *action* of God or the *status* that he will confer on people, which they cannot gain by observing the law. To be justified is to be put into a right relationship with God; when the sins that people have committed are no longer counted against them, they can enter into a relationship with God characterized by peace and not by wrath.

Justification is motivated by God's *grace*, his merciful attitude toward sinners. It entails an act of "redemption" or "deliverance" from enslavement both to sin and to its attendant consequences (cf. Rom 6:23).

Redemption comes about through God putting Jesus forward "as a *sacrifice of atonement*" *(hilastērion)*. This term may be (1) a noun signifying the lid on the ark of the tabernacle, on which was sprinkled the blood of sacrifices making atonement for the people's sins (Lev 16:14); or (2) an adjective signifying the effect of that blood in bringing an end to God's wrath against sin. God himself provides this remedy for the sins committed against himself, thereby delivering sinners from his wrath, to which they would otherwise be exposed. The death of Jesus (symbolized here by "blood") functions like the animal sacrifices, thus making the latter redundant.

Finally, it is through the *faith* of individuals that justification becomes a reality in their lives. Since justification does not depend upon observance of the Jewish law (in particular circumcision), there is no place for "boasting", a term that combines the nuances of trusting or being confident in something, regarding it as a human achievement, and thinking oneself superior to other people who have not achieved it (cf. Phil 3:3-4).

*The justification of Abraham (Rom 4:1-25).* Now for possible Jewish objections to Paul's teaching! Abraham, the ancestor of the Jewish people, was thought to have been put in the right with God by his "work" when he obeyed God's commands, including specifically circumcision. But Paul interprets the statement "Abraham believed God, and it was credited to him as righteousness" (cf. Gen 15:6) in the light of Psalm 32:1, where God himself freely remits people's sins without their doing anything to deserve it; the conferral of righteousness is a *gift* given by God, rather than an *obligation* that God had to fulfill if somebody had "worked" to deserve it. Abraham's later circumcision was clearly not the means of justification but a confirmatory mark of his new status. So Jews and uncircumcised Gentiles are on the same footing, provided that they both believe. Abraham as a believer is spiritually the father of all believers, both the Jew and Gentile.

Abraham's belief in God's power to do the impossible thing that he had promised (raising the dead) foreshadows Christian belief in the resurrection of Jesus. This event is integral to justification. It is not just simply the restoration of Jesus to life after he has died for our sins but God's justification of him as the righteous one, in whose justification and resurrection life believing sinners can share.

*Justification and future salvation (Rom 5:1-11).* Justification becomes a reality for sinners at the point when they believe. They enter a new relationship of peace with God that replaces the former enmity. They have confidence to come into God's presence in prayer and will share in his glory (contrast Rom 3:23). Although suffering continues to be part of their human existence, they experience God's love through the working of the Holy Spirit. The present reality of God's love is demonstrated and confirmed by the nature of Christ's death: he died for the ungodly and sinners, though usually people give their lives only for the righteous and good. The future hope also rests on Christ's death. If God has acted in him to justify *sinners*, there is all the more reason to suppose that he will save *those who have been justified* from the final judgment. If God reconciled his *enemies* to himself through Christ's death, how much more will he accept his *friends* at the final judgment.

*Adam and Christ: Comparison and contrast (Rom 5:12-21).* The universal provision of righteousness and life for sinners through Christ is paralleled by the lethal effects of Adam's action, whose sin has infected the entire race. Romans 5:12 may simply mean that death came upon all people "because all sinned" in the same way; yet it may contain the deeper thought that all people were somehow "in Adam" when he sinned so that sin passed to them and they were "made sinners" (Rom 5:19). But grace is greater than sin! The effect of Christ's righteous deed far outweighs that of Adam's sin.

*Death and new life for believers (Rom 6:1-23).* If such grace is available to cancel out all sins, are we then free to go on sinning, because the more we sin, the more scope there is for God to be gracious (Rom 6:1)? This objection ignores the fact that justified sinners are under obligation not to persist in sin, and they have freedom not to sin. Baptism "into Christ" brings believers into a close relationship with him. In baptism they can be said to have died and even been buried with him. There is a sense in which, if slaves die, they pass out of the sphere in which their master has authority over them; he can no longer issue commands to them. Similarly, in dying with Christ, believers have died and passed out of the sphere of authority of their old master, sin. They are no longer under any obligation or constraint to sin. Certainly there would be no real freedom if they simply died. But those who are united with Christ in his death also share in his resurrection. Ultimately, they will be raised from physical death. Here and now they are raised up spiritually to live a new life: they are dead so far as sin is concerned, yet alive to God as their new master. Their hidden life with God transforms how they live in the world. No longer enslaved to obey sin, they are under obligation to obey God and therefore must consecrate themselves to him.

Underlying this discussion is the place of the law of Moses (Rom 6:14). For Paul, salvation by grace is salvation by faith and not by law. Not only are faith and works antithetical, but also grace and law oppose each other. The action of God's grace does not require obedience to the law. But if so, what is to stop people from sinning? Paul repeats that believers are now slaves to God and therefore under obligation to obey him (just as Jews were under the obligation to obey the law). Previously they were slaves to sin (because the law was powerless to make them obedient), and their deeds stood under God's judgment. Now, having been set free from sin, they must obey God, doing what is good and right and receiving the gift of eternal life.

*The impotence of the law (Rom 7:1-25).* Similarly, marriage binds a wife to her husband during his lifetime; if he dies, she is legally free of her obligation and may marry somebody else. Jewish believers were formerly under obligation to obey the law. Though in the illustration the husband dies, in the application the wife dies and her husband has no further authority over her; thus the believer, transferred by death and resurrection into a new sphere where the law no longer has force, is now free to "marry" a new "husband": Christ. Formerly under the rightful authority of the law, believers are no longer under it. The law did not in fact succeed in preventing sin; rather, it stimulated sinful passions. There is, however, a new way, that of the Spirit, whereby believers can bear fruit that is pleasing to God.

This does not mean that the law itself is on the side of sin (Rom 7:7). Rather, it brings "dead" (dormant) sin to life so that its sinful character becomes apparent, like covetousness in Paul himself. It was not the law that "killed" Paul but his sinful nature, which the law exposed for what it really was.

Although Paul uses "I" here, he is referring to people generally and not just to himself. The present tense (Rom 7:14-25; contrast Rom 7:7-13) could refer to the life of believers, whether to the "normal" Christian life or to sin making believers abnormally captive. Certainly believers do experience such occasions in their life. Is the description also true of unbelievers? Although some assert that they do not even have the desire to do what is good, this is simply not true. People may know what is good (e.g., from the law of Moses) and want to do it, and yet be unable to do so because they are controlled by sin. Only Christ can deliver them.

*The Holy Spirit and future glory (Rom 8:1-39).* In Romans 8, Paul shows how the conflict is resolved. Believers no longer stand under condemnation to death because of their sin. The death of Jesus as a sin offering delivers them from the death caused by sin. The Spirit comes into all believers, bringing about their adoption into God's family and entitling them to call God "Father". They are enabled to fulfill the law's requirements. People who approve what the law says are now able to put their desires into action. Yet the control of the Spirit is not automatic. Believers still have to be commanded to kill their sinful desires by the Spirit and not to obey their sinful nature.

This does not exempt them from suffering. Paul contrasts their present situation with their promised future inheritance of a share in the glory of Christ, the firstborn Son, when God restores the perishable and fallen world. Although truly experiencing salvation, believers live in the tension of "the now and the not yet": their salvation is not yet fully realized, and they must live by hope. God has predestined them to share the glory of Christ, and therefore he takes the appropriate steps to bring this about. Believers need not fear any force opposed to them; with a loving, faithful God on their side, there is no chance of success for their opponents.

## THE THEOLOGICAL STORY: ISRAEL AND THE GENTILES (ROM 9—11)

Thus far Paul has expounded his gospel and dealt with objections to it arising from the place of the Jewish law. A second problem is that so many of the Jewish people have rejected Jesus. The Jews' unbelief is all the more surprising because they have so many religious privileges, including giving birth to the Messiah as a Jew. Does this unbelief show that God has not kept his promises (Rom 9:6a) and has rejected his people (Rom 11:1)?

Paul's first line of argument is that God never did promise that all Jacob's physical descendants would be included in the people of the Messiah. He is free to choose whom he will favor, and ultimately God's acceptance does not depend on physical descent. Just as believing Gentiles can be regarded as spiritually Abraham's offspring (Rom 4:11), so conversely physical descent is not necessarily a qualification for being part of his offspring. The inheritance is not due to a qualification based on human works but entirely depends on God's call. It is not belonging to the physical nation of Israel that matters but response to God's call (which goes to both Jews and Gentiles).

God is entitled to show mercy to some people and also to harden others so that they do not believe. He has freedom to do as he pleases, like a potter deciding the destiny of his pots. This may seem to challenge human freedom and to take away the blame from human beings who resist God. Yet God actually shows patience toward those who are the objects of his wrath and makes his mercy known to those whom he has destined for glory: believers from both the Jews and the Gentiles. The unbelief of so many Jews is thus consistent with God's promises to Abraham's descendants, since God never intended these promises to include everybody, and God never intended these promises to include every single individual, and he in fact has acted in mercy to save a people composed of both Jews and Gentiles.

Paul's second line of argument is concerned with human response. The Gentiles, who in the past had not sought after righteousness, have now attained it, whereas the Jews, who did seek after righteousness, have failed to attain it. This difference is traced not to divine choice but to the fact that the Gentiles have responded to Christ with faith, whereas the Jews (on the whole) have zealously but mistakenly tried to get right with God by the works of the law. The only way to righteousness for both Jews and Gentiles now consists in believing that Jesus rose from the dead and acknowledging him as Lord.

The fact that Paul can pray for the salvation of Jews shows that the way is still open for them, and the gospel must be preached so as to give people the opportunity to believe. God has not totally rejected his people and prevented them from being saved. When Paul says that the rest of Israel have been "hardened", this is a judgment upon them for their unbelief. There is no barrier to individual Jews hearing the gospel and responding to it, but for the time being, there has been a general hardening of hearts against the gospel, and God has in effect "given them up". The coming of salvation to the Gentiles will make the Jews become envious and thus turn to the same source of salvation. Believing Gentiles are reminded that they have been grafted into the olive tree, which is Israel; unbelieving branches that have been cut off can also be grafted back in. When the mass of the Gentiles have come to faith, the hardening of the Jews will come to an end, and there will be mercy for them. The last word is that God's purpose is to offer mercy to all (whether or not they believe and accept it).

## THE THEOLOGICAL STORY: LIVING THE NEW LIFE (ROM 12—15)

The practical response to the doctrinal teaching about the grace of God is a thank offering: believers must dedicate themselves to God and live in a new way, not dictated by this (sinful) world but by minds transformed by God. Like parts of a body, believers serve one another, using the various gracious gifts of the Holy Spirit given to each of them. The command to love is crucial (Rom 13:8-10). To love is to fulfill the law, since all the commandments can be regarded as the outworking of the law to love one's neighbor. The commandments in mind are all moral commandments; a rough working distinction between the moral commands in the law and the Jewish ritual commands (no longer required) seems to underlie Paul's thought.

The final manifestation of salvation at the coming of Christ is now nearer in time than formerly (Rom 13:11-14). Believers already belong to this new day and should at all times be ready for its arrival lest they be found asleep and are excluded from it. Let them avoid the kind of sins associated with nighttime and put on appropriate clothing for the day.

A specific problem is the existence of different attitudes within the readership to the observance of festivals and to choice of food (cf. 1 Cor 8—10). Where different practices are driven by the desire to honor God, there must be freedom for difference of opinion. Whatever people do, they must so act as to honor the Lord and behave lovingly toward their Christian brothers and sisters. God's kingdom is a community where mutual peace and harmony, doing what is right, and rejoicing in God's gifts, are possible through the influence of the Holy Spirit (Rom 14:17). God's intention, confirmed by Scripture, is that Jews and Gentiles together should glorify God. Christ came as a servant of the Jews, to confirm God's promises to Abraham and their other ancestors, but these promises include admitting the Gentiles among the worshipers of God.

The conversion of the Gentiles is the offering that Paul brings to God as his particular service through Christ, who works in him by the Spirit (Rom 15:14-33). He requests prayer that he may avoid trouble in Jerusalem and be able to travel as a missionary via Rome to Spain. The lengthy concluding doxology focuses on the gospel, which God has long planned, announced through the prophets, and finally revealed so that all the nations might come to faith.

## THEOLOGICAL THEMES

*The main concern: Salvation for Jews and Gentiles by grace through faith.* Jews and Gentiles are all sinners under divine judgment, and all can be justified through faith in Christ without being required to be circumcised and keep the rest of the Jewish law. Christ's death and resurrection constitute an act of redemption, with the power to deal with the sins that make people guilty and liable to God's wrathful judgment. Justification by faith, rather than by obeying the law, does not result in an immoral life of disobedience to God's will; rather, believers are set free from bondage to sin by their union with Christ, receive the gift of the Spirit, and are under obligation to live a new life of obedience to God, which issues in corresponding "fruit". The law expresses God's commandments and exposes the sin that is latent in people's lives, but it cannot enable people to overcome sin; for this to be possible, the power of God's Spirit is needed.

The fact that many Jews have rejected the gospel does not mean that God has rejected his chosen people; instead, they have refused to accept that a right relationship with God comes through acceptance of what he has done in Christ and not through their own efforts to please him by the works of the law. A partial "hardening" has come upon those who have not believed while the mission to the Gentiles is successfully proceeding. Once the full number of the Gentiles has responded to the gospel, most of the Jewish people will see what they have been missing and will then be saved.

Finally, Paul develops an ethic of love for the life of Jews and Gentiles together in the church. This in effect fulfills the law but at the same time allows for diversity in practice on some issues, always provided that diversity is accompanied by mutual loving concern for those who think and behave differently.

*The sovereignty of God, election and faith.* Romans is partly a theodicy, a justification of the God and Father of Jesus Christ and of Christian believers. God is sovereign, with authority and power over the whole universe. Romans is often thought to teach that God has chosen beforehand the individuals whom he intends to save, that he calls them, and then brings about the whole process that leads to their justification and eventual glorification (Rom 8:29-30). The implication is that God chooses not to save other people. His offer of salvation is thus not universal in the sense that he makes provision for the possible salvation of all people: Christ died only for the people chosen by God to be saved, some claim.

This understanding of Romans is problematic. Paul states that the mercy of God and the death of Christ are universal in their scope (Rom 5:18; 11:32). "Double predestination" makes God out to be unjust, arbitrarily dispensing mercy to some and not to others. Certainly, human beings cannot compel God to be merciful, but this does not mean that he is arbitrary in his exercise of mercy (Rom 9:15). If God has predetermined who will be saved, Paul's prayer for Israel (Rom 10:1) would be pointless, unless we argue that Paul's prayers were also preordained, and so were God's own responses to them. In that case, however, prayer is not really prayer. Moreover, God can appeal to the obstinate people and be disappointed by their lack of response, in a way that would be inconsistent with his having hardened them himself (Rom 10:21). Paul also refers to people not persisting in their unbelief as if it were within their own power whether or not to believe (Rom 11:14, 23). Paul never writes as though his preaching would lead to the salvation of a predetermined group of hearers who would certainly believe once they heard the message because God had predetermined it.

Similar problems arise with understanding Paul's view of sin and sanctification. Through faith in Christ, people are delivered from the power of sin; they can be said to be "dead" to its authority over them, and they can now freely obey God through the power of the Spirit (Rom 6:19-23). Their lives are also influenced for good by prayers of intercession (cf. Rom 15:30-32). Yet they may (and do) fall back under the domination of sin. They are controlled by the Spirit of God, without whom they cannot fulfill God's will, and yet they have to be commanded to do so and be warned against the danger of succumbing again to sin (Rom 6:13; 8:12-13; cf. Gal 5:13-26). Here is a tension between divine empowering and the human freedom that can evidently choose not to do righteousness.

Paul clearly teaches the freedom and power of God to will and do as he pleases. He is loving, just and sovereign. God will bring his purpose for his creation to its fulfillment. He treats people as persons and not as things. There is such an activity as prayer, to which God makes genuine responses. He wants all people to be saved and come to a knowledge of the truth. God certainly works in human lives by the Spirit. The tensions in holding these statements together are in principle irresolvable because the origin and nature of evil in a universe created by a sovereign God are incomprehensible to us, as is the relationship between God's action and human response. Any attempt to express the relationship between God and human beings exposes tensions that we cannot fully resolve. What Paul says leaves us with a mystery beyond our total comprehension.

*Righteousness and faith.* Paul's understanding of salvation is expressed in terms of righteousness and justification. But what is meant by *righteousness* and in particular by the *righteousness of God?* Sometimes the phrase refers to the justice and fairness of God (Rom 3:5) or to his action to bring about righteousness. At other times it refers to a quality or standing that God credits to human beings by virtue of which their sins are not counted against them and they have a good relationship with him. Such righteousness is expressed in the doing of what is right in God's eyes as opposed to doing what is evil. According to Paul, the failure of the Jews was that they sought a righteous standing with God by doing the works of the law (Rom 9:30-31), whereas God credits righteousness to those who do not work but trust in him as the one who justifies the ungodly (Rom 4:1-5). Yet this does not mean that people are not obliged to do what God requires and to present themselves to him to do what is righteous (Rom 6:13, 19).

Justification is by faith, whether in God (Rom 4:3, 5, 24; 9:33; 10:11) or in Christ (Rom 10:14). Although the phrase *the faith of Jesus Christ* is sometimes interpreted to mean "faith [or faithfulness] shown by Jesus Christ" (Rom 3:22, 26; cf. Rom 3:3, "the faith[fulness] of God"), it is more likely that it refers to faith in Jesus Christ, in line with Paul's usage elsewhere of phrases with *ek* to signify the quality by which believers live (Rom 2:8; 4:16; esp. 9:30). Such faith is essentially trust in God's promises and hence reliance on him rather than on oneself or one's own deeds.

*Israel and the Gentiles.* Romans is particularly concerned with the unity of the church as composed of believing Jews and Gentiles. The Gentiles should have known God from his revelation in the created order, but have failed to do so and turned to sinful and idolatrous practices that have brought them under God's wrath. The gospel offers them justification and new life, on the basis of faith and not on keeping the Jewish law. They are engrafted into the people of God, Israel. As for the Jews, Paul maintains that they do not have a superior position by virtue of possessing the law unless they keep it, and that they actually are all sinners just like the Gentiles. Physical descent from Abraham and circumcision do not guarantee them a place in the people of God. But since they have fallen under sin and the law cannot save them, they need to be justified by faith, just like the Gentiles. It is impossible to understand what Paul says in any other sense than that Jews and Gentiles alike can be justified only by faith in Christ.

"Israel" is the people of God who begin from Abraham and stretch down through his descendants. However, not all physical descendants of Abraham have lived by faith. Israel is like an olive tree from which God cuts off the Israelites who do not believe and into which he inserts those Gentiles who do believe. This is not supersessionism, with the church replacing Israel as the people of God. Rather, the believing Gentiles are engrafted into believing Israel. The people of God, descended from the believer Abraham, are now defined by faith in Christ and not by the marks of Jewish identity (physical circumcision; Jewish festivals; other Jewish practices). Paul looks to a day when the hardening of unbelieving Jews will cease and they will respond to the deliverer, who will "turn godlessness away from Jacob" (Rom 11:26).

Some have thought that certain passages (Rom 5:18-19; 11:26, 32) imply that God will bring about the salvation of all people by causing them to believe through some kind of postmortem persuasion and reformatory judgment. This implication is never expressed, and the final judgment is never presented as other than final.

*The law of Moses.* The Jews have been distinguished from other people by the covenant that God made with them at Sinai (thus ratifying his earlier choice of Abraham and of Jacob), and with this covenant has come the law committed to Moses, by which the Jews were to live as God's people. But the law cannot put people right with God if they have broken it. What the law cannot do, God has done by sending his Son to deal with sin and by enabling people to live by the Spirit. Jews need to be justified just as much as Gentiles do. Their position as the people of God within the covenant is valid only if they believe in God and accept the Messiah rather than depending on their descent from Abraham or on their doing the requirements of the law. God's requirements are fulfilled by those who live by the Spirit. The law is thus fulfilled by the ones living by the Spirit, whether Jews or Gentiles. Within the church, Jews are free to keep the law (circumcision and so forth) and Gentiles are free from it, but each must respect the other's way of life and live in peace and harmony.

*The Holy Spirit.* Paul refers to the Spirit especially in contexts where he is comparing Judaism and Christianity; the law and the Spirit stand over against one another. There is a contrast between the inability of the law to deliver people from sin and the power of the Spirit to deliver them. If believers are no longer under the law, they live by the Spirit and are enabled to fulfill what the law requires (Rom 8:2-4). The flesh and the Spirit also stand over against one another, the flesh connoting human nature in its weakness, sinfulness and self-confidence, whereas the Spirit indicates the divine power that can transform human nature, bringing life and resurrection.

There are hints of understanding the Spirit as an independent person who resides in believers (Rom 8:9) and who intercedes for them (Rom 8:26-27). Christ and the Spirit are closely associated, so that the Spirit is called the Spirit of Christ (Rom 8:9), and the workings of both in believers are described in the same ways. Being raised to newness of life through union with Christ in his death and resurrection brings deliverance from the power of sin and the capacity to obey God (Rom 6); this is precisely what the Spirit conveys to believers in Romans 8.

## CONCLUSION

Romans is the most sustained doctrinal discussion in Paul's letters. It centers on the place of Jews and Gentiles in God's saving purpose, defends Paul's understanding of salvation by grace, shows how this works out in the new life of those who are justified by faith, explains how God's promises to the Jewish people find their fulfillment in Christ, and applies the gospel to life together in Christian congregations.

# 12

# THE LETTER TO THE PHILIPPIANS

Philippians expresses the affectionate fellowship between Paul and his readers as sharers in the common task of Christian mission (Phil 1:5). They have helped him by prayers (Phil 1:19) and gifts (Phil 4:10-20). Paul shares news about his own situation as a prisoner with the aim of encouraging his readers (Phil 1:12-26) and also writes about other personal contacts with them through colleagues (Phil 2:19-30). The readers need to avoid dissension and so be able to resist temptations to give up their faith (Phil 1:27—2:18; cf. Phil 4:2-9). The congregation is threatened by traveling preachers encouraging Jewish ritual and legal practices as the path to spiritual maturity (Phil 3:1—4:1).

## THE THEOLOGICAL STORY

*Prayer report (Phil 1:1-11).* Paul encourages the readers by telling them that he thanks God joyfully for their own ongoing spiritual progress in love, knowledge, and righteousness and also for their sharing in the task of mission. They are supporting Paul by their gifts and prayers and through his helper, Epaphroditus, and are also bearing their own witness to Christ despite opposition.

*Paul's situation theologically examined (Phil 1:12-26).* A missionary may be "chained like a criminal. But God's word is not chained" (2 Tim 2:9). Paul's imprisonment has led to knowledge of the gospel spreading among the people in the area, and other believers have been encouraged and challenged to fearless witness. The threat of further suffering and death looms over Paul. He is able to recognize that death is a desirable experience in that it opens up the way to being with Christ. At the same time Paul is confidently expecting continued work in this world despite all the harassment and pain that it entails.

*Threats to the congregation (Phil 1:27—2:4).* From the beginning the establishment of groups of believers in Jesus as Messiah and Lord has been opposed by the people among whom they hope to find converts. Such opponents who reject Christ are destined for judgment, and so an obligation rests on believers for sharing their faith as well as holding fast to their own faith despite what it costs.

Suffering for the sake of Christ is part of the believers' life; it is integral to their Christian witness, just as it was for Paul. But for them to survive, there must be unity and harmony within the congregation. This is threatened by selfish aims and objectives, which need to be replaced by having a common goal and consideration for one another's needs rather than their own satisfaction. In short, love for one another should characterize the life of the congregation.

*The example of Jesus (Phil 2:5-11).* To reinforce this point, Paul cites the example of Jesus, whose attitude should also be that of believers. In rhythmical prose Paul describes Jesus' career. He who had the nature of God renounced the privileges of that state and took on the form of a human servant of God, demonstrating an obedience to God that extended to willingness to die the most sordid of deaths. Then God exalted him to the highest conceivable position alongside himself and now requires all creation to acknowledge him as Lord, just as they would acknowledge God the Father (Is 45:22-23).

The self-denial shown by Jesus must be seen in the readers. They are to deny themselves, even though their status is not that of Jesus. He is the Lord before whom all must bow. The readers must deny their own selfish desires and instead obey Christ. Their unity will arise out of their common obedience to Christ and confession of him as Lord.

*Application to the congregation (Phil 2:12-18).* In the light of the story of Jesus Christ, the readers are specifically called to obedience and to work out in their lives the fact that God is at work "in them". Practically this means a life free from selfish desires and moving toward perfection and freedom from fault. Paul hopes that he will be able to exult at the judgment day, when his work as a missionary among them will be vindicated. Although he is presently expending his life, like a sacrificial offering, he rejoices over the congregation in Philippi.

*Fellow workers (Phil 2:19-30).* As Paul mentions travel possibilities for his colleagues and himself, he stresses the overruling providence and goodness of God and his own consequent confidence for the future. The Christian quality of his helpers is described in terms of total commitment to Christ, to Paul himself, and to the welfare of the congregation.

*The threat from Judaizers (Phil 3:1-21).* A command to "rejoice in the Lord" is followed almost immediately by reference to exultant confidence (to "boast", NRSV and TNIV) in Christ Jesus. A group of people are exulting and placing their confidence in their human credentials ("the flesh"), such as Jewish racial superiority, religious rituals (including circumcision) and pious zeal. Paul encourages the readers to put their confidence solely in Christ and not in themselves, their status or their achievements. Christ is the source of true righteousness with God, the proper standing with God in which the problem of sin is dealt with. This new way of attaining righteousness cancels out the old way of justification by following the dictates of the Jewish law. Righteousness comes from God as his gift received by a faith that accepts what God does for us. Paul now regards whatever he has inherited or achieved under the old way as a positive liability.

The thought, however, goes deeper. Gaining the righteousness that Christ provides is part of a total experience of which the essence is to "know" Christ. The longing expressed in Philippians 1:21-23 thus returns to the center of focus. Paul wants to know Christ and to gain Christ. Justification cannot be separated from knowing Christ. This experience includes sharing in the sufferings of Christ, becoming like him in his death on the cross (Phil 2:8!), experiencing the power of his resurrection, and attaining to the resurrection from the dead.

The death is dying to sinful and selfish motives and actions, and the resurrection is to a new life of obedience to God; yet supremely there is the experience of knowing Christ himself, a relationship akin to knowledge and love of a human being, which results in the transformation and salvation of believers. There is progress and development in this relationship, leading to "perfection" or "maturity".

The "enemies of the cross" (Phil 3:18) are probably the same as the people described in such strong language at the beginning of the chapter. The cross and people's attitude to it acts as a kind of litmus paper, bringing out into the open the real nature of their relationship with God. Yielding to passion and desire, or perhaps glorying in the fulfillment of religious duties, is incompatible with the cross. True believers are like resident aliens in the world, conforming themselves not to its ways but to the pattern of the kingdom and the King to whom they truly belong. They eagerly look forward to the time when Christ will come and the kingdoms of the world will become the kingdom of God.

*Joy, confidence and generosity (Phil 4:1-23).* The letter concludes on a practical and personal level. The readers are encouraged to put their confidence in the Lord and, if they rejoice or exult in anything, to do so in him. God will provide for all their needs and keep them from anxiety. Finally, Paul thanks the readers for their gifts to him, which are like a thank offering made to God.

## THEOLOGICAL THEMES

*The believer's relationship to Christ.* Paul's central concern is the advance of the gospel, through which people come into an ongoing relationship with God through Jesus Christ and form a congregation (Phil 1:5, 12, 27). At the outset he refers to Jesus Christ to define his own role as his servant and the Christian status of the readers (Phil 1:1). "Saints in Christ Jesus" picks up on Old Testament language to identify them as God's people, showing that they owe this status to their relationship to Jesus Christ, who is named right alongside God the Father as the source of salvation (Phil 1:2; cf. Phil 4:19).

The significance of Christ for the readers is expressed in the phrase *in*

*Christ*. It can be the natural complement to a verb, such as to rejoice or be confident on the basis of Christ (or the Lord) and who he is (Phil 2:19, 24; 3:1). Christian conduct should be "in the Lord", determined by the fact that Christ is the Lord of his people and requires a certain manner of behavior from them (Phil 2:29; 4:2). God acts "in [through] Christ" for the good of his people (Phil 3:14; 4:7, 19). The readers have a close relationship with Jesus through their faith in him (cf. Phil 3:9b), so that Paul can say that they are in Christ (Phil 1:1, 14; 3:9a; 4:21). This is like the way in which he can speak of believers as parts of the body that belongs to Christ and of which he is the head, or again the way in which John writes of believers being in Christ and Christ being in them.

Paul's desire to know Christ and the power of his resurrection and to participate in his sufferings (Phil 3:10) is concerned not simply with knowledge about somebody but with a personal experience in which he shares the actual events of Jesus' life. Being united with Christ in his death and resurrection is the experience of all believers (Rom 6:1-14; Col 2:20—3:4). They share in the resurrection life of Christ both now and after physical death. They also share in the sufferings of Christ. These include the pains and hardships associated with the Christian existence of all believers (Phil 1:29-30) and of missionaries (cf. 2 Cor 11:23-33).

Paul has been going through some situation in which the possibility of his own imminent death is very real. This raises the question of what matters most to him. If for him "life is Christ", as the opportunity to know Christ and experience his love (Phil 1:21), it follows that physical death is a better state, since it brings a believer into even closer union with Christ.

*Christ's humility and exaltation*. What kind of person could Jesus be for Paul to talk about him in this astonishing way? How can this person be the channel through whom God operates, a person with whom one can have this kind of spiritual relationship? He is a person who has existed in the form of God and did not regard his equality with God as something to be held on to or exploited (Phil 2:5-8). Such language sets Jesus on the same level of authority as God the Father. The use of the verb "being" and the clear contrast between the original state of Jesus and the way in which he then took the nature of a servant and adopted a human likeness and appearance show that Paul is describing the "preexistent" state of Jesus, when he was with God the Father before God sent him into the world to be born of a woman (Gal 4:4) and live a human life. This ties in with the earlier description of Jesus as the one Lord alongside the one God the Father (1 Cor 8:6; cf. Col 1:15-17).

The point, however, is to contrast the position of supreme authority enjoyed by Christ with the way in which he became a human being who plumbed the depths of obedience to God by being prepared to die. Elsewhere the character of his death as a means of salvation is often stated (e.g., Rom 3:25; 5:6-11), but here Paul stresses the willingness of Jesus himself to "do nothing out of selfish ambition or vain conceit"—the very thing that is spoiling the life of the congregation in Philippi (Phil 2:3). Such saying "No" to self is what God approves.

Because Jesus was prepared to die, God subsequently exalted him to the highest place in the universe, where he had been previously, but also made him the object of universal worship by all people. The language used here (cf. Is 45:22-23) shows that the term *Lord* here is the title of God the Father himself, now bestowed on Jesus.

As a result of this V-shaped career (from God "down" to earth and back "up" again) Jesus has a "postexistence" in which, without losing his humanity, he is now an omnipotent (Phil 3:21) spiritual person, able to enter into relationships with those who believe in him. Consequently, he is able to act as the mediator of God's blessings to his people. To say "The Lord is near" (Phil 4:5) means acknowledging his availability to help his people in their needs. Such relationships will be fully realized when he returns in a glorious bodily form from heaven to earth, to be the Savior of his people from their imperfect life in this corruptible world and to share his new existence with them (Phil 3:20-21).

*The Holy Spirit.* Jesus is the dispenser of the Holy Spirit (cf. Acts 2:33); the blessings bestowed by God on his people may be attributed both to him and to the Spirit. The help given to Paul in his present sufferings comes by the Spirit of Jesus Christ (Phil 1:19). Believers should "stand firm in the one Spirit" (Phil 1:27). "Sharing in the Spirit" (Phil 2:1) is strikingly similar to sharing in Jesus Christ (1 Cor 1:9). Christian worshipful service of God takes place through the agency of the Spirit (Phil 3:3).

*God the Father.* The significant roles of Christ and the Spirit should not be allowed to overshadow the place of the Father in Paul's theology. The letter reaches its climax in a statement of the extraordinary generosity of the God who acts in Jesus and in a doxology to God (Phil 4:19-20; cf. Phil 2:11). Throughout the letter, God initiates the action and is at work in believers (Phil 2:13; cf. 3:15) to protect and overrule in their lives (Phil 2:27).

*New life in Christ.* The new life in Christ is one of spiritual growth and progress. The readers are to grow in love, knowledge, purity and righteousness right up to the day of Christ (Phil 1:9-11). Great importance is attached to being blameless on the day when Christ comes. If there is tension between statements that believers have nothing to fear on that day (Rom 5:1-11) and other statements in which growth in holiness is a condition for blamelessness on judgment day, it disappears when we recognize that God himself will achieve this blamelessness in the lives of his people; God is faithful and he will do it (Phil 1:6).

The term "fellowship" *(koinōnia)* is used for the participation of believers in God's blessings, in the Holy Spirit (Phil 1:7; 2:1) and in the work of the gospel (Phil 1:5); this brings them into a relationship with one another and with Paul (Phil 4:14-15). Such a sharing includes participation in the sufferings of Christ (Phil 3:10), but this also carries with it the hope of sharing in his resurrection. On a practical level, the congregation's ongoing work of mission includes supporting Paul's own work through prayer, tangible gifts of money, and sending colleagues; it also involves the local activity of striving together for the faith of the gospel and in holding out the word of life (Phil 2:16).

## CONCLUSION

Philippians shows the way in which Paul understood his own circumstances theologically. A personal relationship of knowing Christ lies at the heart of Paul's religion. Christ himself is seen not merely as the Savior but also as the pattern for Christian living. Believers must put their confidence solely in Christ for salvation and not in any human achievements, and their lives must be conformed to Christ and his cross.

# 13

# THE LETTER TO PHILEMON

Paul's shortest letter is about the real-life situation of a master whose slave has apparently run away after some wrongdoing, but has met with Paul in his prison and has become a believer. Paul has developed an affection for him and wishes to have him stay with him as a helper, but he cannot do so without first sending the runaway back to his master. He asks the master to receive Onesimus back as a Christian brother and forgive whatever wrong he has done.

The whole of this appeal is based upon the gospel and the fellowship that results from it. So Paul begins by referring to Philemon's faith and love toward Christ and God's people. As Philemon and other believers share their faith with one another, they all grow into a fuller knowledge of the good things that God intends believers to have. On the basis of this common life dominated and determined by their relationship to Christ crucified and risen, Paul makes his appeal on behalf of the "son" whom he has spiritually fathered. He asks Philemon to receive back Onesimus as more than a slave, as a beloved brother "in the Lord" but also "in the flesh", meaning on a human level (Philem 16). Philemon is to welcome his slave back in the same way as he would welcome Paul himself. Such a statement will eventually be recognized to imply that one can no longer treat a brother as a slave and hence that slavery is incompatible with Christianity. Although this is put in terms of Christian love, behind it lies the authority of the Lord, whom Christians must obey. Here is a theology of Christian action showing how an ethical appeal can be based on the gospel and demonstrating the effect that it has in the lives of those who accept it.

# 14

# THE LETTER TO THE COLOSSIANS

The recipients of Colossians were in danger of being misled by a "philosophy" that assigned great significance to spiritual powers threatening human life; these had to be warded off by ascetic practices. Christ was assumed to be no stronger than these other powers. Paul's letter focuses on this danger.

## THE THEOLOGICAL STORY

*Prayer report (Col 1:1-14).* Paul thanks God for the spiritual progress of the congregation in terms of the familiar triad of faith (in Christ), love (for one another) and hope. "Hope" refers concretely to what is already waiting in heaven for believers: the glory already bestowed on Christ, which will be shared with his people (Col 1:27). This hope inspires their faith and love. Their knowledge of it has come from the preaching of the gospel, which is likened to a plant that spreads and grows and bears fruit in conversions to the faith.

The need for power and perseverance so as to combat the principalities and powers is particularly prominent in Colossians and Ephesians. The readers should give thanks for the new life that they experience in the kingdom of Christ after being rescued from the kingdom of darkness and forgiven for their sins.

*A celebration of Christ (Col 1:15-20).* Paul develops the theme of Christ and his functions in a passage of exalted prose (cf. Phil 2:5-11). The supremacy of Christ is seen in relation to the universe and then to the church. He is the visible image of God and "the firstborn of all creation" (NRSV), a phrase meaning that he is prior to creation and superior to it. Hence he is superior to all the authoritative beings in the universe.

Christ is also the head of the body, the church. (Here, in contrast to 1 Cor 12, the head is distinguished from the church as the body.) As the beginning, as the first to be raised from the dead, Christ is supreme over all. All the power of God resides in him; it is not distributed among other entities. And God has appointed him to reconcile the entire universe to God by making a peace offering through his death.

*The consequences of Christ's superior status (Col 1:21—2:7).* God's offer of reconciliation becomes effective only when the estranged parties make their peace with him. The readers have shared in this hostility, but now they have become God's friends through their faith in Christ, who has died for them. As a servant of this gospel intended for the whole world, Paul not only proclaims it but also suffers for its sake and for the church. He reveals God's plan whereby Christ offers the hope of glory to all people. Hence Gentiles do not need to follow some other route to salvation. All the saving knowledge that people need is to be found in Christ, no matter what the "philosophers" may say on the basis of their visions.

*Response to the false teaching (Col 2:8-23).* Over against the assertions of the syncretistic "philosophy", Christian believers have received the fullness of God, since they have received Christ, in whom all of this fullness resides. This is the logical outcome of their being united with Christ, putting on Christ, Christ living in them (Gal 2:20), and receiving the Spirit. What is new is the way in which Paul describes Christ as incorporating God in his body. The threat posed by the false teaching about the principalities and powers, perhaps with divine powers distributed among them, may have led Paul to draw the logical conclusions from his earlier teaching and recognize that God is uniquely present in Christ, and through him the divine power is conveyed to believers.

Physical circumcision is an outward symbol of cutting sin away from the heart; it is effectively replaced by Christian baptism as a symbol of cleansing from sin and of union with Christ in his death and therefore signifies death to sin.

Baptized believers share in Christ's burial and resurrection (Rom 6:11; cf. Gal 2:19-20; 6:14). Paul uses the term *death* to refer to two different experiences: the situation of people who are "dead in sins" and therefore deaf so far as responding positively to God is concerned (Col 2:13), and then the situation of believers who die to the world (Col 2:20) and are "buried" (Col 2:12) through union with Christ in his death and become alive to God. This experience is accompanied by forgiveness of sins (cf. Col 1:14); it is as though a list of their sins has been nailed to the cross on which Christ has died (Col 2:14; cf. Mk 15:26). At the same time by dying on the cross Christ triumphed over the principalities and powers. Whether Paul means that he "disarmed" these enemies or "divested himself of" them (NRSV note), he in any case defeated them; then, like a Roman general celebrating with a triumphal procession, he led them in chains to execution (Col 2:15).

*Life as God's chosen people (Col 3:1—4:1).* If all this is true, believers do not need to yield to demands that Jewish practices be observed. Regulations about foods and festivals are no longer required; they used to point forward to Christ, but now they are no longer needed. Practices like worship of angels have nothing to do with Christ, who is the true source of spiritual growth in the church. In fact, they threaten his position as the only Savior. Positively, Paul urges the readers to progress in their life in union with Christ by adopting the way of living associated with their future (and still hidden) hope of glory, expressing it here and now in this world.

Believers who have died with Christ to the world must put to death their old way of life. They must put off their old self and put on a new nature, like a person taking off dirty clothes and putting on clean ones. Believers are being made new with regard to their knowledge of God and how he wants people to live, by contrast with the sinful world that does not know (or chooses not to know) what God requires. Specifically, in the church no distinction counts any longer between people of different races or between slaves and free people, since Christ is in them all.

Believers are God's chosen people, called to be holy and loved by him. Themselves forgiven, they must show forgiveness to other people. As members of one body, they must live at peace with one another. They must let the living word of Christ live in them. Whatever they do must be appropriate to being done "in the name of the Lord Jesus". The similar formula *in the Lord* (cf. *in Christ*) expresses the requirement of obedience created by their acceptance of Christ as Lord of their whole lives. The behavior commended is to be practiced not simply because it will commend believers to other people, but also because it is an expression of obedience to the Lord (Col 3:22), who will reward it.

*Paul and his colleagues (Col 4:2-18).* Finally, the importance of prayer, including prayer for Paul himself, is inculcated. Opportunities for Paul to evangelize even while chained in prison will not arise without the prayers of God's people for him.

## THEOLOGICAL THEMES

*Jesus Christ.* In Paul's later letters there is a rich understanding of Christ's preexistence and his present and future power and supremacy over all created entities, including extraterrestrial powers. It is not just that the implications of Christ's resurrection and exaltation are brought out more fully. Rather, the recognition that his position and authority stretch back to eternity past is powerfully developed. The superiority of Christ to the principalities and powers is grounded in the fact that he is not a created entity but existed before them all as the Son of God, reflecting in his own being the nature of God the Father. He incorporates the divine being in a bodily, human form (Col 2:9), a statement referring to him as he now is in his exalted state, as well as during his earthly existence. His resurrection was bodily; it was not the continuing existence of a heavenly being who temporarily inhabited a human body and then left it behind.

Paul uses the verb "fill" quite naturally of the way in which believers are filled with various qualities and benefits in his earlier letters (Rom 15:13-14; Phil 1:11). Here, however, he speaks of "the fullness" of God dwelling in Christ (Col 1:19; 2:9) and then of believers being filled in Christ, apparently with the same "fullness". In Ephesians, the goal is that believers be filled with the fullness of God and of Christ (Eph 3:19; 4:13), and the church is "the fullness of him of who fills everything in every way" (Eph 1:23). It is not necessary that the term should have the same reference each time it is used. The sense appears to be "the totality of the divine attributes", and as applied to Christ, the term may indicate all the powers and qualities of God, whereas when applied to believers and the church the reference is more to the qualities of God. Nevertheless, in Colossians 2:10 the implication is that a power superior to that of the principalities and powers is present in Christ and is effective in believers, so that they are not subject to these alien powers.

*Reconciliation.* In Colossians we have an understanding of humanity with two aspects. First, human beings are sinners (Col 2:13), alienated from God and at enmity toward him (Col 1:21); they belong to a world characterized by darkness (Col 1:13), from which they cannot deliver themselves. Christ's coming is a rescue operation, setting them free and bringing forgiveness of sins (Col 1:14; 2:13). The same action of Christ is also described as reconciliation or making peace. It embraces "all things", the implication being that there is no other mediator needed for anybody. The subjective experience of being forgiven and reconciled is also expressed in terms of dying and rising with Christ, and this is fully developed for its practical ethical implications. God's purpose is to create a holy people (Col 1:12), whose character befits them as God's people.

Second, some of the addressees believe that the world is dominated by supraterrestrial beings that have to be placated or obeyed. Since the law of Moses was given by angels (Gal 3:19), it could be that obedience to this law is thought to be part of the requirements on believers. At the same time these powers doubtless rule over the dark world of sin, and at least some of them are clearly opposed to God and Christ; otherwise, there would not be a description of their defeat. Whatever the situation, Christ has defeated them, and therefore believers are to let nobody condemn them for not fulfilling the various commandments being imposed upon them.

## CONCLUSION

In Colossians there is a much more explicit understanding of the position of Christ as head over all things and as being filled with the fullness of the

Deity. He is the head of the church, which is clearly conceived as a cosmic entity. Believers are redeemed, forgiven and reconciled to God; they have died and been raised with Christ, although their new life is hidden with Christ and is yet to be revealed.

# 15

# THE LETTER TO THE EPHESIANS

Ephesians expounds the nature of Christian salvation with respect to the church composed of Jews and Gentiles and then the character of the new life that flows from this. Its style is that of prayer and meditation.

## THE THEOLOGICAL STORY

*An ascription of praise (Eph 1:1-14).* Paul begins the first part of the letter by calling his readers to praise God for what God has done and will do for his people. God is identified as the Father of Christ; to praise God for what he has done is associated with Christ as his agent; there is also a reference to the Holy Spirit. The thanksgiving has a three-part structure, each part ending with "to the praise of his glory" (Eph 1:6, 12, 14). God has blessed his people "in the heavenly realms" (cf. Eph 1:20; 2:6). There has been a spiritual resurrection of believers so that they are now alive to God and therefore in a spiritual sense are already in heaven, but this does not free them from attack by the powers of evil, both in the world and in heaven (Eph 3:10; 6:12).

Salvation is rooted in the purpose and initiative of God. Before the world was even created, God planned to have a holy people, and he further

destined them to be his children. Their adoption would take place through
Christ, but also his choice of them took place "in Christ". All of this should
move believers to praise God for his grace to them. This plan was realized
through God's acts of redemption and forgiveness through the blood of
Christ. Grace is also at work in the way in which God conveys knowledge
to his people, specifically of his plan to bring together the whole universe
in unity in Christ. The divisions brought about by sin and rebellion and
enmity between sinners and sinful powers will be brought to an end. But
already believers have become God's property, marked as such with the
Spirit, the first installment of their inheritance, until God fully redeems
his people.

*Prayer report (Eph 1:15-23)*. Paul moves to intercession that his readers
may know the greatness of the power that God exercises for them over
against the hostile powers. God's power was especially displayed in the
exaltation of Christ, who has been made head over everything for the
church; his authority and power are exercised for their sake. Christ and
the church are related as head and body. Christ, who fills the universe
with his power, is also fully present in the church; thus the church itself
has the power to overcome any forces arrayed against it. Through its Head
the church is able to overcome all evil opposition in a hostile universe.

*Jews, Gentiles, salvation and reconciliation (Eph 2:1-21)*. Paul now
focuses on the relationship between Jewish and Gentile believers. Before
their conversion, both groups were sinners, whose life was governed by
the world; they were dead as far as responding to God was concerned and
destined to his wrath. At their conversion, God raised them from their
old life and brought them into a new "heavenly" existence, in which they
are alive to him. This was entirely due to his gracious initiative and action through Christ and did not depend upon any kind of human works
that might inspire self-confidence. Rather, good works are what God has
planned for believers to do as part of their new life.

If some Gentiles are in danger of thinking of themselves as independent
of Jewish believers, Paul reminds them that through Christ those who
were "far off" have been brought near to God's people. The barrier created by the law of Moses has been broken down. There is now one people
of God, since through Christ both Jews and Gentiles now have access to

God the Father. In effect, Israel is enlarged to include believing Gentiles. The new house (or better, household) of God is built upon the foundation that consists of (the teaching of) the apostles and (Christian) prophets, with Christ as the controlling stone. This building is a temple or place in which God is present, and the Gentiles form part of it.

*Apostleship to the Gentiles (Eph 3:1-21).* Paul confirms the position of his Gentile readers by referring to God's previously hidden plan, affirming that Gentiles and Jews together form one people of God, sharing the same divine promises. This united church is to bear witness to God's wisdom to the cosmic powers. Paul then prays to God as the Father for the spiritual strengthening of the readers, for Christ to live in them, and thus for them to grasp and experience the love of Christ in all its fullness.

*Unity and diversity in the church (Eph 4:1-16).* The second part of the letter inculcates conduct appropriate to this gospel. The church must manifest its unity, based on having one God and one hope for the future. Unity is inclusive of the rich provision that God has given for building up the church toward love and maturity. Different individuals receive different spiritual gifts; their recipients are themselves God's gifts to the church. Apostles and prophets form the foundation of the church, with their revelations of God's mysteries and other teaching; evangelists maintain the missionary outreach; pastors and teachers, linked together as a pair, undertake the two main tasks in local congregations.

*The old life and the new; family relationships (Eph 4:17—6:9).* The former sinful way of life must be replaced by a new pattern of behavior. Unchristian, immoral conduct arose from impenetrable Gentile ignorance of divine teaching; Christian believers learn about Christ, his character (cf. 2 Cor 10:1) and teaching. Their old nature must be shed like dirty clothes and replaced by the new nature. Sinful conduct grieves the Holy Spirit—a casual indication that the Spirit is understood as a personal being.

Divine forgiveness entails human forgiveness, as Christ taught. Love for one another is rooted in the love that he has demonstrated in giving himself as an offering to God. People who practice worldly, sinful behavior have no place in the kingdom of God; such people will face the wrath of God. Intoxication is contrasted with the joy and thanksgiving expressed in songs of praise, which goes along with being filled with the Spirit.

Believers are to subject themselves to one another. This is not one-sided (cf. Gal 5:13; Phil 2:3), but nevertheless three groups of people are singled out (wives, children, slaves). The wife's submission and respect for her husband are related to the submission of the church to Christ. There is an analogy between the church's dependence for care and support on Christ as its Head and Savior and that of the wife on her husband. However, the husband is counseled *at much greater length* to love his wife, just as Christ left his Father (cf. Gen 2:24), loved the church, and gave himself for it, so that the church might be pure and holy.

The corollary of the fact that Christian slaves and masters are brothers with the same heavenly Father is that this Master administers justice impartially, treating slaves and their masters alike.

*Spiritual battle (Eph 6:10-24).* Finally, believers must prepare themselves for what is not so much a moral struggle as a spiritual battle. They must put on Christ (Rom 13:14), a metaphor developed here (cf. 1 Thess 5:8) with the traditional picture of a suit of armor, with each part representing a Christian quality (faith) or a spiritual gift (truth, righteousness, salvation, the word of God).

## THEOLOGICAL THEMES

*Prayer and worship.* The letter emphasizes the love and the power of God, both of which are described in superlative terms. The mood of worship and praise dominates the presentation. Ephesians glorifies God the Father for his greatness, demonstrated in his blessings bestowed on his people. It is easy to overlook this element in expounding New Testament theology and try to reduce everything to cold, systematic, propositional form. Ephesians reminds us that New Testament theology is expressed in worship.

*Jews and Gentiles in the church.* One central concern of the letter is the relationship between Gentiles and Jews in the church. Jews and Gentiles have been reconciled by the death of Jesus and form one people and one temple for God to dwell in. This motif is based on the divine revelation given to the apostles and prophets, with Paul as the apostle specially commissioned to take this message to the Gentiles. There is a practical emphasis on maintaining this unity in the church's manifold life and ministry. The concern has broadened out from the issue of Jews and Gentiles, now stressing the unity of all believers with one another in love and the development of spiritual maturity.

In Paul's earlier letters the term "church" *(ekklēsia)* is mainly used for individual congregations or local groups of believers. Yet Paul could also refer to "the church" as an entity that exists across time and comprises the whole of the new people of God at any particular moment (1 Cor 10:32; 12:28; 15:9; Gal 1:13; Phil 3:6). This motif develops in Colossians and Ephesians. Each of the nine uses in Ephesians refers to the church as a whole rather than to an individual congregation. This cosmic entity is the object of Christ's love (Eph 5:25, 29). He is the head over the whole church, which can therefore be thought of as his body (Eph 1:22; 5:23). However, the church is not seen as a universal, organized world institution.

Ephesians distinguishes between church leaders who form the foundation of the church and are responsible for its mission (apostles, prophets and evangelists) and those who are active in local congregations (pastors and teachers). A mission (or rather missions) goes on alongside and in conjunction with local congregations but is separately organized to plant new congregations.

The stress on unity in the church goes beyond the exhortation that people should have the same mind and purpose in the local congregation (Phil 2:1-4) to the insistence that all Christians (both Jewish and Gentile) have one God (Spirit, Lord and Father—implicitly trinitarian) and one way of salvation through faith and baptism, and one hope. Yet there is variety in the church in the different gifts of grace that Christ gives to different individuals, for the one aim of building up Christ's body.

*Principalities and powers: The lordship of Christ.* A second central theme is the problem of the principalities and powers that dominate the world of darkness and threaten believers. Despite Christ's supremacy over them from his throne beside God, they are still active, and believers must oppose them. The fact that God has raised believers to the heavens does not insulate them from opposition. The hope of Christians is oriented not just toward the future and the end of the world when Christ returns (Eph 1:10), but also upward to the heavens, where Christ now sits enthroned and from where he empowers his people. The present lordship of Christ is of vital importance. The important statement in Ephesians

4:9-10 affirms the descent and ascent of Jesus and is best understood in terms of the V-shaped trajectory in Philippians 2:6-11: the "lower, earthly regions" (TNIV) refers to the earth rather than the underworld (NRSV). On his ascent, Christ bestowed the gifts of the Spirit on his people (cf. Acts 2:33). He himself is now said to fill everything. The church is then "the fullness of him who fills everything in every way" (Eph 1:23). The divine characteristic of being everywhere present is now manifested in the exalted and omnipotent Christ (Eph 4:10). What is said in Philippians 2:9-11 in terms of lordship is here stated in terms of omnipresent rule and authority and influence. Paul also prays that believers will be filled with all the fullness of God (Eph 3:19). They are engaged in a struggle with the opposing powers, and for this task nothing less than God's power is adequate. That power was seen in Christ and continues to be present in him, and through him it is conveyed to his church and to the individuals who compose the church.

*The Holy Spirit.* Alongside this strong emphasis on Christ and the way in which he fills the church and individual believers, there might seem to be no role for the Holy Spirit. However, the Spirit is the seal placed by God upon his people (Eph 1:13). Through the Spirit's influence, believers are strengthened with divine power (Eph 3:16). They are to seek to be filled with the Spirit (Eph 5:18). Through the Word of God the Spirit equips them for their battle with the powers. The Spirit is active in the church in producing oneness, since all Christians share in one and the same Spirit (Eph 2:18; 4:3-4). The Spirit is also associated with revelation, wisdom and knowledge (Eph 1:17).

## CONCLUSION

Alongside the understanding of Christ's work in terms of forgiveness of sins and raising up believers to new life in the Spirit's power, there is also a conception of Christ as the omnipresent, supreme manifestation of God's power, through which the forces hostile to God will be overcome. The victory of Christ is an indispensable part of understanding his death and resurrection. At the same time the death of Christ brings about reconciliation between Jewish and Gentile believers and forms the foundation for the church's unity in the Spirit.

# 16

# THE LETTERS TO TIMOTHY AND TITUS

The two letters to Timothy and the one to Titus (collectively known as the Pastoral Letters or Epistles) can be discussed together because, despite their significant individual emphases and characteristics, they stand quite close to one another in their discussion of Christian leadership at the point of transition from the living presence of Paul to dependence on the memory of his example and teaching. They differ from the earlier letters in being addressed to the leadership, although they are also meant for the congregations to read. Although their style raises some doubts as to whether they have come to us directly from Paul's own pen, we treat them here as part of his legacy to the church.

## THE LETTER TO TITUS: THE THEOLOGICAL STORY

*Greeting (Tit 1:1-4).* Titus begins with a lengthy greeting that spells out three things. Paul has been appointed an apostle in order that through his preaching he might help people with the two stages in the Christian life:

the moment of conversion and the growth in godly living. The gospel that lies behind this process is analyzed in terms of promise and fulfillment: God's premundane promise of eternal life, and the realization of that promise through the apostolic proclamation of the gospel. The stress rests upon the word of God and its proclamation; Titus must continue this apostolic task, although neither he nor Timothy are called apostles. This greeting puts all the practical and ethical instructions that follow into a spiritual context.

*The appointment of elders (Tit 1:5-16).* Titus is to complete the unfinished task of consolidating the infant congregations in Crete (Tit 1:5a), including the appointment of leaders (Tit 1:5b). The essential characteristics to be sought in these leaders are sound belief and Christian behavior, although the ability to lead and to teach is implicit in the description. They must be able to rebuke those who promulgate false teaching and those who are deceived into accepting it.

*The teaching that Titus is to give (Tit 2:1—3:15).* Titus is to teach the truth. Specific applications are made to different groups in the church, adapted to their particular needs and temptations, but sufficiently general to apply to everybody. The outstanding requirements are personal self-control and good behavior in society. The teaching is backed up by two doctrinal statements that give a basis for abandoning sinful behavior and living godly lives (Tit 2:11-14; 3:3-8). Believers live between the first appearing of God's grace and the future glorious revelation of Christ; they are redeemed from sin and live in hope. Living in this context, they must eschew their former wickedness and lead lives dedicated to God and filled with good. Their conversion was a divine act of grace, which has powerfully renewed them through God's bestowal of the Holy Spirit.

Throughout, practical instruction is thus based on the gospel. The two main positive motifs, right belief and godliness of character, are closely related to each other. Since the false teaching lies more in the area of ethical slackness than in doctrinal error, the antidote is primarily giving a reminder of the basis for ethical living and showing how it necessarily arises out of the gospel.

## THE FIRST LETTER TO TIMOTHY:
## THE THEOLOGICAL STORY

Like Titus the first letter to Timothy is primarily concerned with church life threatened by the activity of opponents.

*Timothy's commission (1 Tim 1:1-20).* Paul renews his commission to Timothy for using his authority to restrain the opponents' efforts. They are teaching foolish and futile doctrines based on a misuse and misunderstanding of the law contained in the Old Testament Scriptures. This law properly understood and used has its place in the context of the gospel. Paul outlines the gospel by describing his own commissioning to be God's servant in the gospel; this has taken place despite Paul's previous sin, as a result of divine grace and mercy displayed toward sinners. Timothy too must "fight the good fight" (1 Tim 6:12) despite the opposition as he holds on to faith and keeps his conscience pure, unlike some who have gone astray.

*Prayer in the congregation (1 Tim 2:1-15).* First, believers must intercede for all people and specifically for peaceful conditions to spread the gospel, since God wants all people to be saved and Christ gave himself as a ransom for them. Effective prayer is hindered by inappropriate behavior, whether by men or women. The proper demeanor of women must be shown in their outward appearance. An addendum stipulates that they must not teach men. We may surmise that congregational prayer was suffering because of dissension in the meetings and that some of the women were affected by the teaching of Paul's opponents and needed to be restrained.

*The appointment of leaders (1 Tim 3:1-16).* Second, godly leadership is essential. Not everybody is spiritually and otherwise qualified for these tasks. The qualifications listed apply both to candidates and those already doing the work. One implied purpose of leadership is to counteract the work of the opponents (cf. 1 Tim 3:9). Positively it enables the congregation to be a buttress that upholds the truth. Paul succinctly expresses the wonderful heart of that truth as what took place in the bodily appearing and subsequent glorification of Jesus. This is the glorious divine "mystery" revealed and committed to the church for safekeeping and for proclamation to all people (1 Tim 3:16).

*How the church leader is to behave and teach (1 Tim 4:1—6:21).* After a prophecy of false teaching and practice, which is already coming true, and a rebuttal of one aspect of the heresy concerning marriage and asceticism, Timothy himself (typifying leaders generally) is called to act in a godly way, avoiding error and teaching the truth (1 Tim 4:1-16). After some practical instructions to him concerning pastoral care, Paul turns to the dangers caused by love of money and instructs Timothy personally regarding his stance amid these temptations. The point is backed up by reminders about God and Jesus.

As in Titus, practical instructions are followed or preceded by theological "warrants": referring to Paul's own conversion and status as an apostle, restating the content of the gospel, placing the opposition in the context of prophecy, putting Timothy under the judgment of God, and reminding Timothy of his own conversion and commission.

## THE SECOND LETTER TO TIMOTHY:
## THE THEOLOGICAL STORY

Second Timothy concentrates on Timothy himself as a leader and his personal behavior.

*Encouragement to a church leader (2 Tim 1:1—2:26).* Timothy is encouraged to overcome timidity and a temptation to weakness in the face of possible suffering. Equipped with the gift of the Spirit, he is called to fearless presentation of the gospel; he must preserve and teach the apostolic deposit faithfully. Timothy must also entrust the message to faithful people who will continue the task. These injunctions are backed up with a doctrinal argument that refers in turn to Jesus and his resurrection, God's purpose for his people, and the promises given to those who are prepared to be identified with Jesus.

*Opposition and steadfastness (2 Tim 3:1—4:8).* As in 1 Timothy, the context includes the dangers of apostasy afflicting the church in the last days. Timothy is reminded of Paul's own example of patience and suffering, and of the need to hold fast to what he has learned from the Scriptures (provided they are rightly understood!). The strength of the opposition appears to be the greatest threat to Timothy, but it is counterbalanced by reference to what he has learned from Scripture and by Paul's own example of steadfastness.

*Paul the missionary in prison (2 Tim 4:9-22).* Finally, there is a section of personal news and instructions about how Timothy is to help Paul in his own mission while he is imprisoned. Paul's consciousness of divine help and his ongoing concern for evangelism are vividly depicted.

In summary, Timothy is assured of the Spirit's help. He is reminded of the examples of Christ and Paul himself. He is told to expect opposition, persecution and suffering, yet he is to stand firm, avoid evil, preach the gospel, rebuke heresy, and hope that some heretics may repent.

## THEOLOGICAL THEMES

*Traditional features.* Some of the doctrinal statements that back up the practical teaching and exhortation are described as "trustworthy" sayings (1 Tim 1:15; 3:1; 4:9; 2 Tim 2:11; Tit 3:8). These and other statements may rest on traditional formulations (e.g., 1 Tim 2:6 and Tit 2:14 clearly echo Mark 10:45).

The main features of Paul's theology as we know it from his earlier letters reappear. Justification is by grace through faith and without any works (Tit 3:5; 2 Tim 1:9); Christian salvation is mediated "in Christ" (1 Tim 1:14; 3:13; 2 Tim 1:9, 13; 2:1, 10; 3:12, 15). Believers are identified with Christ in his death and new life (2 Tim 2:11-13). There is universal provision of salvation for all people (1 Tim 2:6; 4:10; Tit 2:11), with special emphasis on the inclusion of the Gentiles (1 Tim 2:7; 3:16; 2 Tim 4:17). The Spirit is the agent in new birth (Tit 3:5), the source of power for Christian living (2 Tim 1:7, 14), and the source of charismatic gifts for ministry (1 Tim 4:14; 2 Tim 1:6). The Christian life is characterized by strength in weakness, and the life of the missionary in particular is one of suffering and imprisonment and even death, although the triumph of the gospel is assured. Alongside these familiar theological traits, there are some fresh, or developed, features.

*Jesus and God.* The term *epiphany* (or *appearing*) was used in the ancient world for visitations by God that were in some way visible and salvific. In the Christian circles, it has come to be used for the future coming of Christ (2 Thess 2:8; 2 Tim 4:1, 8; Tit 2:13). Now it is also used to refer to the earthly life of Christ (2 Tim 1:10). His incarnation is envisaged as such a visible, saving action of God. First Timothy 3:16 speaks of the One who appeared in flesh and was vindicated "in spirit" (*or* "by the Spirit"). His coming into the world (1 Tim 1:15) carries resonances of similar incarnation language in John. The insistence that Christ Jesus was himself "human" (1 Tim 2:5) would be unnecessary if he were not already thought of as divine. The language of epiphany was used in Judaism of the time, but here it may express the gospel in a way that would be intelligible in the Greek-speaking world of Ephesus and Crete.

This concept of epiphany is extended to include the whole of God's saving action in and through Christ. "The grace of God has appeared" and "the kindness and love of God our Savior appeared" (Tit 2:11; 3:4). The saving event comprises not only the coming of Christ but also the pouring out of the Spirit and the apostolic testimony to Jesus' significance (cf. 1 Tim 2:5-6, which links the self-giving of Christ and the testimony to it); similarly in 2 Corinthians 5:18-21, the reconciling action of God in Christ and the message of reconciliation belong together.

In his death, Christ gave himself in order to redeem sinners (Tit 2:14). Little is said about his resurrection in relation to salvation, although it is stressed in connection with believers' resurrection (2 Tim 2:8-13) and implied in a reference to him as the destroyer of death (2 Tim 1:10). He will come as the Judge and Savior (2 Tim 1:10; 4:1).

*Savior* aptly sums up the person of Jesus in these letters. Not only does it emphasize the fundamentally salvific character of the theology, but it also is a title shared by Christ (Tit 1:4; 2:13; 3:6; 2 Tim 1:10) with God (Tit 1:3; 2:10; 3:4; 1 Tim 1:1; 2:3; 4:10). Christian hope rests on "the appearing of the glory of our great God and Savior, Jesus Christ" (Tit 2:13; there is debate whether "Jesus Christ" stands in apposition to "our great God and Savior" or to "the glory"). There is thus a functional equivalence between Christ and God; the Old Testament concept of the "coming" of Yahweh (or of his "glory") is here interpreted in terms of Christ's coming in the same way as the title *Lord* (= *Yahweh*) is also transferred to him.

The concept of God that stands alongside this picture of Christ has sometimes been thought to be somewhat remote and lofty (cf. 1 Tim 1:17; 6:15-16). The term *Father* is rarely used with reference to God, whether in his relationship to Christ or to believers, and the terms *son* and *child* are not used for relationships with God. However, this impression is offset by the use of the term *Savior* and the reference to God's "kindness and love" (Tit 3:4).

*The life of believers.* Entry into the people of God rests entirely on God's action through Christ as Savior (1 Tim 1:15; 2:4; 2 Tim 1:9; Tit 3:5). Human beings are sinners, characterized by wickedness, ungodliness and futility (Tit 2:11, 14; 3:3). Salvation is deliverance from such a state to a new quality of life here and now (cf. 1 Tim 4:8) and to eternal life in God's heavenly kingdom (1 Tim 1:16; 2 Tim 1:10; 4:18; Tit 1:2; 3:7). References to the day of judgment (1 Tim 5:24; 2 Tim 1:18; 4:8) imply that, unless they have been saved, sinners face condemnation and loss (1 Tim 6:9).

Salvation is also spoken of as justification (Tit 3:7). The language of rebirth and renewal (Tit 3:5) expresses a fundamental transformation through the working of the Holy Spirit, who is lavishly outpoured on believers (Tit 3:6); creates power, love and self-discipline (2 Tim 1:7); and provides help to believers in their custody of the gospel (2 Tim 1:14). The Spirit also gives appropriate endowments to church leaders (1 Tim 4:14; 2 Tim 1:6-7).

The life of believers is one of identification with Christ (2 Tim 2:11-13) and is empowered by his grace (2 Tim 2:1). They share in the death of Christ; conversion is regarded as a metaphorical death to the old life, entailing the readiness even for martyrdom as the extreme possibility facing believers. The ongoing nature of this life appears in the need to be ready for endurance and faithfulness, despite temptations to apostasy and unfaithfulness.

The inner basis of the Christian life is "a pure heart and a good conscience and a sincere faith" (1 Tim 1:5). The *heart* refers to the seat of motives and is to be pure and single-minded in devotion to God (1 Tim 1:5; 2 Tim 2:22). The word *conscience* is used in much the same way, as the organ that adjudges conduct (or planned conduct). It can be described as "good" (1 Tim 1:5, 19) or "clean" (1 Tim 3:9; 2 Tim 1:3). The contrasting condition is when the conscience is not working properly (1 Tim 4:2; Tit 1:15), giving false judgments (or no judgment) instead of condemning conduct that is wrong by God's standards.

*Faith* is the most conspicuous theological term in the Pastoral Epistles. It is closely linked with knowledge (Tit 1:1) and the corresponding stress on sound teaching in the church. Consequently, the notion of faith itself broadens to include "the faith" as the objective expression of what Christians should believe and as the act of accepting this creed (1 Tim 3:9; 6:21; 2 Tim 2:18). Faith certainly remains basically trust in God or Christ and commitment to him (1 Tim 1:16; 3:16; 2 Tim 1:12; Tit 3:8). Although closely associated with conversion (1 Tim 1:14; 5:12; 2 Tim 1:5; 3:15), faith is an ongoing attitude, involving faithfulness and perseverance (1 Tim 2:15; Tit 3:15). The standard term for "Christians" is *believers/ faithful* (1 Tim 4:3, 10, 12; 5:16; Tit 1:6).

In the lists of vices and virtues that are typical of the Pastoral Epistles, faith is most frequently linked with *love* (1 Tim 1:5, 14; 2:15; 4:12; 6:11; 2 Tim 1:13; 2:22; 3:10-11; Tit 2:2). Love in turn is expressed in "good" or "beautiful" deeds (cf. Tit 2:14; 3:8, 14). Another general concept used to sum up Christian behavior is *piety* (*eusebeia*), a current term for describing the type of life determined by a right attitude to God or the gods. Within Judaism, piety meant the "fear of the Lord" and combined both reverent knowledge of God based on his self-revelation and conduct in the light of that knowledge. It was thus a comprehensive term for "religion" in all its aspects. For Christians, religion is shaped by Christ (1 Tim 3:16), expressed in a life "in Christ" (2 Tim 3:12). It includes living an orderly life, characterized by sobriety, moderation, dignity and self-control.

*The church.* There is a strong stress on the church, largely because of the need to develop alternative forms of leadership for the period after Paul was no longer active. The church needed leaders to cope with the spread of certain teachings in conflict with Paul's understanding of the gospel. There is a stress on the importance of teaching in conformity with the gospel of Paul himself; the "deposit" handed down from Paul was to be preserved carefully by his successors and passed on to other people who would make it the basis of their teaching (1 Tim 6:20; 2 Tim 1:13-14; 2:2). It was necessary to appoint local church leaders who would hold fast to the gospel and also, in terms of character and gifts of leadership, be fit to guide the congregations (1 Tim 3:1-12; Tit 1:5-9). Although the local congregations are under the care of Paul's colleagues, Timothy and Titus, they must facilitate the development of local leadership. The structure of the local leadership is still in process of evolution; *elder* and *overseer* can apparently be used for the same groups of people, and there are *deacons* in 1 Timothy but not in Titus.

In Paul's earlier writings, the congregation is seen as the body of Christ, in which all the members have their respective functions (1 Cor 12; Rom 12). Here the dominant motif is rather that of the church as a household (1 Tim 3:15). This metaphor brings out more the idea of rule and direction, which seems to be needed in the situation. It may also convey the thought that people have different assigned roles and positions within the household, with corresponding duties, just as in an ordinary household there are various roles for the wife, children, slaves and other members (cf. Tit 2:2-10; 1 Tim 6:1-2).

A second, closely related picture sees the church as the pillar and bulwark of the truth (1 Tim 3:15). There is probably a combination of ideas here: the church is to be a guardian of the truth, or firm basis for the truth, and also a freestanding pillar (such as stood outside the Solomonic temple; 1 Kings 7:15-22), which bears testimony to the truth. Thus the church is assigned a central role in preserving and proclaiming the gospel.

The church is also identified as "the church of the living God" (1 Tim 3:15). God is powerfully present in the church, and the whole phrase echoes the description of Israel as the "assembly of Yahweh". Without using the word *temple*, the author conveys the idea of the congregation as the group of people who belong to God (cf. Tit 2:14), within whose assembly he is present, and who form his "house". This leads to a much more dynamic concept of the church than the household metaphor might have suggested. The church is far from being a static institution.

## CONCLUSION

The Pastoral Epistles provide resources for ensuring that congregations remain faithful to Paul's model of belief and life in the face of an opposition representing a reversion to a peculiar type of ascetic Jewish Christianity, which was in danger of losing itself in speculation. There is a powerful stress on the need for teaching in accordance with the deposit of faith handed down in the church and for a church polity to ensure that this takes place, all of which depends upon godly leadership and sound teaching.

# 17

# THE THEOLOGY OF THE PAULINE LETTERS

## THE CENTRAL THEME OF PAUL'S THEOLOGY

As with the other New Testament authors, the framework of Paul's theology is constituted by Judaism. The main influence is the Old Testament itself, seen in the formal citations (mostly in Romans, 1 and 2 Corinthians, and Galatians) and the frequent allusions. Paul is also influenced by the Jewish theology of his time. He is less shaped by the kind of religion centered on exposition of the law, as found in the rabbinic literature, and is much more at home in apocalyptic theology, centered on God's intervention in history through the Messiah and the life of the world to come. From his conversion onward, his own Christian experience plays the decisive part in the development of his theology. This includes occasions when he receives prophetic visions and messages from the Lord. His thought is also shaped by that of the earliest Christians who were his contemporaries and were developing their theological understanding of the gospel alongside him. He has close personal contacts with other missionaries and leaders associated with Jerusalem and Antioch. He quotes traditions handed down within early Christian circles, including accounts of things said and done by Jesus.

Paul is primarily a preacher and teacher. He sums up his evangelistic message: "Christ died for our sins according to the Scriptures, . . . he was buried, . . . he was raised on the third day according to the Scriptures, and . . . he appeared to Cephas, and then to the Twelve. . . . Last of all he appeared to me also" (1 Cor 15:3-5, 8). Those who believe this message experience salvation; God calls them into the church, the company of people who receive the Holy Spirit. They live a new life in union with the crucified and risen Christ, a life expressing itself in holiness and love, and they look forward to the (second) advent of Christ and the resurrection of the dead.

We have expressed this central theme in the form of a doctrinal statement because this is what Paul himself does. A current theological fashion is to say that Paul tells a story (or narrative) whose plot can be reconstructed. Certainly the Jewish Scriptures tell the story of the ongoing interrelationship between God and humankind from the creation of the world and Adam and Eve. Early Christians such as Paul do take over this story, and in a new way they understand it in the light of how it continues in their own time. Paul, however, does not so much narrate a story as rather comment on the story and its implications.

## SPECIFIC ELEMENTS IN PAUL'S THEOLOGY

*God—the Father.* God the Father is the initiator of the action in the story. He is the sovereign ruler, carrying out his purpose through the mission of his people and specifically of those called to be witnesses and apostles. The gospel is the gospel of God (Rom 1:1). God the Father is the one God and Creator of the universe (1 Cor 8:6; cf. Eph 4:6), and human beings are made in his image (1 Cor 11:7). He expects their worship and their willing obedience to his way of life for them (cf. Rom 1:21). God is living and active, by contrast with the idols worshiped by the Gentiles (1 Thess 1:9). He will judge the world for its sinfulness (Rom 2:5); indeed his wrath is already being revealed in the way in which human sin leads to human misery (Rom 1:18). God was active in the history of Israel, the nation called to be his people, who turned out to be generally rebellious against him (Rom 9—11). God sent the Messiah to the Jewish people

(Rom 9:5). And now he is active in initiating and effecting salvation for Jews and Gentiles alike. He is faithful to the people whom he has called and who have responded to his call (1 Cor 1:9; 1 Thess 5:24). The word *Father* expresses his caring relationship for believing people (2 Cor 6:18, citing 2 Sam 7:14), and they have the privilege of praying to him as "Abba, Father" (Rom 8:15; Gal 4:6).

*God—the Son.* God is, however, supremely Father as the Father of his Son, revealed and manifested in the human person Jesus (Rom 15:6; 2 Cor 1:3), through whom believers come into a similar relationship of sonship (Rom 8:29; Gal 4:5-6). As Son, Jesus is the image of God (2 Cor 4:4; Col 1:15), and believers are being transformed to bear the same image (Rom 8:29; 1 Cor 15:49; 2 Cor 3:18; Col 3:10).

That Jesus was truly human, with a human body, was scarcely disputed (1 Tim 2:5). Plenty of people could testify to his life and death. Paul describes him as the heavenly man (1 Cor 15:45-49) whom God sent from heaven to be born of a woman (Gal 4:4). It is not that a human being ascended to heaven and became a heavenly being, but that a heavenly being became human (2 Cor 8:9; Phil 2:6-8). The human character of Jesus is theologically significant because it enables Paul to compare him with Adam (Rom 5:12-21; 1 Cor 15:22, 45-49) and to state that he was born and lived under the law and came under its curse to deliver humanity from it (Gal 3:13). He is the "one man" whose righteous act undid the effects of that other man, Adam (Rom 5:15). His Davidic sonship qualified him to be the Messiah.

Alongside his human descent and nature, Paul stresses his position as Son of God with power at the resurrection (Rom 1:3). He was Son of God throughout his career (Gal 4:4) but after the resurrection has become the enthroned Son of God. At Paul's conversion, God the Father revealed Jesus Christ as his Son to him (Gal 1:16), and Paul expresses his faith in God's Son, "who loved me and gave himself for me" (Gal 2:20) and for all sinners (Gal 1:4; Eph 5:2, 25; 1 Tim 2:6; Tit 2:14). The use of "Son" expresses the greatness of God's gift in sending Jesus to die for sinners (Rom 5:10; 8:3, 32).

Paul names Jesus alongside God as the source of spiritual blessings (e.g., Rom 1:7), thus implicitly assigning to Jesus the same role as that of

God the Father. Alongside the Jewish confession of the one God, Paul also affirms the one Lord, Jesus Christ (1 Cor 8:6). The association of the Son with the act of creation is developed to show his supremacy over all that has been created, specifically over the principalities and powers that threaten human existence (Col 1:15-20; cf. "raised" to God's right hand: Rom 8:34; Eph 1:20; Col 3:1). The Son thus existed as Son before creation. God's judgment seat (Rom 14:9-12) is also identified as Christ's (2 Cor 5:10; Phil 2:10-11). Paul did not receive his gospel from a human source, (literally) "from a man", but from a revelation of Jesus Christ (Gal 1:11-12). Both Jesus and God are the objects of faith (Rom 4:24; 10:9, 11). Hence it would not be surprising if Christ is actually referred to as "God"; however, the interpretation of Romans 9:5 and Titus 2:13 is debated. The later letters bring out the way in which the fullness of Deity is present in Christ (Col 2:9) and through him is conveyed to believers (Eph 1:23). Even so, God the Father remains the supreme being in the universe, so that ultimate obedience is given to him even by Jesus, who fully shares his authoritative position over the universe (1 Cor 15:28; Phil 2:9-11).

*God—the Holy Spirit.* Paul describes the Spirit both as a power operating in believers and also in more personal terms. The Spirit intercedes for believers with the Father (Rom 8:26-27) and can be grieved by their sin (Eph 4:30). The same effects in the lives of believers are attributed to both Christ and the Spirit (cf. 1 Cor 12:4-6), and Paul identifies "the Lord" in Exodus 34:34 as the Spirit (2 Cor 3:18) in the same way as he interprets other Old Testament occurrences of "the Lord" as references to Christ. Paul links together the Lord Jesus Christ, God and the Holy Spirit in a benediction (2 Cor 13:14). The Spirit can be placed alongside the Father and the Son in an incipient trinitarianism; there is an understanding of Father, Son and Spirit each as personal and sharing similar functions in such a way that the later church recognized them as equally divine and sought for a way of expressing their interrelatedness that did justice to their unity as well as their individuality.

*The gospel—the need for salvation.* Although Paul's mission is to make known the gospel as good news for humankind (Rom 1:1, 9; 15:16; 1 Cor 1:17; Gal 1:16; cf. Eph 3:8), his ultimate concern in so doing is to glorify God (cf. Eph 1:6, 12, 14). *Glory* can refer to the praise and worship that people should offer to God or to God's exalted state and its visible accompaniments, a throne and dazzling light. The final aim of all human endeavor must be to glorify God in word (Rom 11:36; 16:27; Gal 1:5) and deed (1 Cor 10:31). The Son glorifies the Father, even when he himself is being glorified (Phil 2:9-11). Ultimately God alone is to be glorified; nevertheless he shares his glory with his people (Rom 8:30; 1 Thess 2:12; 2 Thess 2:14).

The need for the gospel arises from humanity's failure to glorify God (Rom 1:21), and the effect of bringing salvation to people should be that they offer praise to God (Rom 15:9; Gal 1:24). Good news presupposes a lack in the human situation, for which the gospel provides a welcome remedy. If people are unaware of their need, their position needs to be made clear to them. Consequently, Paul begins by announcing God's negative reaction of wrath (Rom 1:18), which is linked to a future occasion when God will impartially judge humanity for its wrongdoing and express his anger against sinners who disobey him (Rom 2:5; 5:9; cf. Eph 5:6). The content of judgment is death (Rom 5:12-21; 6:23) and destruction, in other words, separation from God and his kingdom (2 Thess 1:9).

Judgment is necessitated by sin. Though other New Testament authors tend to use the term "sin" for individual sinful acts, Paul more commonly refers to sin as a kind of force or power that enters and overcomes human beings (Rom 7:17, 20) or the state of sinfulness that results from it (Rom 6:1). Humanity in general is under the control of sin (Rom 3:9; Gal 3:22); sin is a baleful influence that made its entry into the world through Adam (Rom 5:12). There is no escape from its control (Rom 7:14). Sin is like a terminal disease, leading inexorably to death (Rom 5:12; 7:13; 8:2; 1 Cor 15:56). Paul can write as though the sentence of death has already been executed (Rom 7:11; Rom 8:10).

Paul uses the word *flesh*, a term in itself neutral, in referring to human nature as inevitably sinful and opposed to God. The desires or actions of the flesh characterize humanity following its own desires in rebellion against the commands of the Creator and the guidance of the Spirit (Rom 8:4; Gal 5:17). Salvation issues in setting the sinner free from the flesh's power, free to be led by the Spirit (Rom 8:1-13; Gal 5:16-26). Since *flesh* (as defined above) is the space occupied by sin, the flesh is incapable of redemption; rather, the sinner is delivered from its domination. Paul also speaks of the human "body" as being subjected to the hostile power of sin (Rom 6:6; 7:24), but it can be redeemed and transformed (Rom 8:23; 1 Cor 15:44, 51).

The Jewish people received the law of Moses from God, and it could well be thought that obedience to its commandments would lead them to life (Rom 10:5; Gal 3:12). Paul agrees that the possession of the law makes clear to people just which forms of conduct are sinful (Rom 7:7). It brings sin to light. The sinful impulses already in a person come to life and issue in sinful desires and actions (Rom 7:7-11). The law is obviously not the cause of sin, but rather it functions as the indicator that registers the presence of sin. The law cannot give a person the power to overcome sin and cease to sin.

Paul attacks the view that people may get right with God by (what he calls) the *works of the law*. This phrase signifies obedience to the precepts of the Mosaic law, with circumcision, observance of festivals and food laws being the aspects that are to the fore. Paul attacks these observances as works in which people may put their confidence ("boast") and rejects them as being unable to fulfill this function. To adopt them is to misconceive the Mosaic law as a means of justification. This is not the intended purpose of the law. Paul's opposition is related to the way in which some people are requiring Gentile Christians to do these works of the law in order to be justified and to enable fellowship between them and Jewish Christian believers. Many of the latter continue to regard Gentiles who do not keep such aspects of the Mosaic law as unclean and their foods as unclean.

*The gospel—salvation by grace.* The gospel announces what God has done to save humanity from its plight. Salvation rests on God's action in Jesus Christ to deliver people from the wrath to come (1 Thess 1:10; 5:9). Some claim that Paul portrays an act of Christ's mediation between sinners and a hostile God, who needs to be persuaded to forgive them; this caricature is a travesty of Paul's teaching. There is a persistent stress on the love, grace and mercy of God toward sinners. Paul's characteristic term *grace* conveys the fact that God shows love to those who do not deserve it. He is compassionate to those who are suffering as a result of sin;

they cannot deliver themselves and have no specific claims to God's favor. Grace is operative in the initial saving action of God but also throughout the subsequent lives of God's people and in the work of missionaries (Rom 1:7; 15:15; Gal 2:9).

*The saving event.* The central event in the gospel is the death and resurrection of Jesus. These two actions belong closely together (Rom 4:25; 8:34; 1 Cor 15:3-5; 2 Cor 5:15; Phil 3:10; 1 Thess 4:14), but the weight lies on the former. The death of Jesus was concerned with sin (1 Cor 15:3; Gal 1:4; cf. Rom 8:3; 2 Cor 5:19-21) and is for all people (2 Cor 5:14-15; cf. 1 Tim 2:6), specifically as sinners (Rom 5:6); it is confessed by the people who have actually benefited from the death as being "for us" (Rom 5:8; 2 Cor 5:21; Gal 2:20; 3:13).

These phrases ("for all" and "for us") might simply mean that Christ died for our benefit without implying that he did something so that other people would not have do it, specifically that he died in order to save them from having to die. However, when Paul says that Christ has delivered us from the curse imposed by the law upon those who do not observe it by himself becoming a curse for us in his death (Gal 3:10-14), this can only mean that Christ bore the curse instead of us. The thought of the scapegoat who bears all the sins of the people away (Lev 16:20-22) may be present. Christ died the death that is due to sinners because of their sin.

Further, having written about Christ dying for all (2 Cor 5:14), Paul says that the good news of reconciliation rests on the fact that "God was reconciling the world to himself in Christ, not counting people's sins against them. . . . God made him who had no sin to be sin for us, so that in him we might become the righteousness of God". The sinless Christ became "sin" so that sinners might become "righteousness"; in other words, he became one with sinners so that they might become righteous. He became the representative of sinners and died on their behalf so that they might be delivered from their sins and have the status of righteous people (2 Cor 5:18-21). People are put in the right with God because he "presented Christ as a sacrifice of atonement, through the shedding of his blood" (Rom 3:25). Just as the offering of sacrifices canceled out sin under the old covenant, so the offering of Christ, provided by God and not by human beings, cancels out sin (cf. Rom 8:3 TNIV; 1 Cor 5:6-8; Eph 5:2).

*The nature of salvation.* Four main images express the results of what Christ did by his death and resurrection. They belong together and mutually condition one another. No one single picture is adequate to explain the cross.

*Salvation* may refer to healing from illness and to rescue from other life-threatening dangers, but also more generally to the benefits brought to a people by a ruler (*Savior* was a common title for such). Paul uses the term particularly for deliverance from God's wrath at the final judgment (Rom 5:9; 13:11; 1 Cor 5:5; cf. Phil 1:28; 1 Thess 5:8-9), but it also sums up broadly the benefits brought by the gospel here and in this world (Rom 1:16; 8:24; 1 Cor 15:2; 2 Cor 1:6; 6:2; Eph 1:13; cf. the use of the present participle "the saved": 1 Cor 1:18; 2 Cor 2:15; Acts 2:47).

*Redemption* covers two related Pauline metaphors. One is the deliverance of captives from bondage, whether by the payment of a ransom (Is 43:1-4; 52:3) or the exercise of superior power (Deut 7:8). God delivers those who were under the law and its curse (Gal 3:13; 4:5). Hence *redemption* is the key term in explaining justification (Rom 3:25). The redeemed people experience freedom. The other metaphor is of the purchase of people so that they belong to God; here the thought is more of a change of master, with the obligation now to serve God (1 Cor 6:20; 7:23). The purchase involves a cost to God, his self-giving in his Son.

*Justification* is concerned with righteousness. In the Old Testament the corresponding verb is used in a legal setting for the action of a human judge, whose duty is to acquit, or "justify", the innocent who are wrongly charged with some crime or wrong and to condemn the guilty: he is unrighteous if he does otherwise. Theologically, justification is concerned with the relationship of sinners to God. One theoretical way to be in the right with God is through keeping his law (not just possessing it, as some Jews apparently thought). So Paul contrasts two ways of being justified, either by works of the law (Rom 3:20; 4:2; Gal 2:16; 3:11), which is impossible, or by faith (Rom 3:26, 28, 30; 5:1; Gal 2:16; 3:8; 24). Behind this contrast lies the fact that God confers justification by Christ (Gal 2:17; cf. Rom 5:9). It is thus to be seen as a gift (Rom 3:24), God acting by grace (Rom 3:24; cf. Tit 3:7) through the act of deliverance "in Christ", the Christ who died sacrificially (Rom 3:24). The implication is that Christ's death takes away the sin that human beings have committed, so that God is righteous in justifying them and not like a judge who acquits the guilty. Consequently, justification is bestowed in the manner of a gift and not as something that God is obliged to give, like an employer paying a wage to somebody who has done satisfactory work.

People receive justification by faith in God himself (Rom 4:24-25; so also with Abraham; Rom 4:3). Where no object is supplied, faith as such is contrasted with working as the means of justification (Rom 3:28; Gal 3:5). Sometimes Paul refers to faith in Christ (Gal 2:16) as the agent through whom justification takes place. The phrase *the faith of Jesus Christ* is widely thought to mean "the faith[fulness] shown *by* Jesus Christ" (Rom 3:22; cf. Rom 3:26; Gal 2:16, 20; 3:22): the basis for justification is in Jesus who trusted in God (cf. Mt 27:43) and was obedient right through to the point of death (cf. Phil 2:8). True though this statement is, it is more likely that the phrase signifies "faith *in* Jesus Christ". Although *repentance* is the flip side of faith in Luke-Acts, it is generally not part of the vocabulary of conversion in Paul; occasionally he mentions it in relation to backsliding believers (2 Cor 7:9-10; 12:21).

Justification is closely tied to the believers' relationship to Jesus, in which they are joined to him in his death and resurrection (Gal 2:20; cf. Gal 6:14; Rom 4:25). It has a negative and a positive aspect in that it sets believers free from sin and its consequences and brings them into a new relationship with God (cf. the new creation in 2 Cor 5:17). Justification takes place "in Christ" (Gal 2:17). This might simply mean "by Christ" (in contrast with "by the law"; Gal 3:11; 5:4), but there may well be a deeper nuance. Justification exists when a person is so united with Christ by their faith that they share in his new life. Consequently, justification is not a mere declaration of pardon that could be bestowed without any real change following it in the sinner. It is inextricably linked to the change in character that comes about through being united with Christ.

*Reconciliation* is the fourth main image used by Paul. As a metaphor based on human relationships, specifically diplomacy, it might well be thought to be more personal than language drawn from law courts, slave markets and even rescue operations. Reconciliation is the establishment of peace between two opposing or warring groups or individuals. Since

Paul stresses that God in his grace sent Jesus his Son, it follows that Jesus acts as the envoy of God in bringing the offer of peace to God's enemies and not as a third-party mediator who has to persuade God and humanity to come together (2 Cor 5:18-21). But it is not that God could simply overlook the sins. The statement that God made Christ to be sin for us so that we might become righteousness through Christ shows that God was prepared to treat sinners as righteous, but only as the result of his making Christ to be sin for them, to be the bearer of their sins.

Reconciliation is closely linked with justification as another way of making essentially the same point. If sinners have been justified by the blood of Christ, they will all the more be saved from God's wrath at the final judgment through Christ. Similarly, if God's enemies were reconciled by God giving his Son to die, how much more will God deliver his friends who put their confidence in him! (Rom 5:9-11). God makes peace through the blood shed on the cross and thus reconciles all things to himself, including specifically the readers who had been enemies of God but have now been reconciled through Christ's death (Rom 5:1; Col 1:20-21; Eph 2:16-18). The concept of reconciliation particularly brings out the fact that racial and other distinctions are overcome in the creation of the one people of God; in being reconciled to God, we are reconciled to one another.

*Election and calling.* Sometimes Paul refers to those who have believed and been saved as "the elect" (Rom 8:33; 16:13; cf. Col 3:12; 2 Tim 2:10; Tit 1:1). This language reflects God's deliberate choice to create a people for himself and to deliver them from their sin. This purpose found its realization as God called Abraham and subsequently his offspring. This making of a relationship between God and human beings rests entirely on God's initiative, not on the display of any people's particular qualities that might be thought to entitle them to God's favor (Rom 9:12) or make God prefer one person against another (cf. 1 Cor 1:26). In his mercy to the undeserving, God issues his call, and the appropriate response by those to whom it is made is faith. Consequently salvation depends on God and not on the good works of the recipients (Eph 2:5).

God's calling is corporate, expressing his determination to have a people encompassing both Jews and Gentiles (Rom 9:24), for whom he has further particular purposes (cf. Eph 1:4-5, 11-12). He is also said to call specific individuals (Gal 1:15). Paul does not say that God's calling makes the human response inevitable, or that this calling implies the passing over of other people whom he has decided not to save. Those who are saved confess that God has graciously called them (Rom 9:24; 1 Cor 1:9; Gal 1:6; Eph 4:1, 4; 1 Thess 2:12; 2 Thess 2:14; 1 Tim 6:12) to be a people who reflect the holy character of their God (Eph 4:1; 1 Thess 4:7; 2 Tim 1:9).

Therefore, a vital part of the process is the verbal proclamation of the gospel, through preachers called by God and empowered by the Holy Spirit (Rom 10:8, 14-15; 1 Cor 1:23; 2 Cor 1:19; 4:5; Gal 2:2; Phil 1:15; Col 1:23; 1 Thess 1:5; 2:9; 1 Tim 3:16).

*The human response—faith, not the works of the law.* The human response of faith (1 Cor 15:2; 1 Thess 1:8) includes accepting the message that God raised Jesus from the dead as true and confessing Jesus as Lord (Rom 10:9-10). Faith is primarily the expression of a dependence upon God for salvation and not upon one's own qualities or position. It comprises a new way of living appropriate to God's people. The terms *holiness* and *love* express this ideal. Hence Paul can speak of the "work of faith" (1 Thess 1:3; 2 Thess 1:11). Yet he also places faith and works in sharp contrast. He may have had more specifically in mind the outward observances commanded in the Mosaic law that were characteristic of Judaism; there is debate as to whether *works of the law* refers specifically to these or should be understood more widely. Paul fears that people may put their confidence in what they themselves are doing rather than exclusively in what God has done in Christ (1 Cor 1:29-31; Eph 2:9), as he himself had once done (Phil 3:1-11). Justification, however, is not a reward or payment for deeds done but a gracious gift (Rom 4:1-8; cf. 6:23); righteousness is attained not by doing what the law requires, but through faith in Christ (Phil 3:9; cf. Eph 2:8; 2 Tim 1:9; Tit 3:5). There is a clear antithesis between grace and works (Rom 11:6). Christ is thus the end of the law (Rom 10:4).

What, then, was the law all about? It expressed concretely how God wanted people to live, and specifically the Jews; there was recognition that some elements of the law were also meant for Gentiles. But nobody ever actually kept the law fully (cf. David: Rom 4:6-8), and Paul seems to have deduced that consequently the law was not given as the means by which people could gain and maintain life. On the contrary, the law was meant to expose the sinfulness of their hearts by bringing it out into the open in specific actions, thus making people aware of their need for forgiveness. It was a guide to lead people to their need for justification by Christ. Then, once Christ has come, the supervision of the law is no longer needed.

Believers are no longer under the law, but under grace (Rom 6:15; 7:4-6). Their relationship with God depends on his grace, not on their fulfillment of the law. In practice, however, some of the law became obsolete for Jewish believers. The fact that Paul never mentions the temple and its ritual suggests that it has no significant role for him. Once Paul has argued that spiritual circumcision is what matters, the outward ritual becomes unimportant (Rom 2:25-29). And the coexistence of Jews and Gentiles in the same congregations must have led to some indifference regarding food laws (Rom 14—15).

Yet this does not prevent Paul from making positive reference to the law and expressing obvious approval of some of its commandments (Rom 7:12). He speaks positively of love as fulfilling the law and exhorts Christians to love (Rom 13:8-10). Though the law could not engender obedience in its hearers, the Spirit can produce just that. Believers who live by the Spirit will do what the law requires (Gal 5:16, 18, 22-23). The Spirit guides believers as to how they are to live and gives them the power to do so (Rom 8:1-13).

As for the question of future judgment, those who are justified have peace with God, and there is no longer any condemnation for them (Rom 5:1; 8:1). They are confident in their hope of sharing in the glory of God (Rom 5:2) and will be delivered from his wrath (Rom 5:9). Yet Paul also insists that everybody must appear before the judgment seat and give account of themselves to God or to Christ (Rom 14:10; 2 Cor 5:10).

How is the dilemma to be resolved? There is judgment here in this life upon those who sin, perhaps even the infliction of illness and death; the aim of that judgment is to bring about repentance here and now, so that people may enter into a restored relationship with God before it is too late (1 Cor 11:29-32; cf. 1 Cor 5:5). There are also judgments after death that fall short of exclusion from salvation (1 Cor 3:10-15). Even a person who has preached the gospel to others might end up being excluded from the prize because of lack of self-control (1 Cor 9:24-27). There are inducements and warnings to believers, encouraging them to a life of faith working by love and to good works. Paul can see his own missionary work as what Christ has accomplished through him, and therefore he has grounds for confidence in Christ (Rom 15:17-18). Believers' confidence at the judgment will thus rest on indications that Christ has been working through them, which will be the evidence of their justification. And this result ties in with the promises that God who has started a good work in believers will accomplish it in the day of Christ (Phil 1:6; cf. 1 Cor 1:8-9).

*The ongoing work of God in the believer.* The life of believers is controlled by the fact of Christ, crucified and raised. Teaching as to how to live is given "in the Lord" (Phil 2:29; 1 Thess 4:1); believers' lifestyle is determined by the pattern of Christ himself and rests on Christ's authority as Lord. *In Christ* also expresses the way in which God conveys blessings to believers through the agency of Christ (Rom 6:11; Gal 2:4, 17; Phil 4:13), not just through his action in dying for them (and being raised), but also through his continuing relationship with them and his future role at the judgment. In such contexts the phrase expresses a close bond between believers and Christ (Rom 8:1; Phil 1:1). They have died with Christ, been buried with him, and been raised to new life (with the hope of future resurrection of the body; Rom 6:1-11; Gal 2:20; 6:14; Phil 3:10; cf. Col 2:12; Eph 2:5-6; 2 Tim 2:11).

The Spirit is the powerful divine gift granted to believers (Rom 5:5; 1 Cor 2:12; 2 Cor 1:22; Gal 3:2, 14; 4:6; 1 Thess 4:8). It is a continuous, lasting endowment rather than just a momentary inspiration for a specific purpose. Through the Spirit people are adopted as God's children (Rom 8:14-15; Gal 4:6) and have God's seal upon them (2 Cor 1:22; cf. Eph 1:13-14). The Spirit guides them to holy living (1 Cor 6:19; 1 Thess 4:8); they develop qualities of character, such as self-control and gentleness, and at the same time they are able to withstand temptations to show sinful qualities (Rom 14:17; Gal 5:22-23). The Spirit makes them subjectively aware of God's love for them (Rom 5:5; cf. Rom 8:16) and fills them with joy (Rom 14:17; Gal 5:22; 1 Thess 1:6); they have the basis for an assurance that what they have received is only the beginning of God's blessing upon them (Rom 8:23).

*The communities of believers.* Believers lead their lives in local communities. The term *church* (congregation) can refer to all believers as a totality as well as to specific groups. Thus "the congregation in their house" (Rom 16:5) could refer to "those members of the whole church who meet in this particular locality". When Paul thinks of the church as the body of Christ (1 Cor 12:27), he may be thinking primarily of the problems within the one congregation at Corinth, but a reference to the church as a whole is likely. This is certainly so in other letters where the body language is complemented by bridal imagery (2 Cor 11:2; Eph 5:23-32). Christ loved the church and gave himself for it, and the church becomes the means through which God works to reveal his wisdom and the sphere within which he is glorified (Eph 3:10, 21; 5:23-32).

Collectively believers are known as *saints*, a term that implicitly identifies them as standing in continuity with God's ancient people *Israel* (a term generally used by Paul for the Jewish people rather than for the church). The relationship between Israel and the church is sometimes misunderstood as implying that God's covenant with Israel has been replaced by another covenant with a different people. For Paul, a distinction can be made between those who physically belong to Jacob's descendants, and within this larger number, the smaller group (the "remnant") of those who show faith in God and obey God (Rom 9:6, 27; 11:5); the Scriptures plainly enough indicate the coexistence of faithful Israelites alongside those who fell into idolatry and disobedience to the commandments. The coming of Christ has led to two crucial changes. First, since Jesus is understood to be the promised Messiah, it follows that the way to be in the right with God is by accepting his Messiah in faith. Thus the faith in God that has characterized the true people of God from Abraham onward is now seen to include acceptance of the Messiah. So there continues to be a remnant of believing Jews who are truly God's people. Second, this believing remnant is opened up to include Gentiles who shared the same faith. This remnant is thus now embodied in the church. The position of unbelieving Jews is no different from what has always been the case.

Not surprisingly, then, Paul says that believers have been circumcised through their baptism (Col 2:11). Here the concept of a spiritual circumcision, already familiar from the Old Testament, is taken up and applied to the baptized. The spiritual washing in baptism (1 Cor 6:11; cf. Tit 3:5) corresponds to what should happen spiritually in circumcision: having sinful tendencies cut away. Baptism itself is the outward rite of initiation into the one body and is associated with receiving the one Spirit with its diverse gifts (1 Cor 12:12-13; cf. Tit 3:5-6). Specific to Paul is the notion that baptism into Christ symbolizes sharing in his death and burial so as to share in his resurrection (Rom 6:3-5; cf. Col 2:12).

In the Old Testament God's presence is associated with the temple, but now the temple is replaced by the church, not as a material building but as the company of God's people (1 Cor 3:16-17; 2 Cor 6:16; cf. Eph 2:21). If the congregation is the place of God's presence, then God is active in it through the Spirit's various activities in different individuals (1 Cor 12:4-6). The congregation's members work for their common good and thus promote the maturing of its participants in their faith, love and hope. The congregation thus acts as a witness to the world of the divine reality (cf. 1 Cor 14:22-25). It is also the place where prayer is made to God. The reports in the letters show that prayer includes praise, thanksgiving, petition and intercession. Prayer is addressed to God (Rom 1:8; 2 Cor 1:3; cf. Eph 1:3, 17; 3:14), but is directed "through Jesus Christ" and takes place in the Spirit (1 Cor 14:16 TNIV; cf. Rom 8:26-27, 34; Eph 6:18).

At the congregational meal, believers remember the death of Jesus "until he comes", a phrase that implies belief in his resurrection and exaltation. The contrast drawn with having fellowship with demons (1 Cor 10:20) indicates that believers have communion with the Lord. The sharing together symbolizes the fact that they belong to the one body (just as is also symbolized in baptism (1 Cor 12:13; Gal 3:28; cf. Eph 4:5), although the practice does not always measure up to the symbolism (1 Cor 11:18-22).

The Spirit is active in the different ministries performed by the members; in principle each and every believer can contribute in this way and indeed is under obligation to exercise the gifts and functions conferred by the Spirit. Some individuals have particular responsibility for teaching (Gal 6:6) and for leadership, including pastoral care and discipline and therefore involving some measure of authority (1 Cor 16:15-16; 1 Thess 5:12). God's gifts to the church for building it up are apostles, prophets, evangelists, pastors and teachers (Eph 4:11-13). The need for sound teaching is particularly emphasized in 1 Timothy and Titus.

*Theology and behavior.* Throughout the Pauline writings we see a close connection between the gospel and behavior. This is particularly evident in the shape of Romans, Ephesians and Colossians, where the first parts of the letters lay theological foundations for practical teaching in the second parts. Believers are to lead lives worthy of the God who has called them and made them his people (1 Thess 2:12; 4:7; cf. Eph 4:1; 2 Tim 1:9). Whatever they do must glorify God (1 Cor 10:31). The function of judgment, whether by the Father or by Christ, is to stimulate holy living (Rom 13:11-14; 1 Thess 5:1-11). The fact that believers are "in Christ" or "in the Lord" is crucial; it shapes their lives in between their calling and their final judgment (Rom 16:2, 8, 11-13; Phil 2:29; 1 Thess 4:1; cf. Eph 6:1; Col 3:18). They are under the law of Christ (1 Cor 9:21); probably this means the command to love. Even if they are not under the law of Moses, they are not free from commandments and patterns to be imitated and followed (cf. 1 Cor 11:1).

This kind of living is most profoundly expressed as one in which believers take on the cruciform shape of Jesus' character through sharing in his death and burial and resurrection, dying to sin and rising to newness of life. They must put off the characteristics of the old, sinful life and put on the character of the new person who has been raised to life with Christ (Col 3—4). Such a life is one of freedom, understood as deliverance from the power of sin that prevents people from being what God wants them to be, and so as having the capacity to do what God requires—not out of the constraint of keeping commandments in order to be put in the right with God, but rather as the expression of love and gratitude to God.

*The future of God and his people.* Paul's theology is concerned with the present existence of God's people and is based on the past act of redemption as proclaimed in the gospel. At the same time Paul's letters constantly make us aware of the future dimension. God is not yet "all in all" (1 Cor 15:28): rebellion against him continues, the creation is subject to bondage and decay, and death continues to reign over humanity. Consequently, there is a forward look to the time when the final victory will be won. The present time is one of conflict between Christ and his enemies, in which they are being defeated; ultimately Christ will return to this world, and his return will involve the raising of the dead, the judgment of all people, and the transformation of God's people as they receive the inheritance that has been promised to them.

The key elements include the defeat of the forces opposed to God. This has already taken place in the death and resurrection of Christ, but nevertheless the victory is not finally consummated. On the basis of what has been done, Paul is sure of the final victory. All the powers in the universe come to the point of accepting that Christ is Lord (Phil 2:9-11). They are not only defeated but also destroyed. Death is singled out for particular mention (1 Cor 15:26). There will be a transformation of the universe (Rom 8:21) and of the people of God (1 Cor 15; 2 Cor 5:1-10; Phil 3:21). At the present time, believers live a precarious, dying existence, "always being given over to death for Jesus' sake, so that his life may also be revealed in our mortal body" (2 Cor 4:11). Paul does not go into any detail concerning this process of transformation. The important thing is the full realization of the life of God's people with him. The heart of the hope for the advent lies in being with the Lord for ever (1 Thess 4:17; 5:10; Phil 1:23).

## PAUL, JESUS AND THE EARLY CHURCH

At the conclusion of our discussion of the work of the three Evangelists, Mark, Matthew and Luke, we summarized their presentations of the earthly mission and teaching of Jesus and then compared this with the depiction of the early Christians' theology as found in Acts. We claimed that the picture of the early church's theology that can be derived from Acts is what might be expected to arise as Jesus' followers continue his mission. Now we must ask how Paul's theology relates to that of Jesus and the early Christians.

*God—the Father.* Paul obviously thinks within the same Jewish frame of reference as Jesus and the Evangelists. They share the same basic understanding of God as he is revealed in the Old Testament, as the Creator of the universe and in particular the God who has acted in history as the

God of Israel and continues to carry out his plans despite opposition from Satan and sinners.

*Jesus and the Holy Spirit.* Paul's understanding of Jesus develops facets that are not so apparent in the Synoptic Gospels and Acts. His role as Messiah and Lord and his status as the Son of God reappear. For Paul, the Son preexisted the creation of the world and became incarnate in Jesus. In his later letters, Paul speaks of the fullness of God being present in Christ and flowing through him to the church. The way in which all this is expressed goes some distance beyond what we have in the Synoptic Gospels and Acts. Pauline theology without difficulty incorporates teaching found in the Gospels and Acts, yet it also includes implications and developments that go beyond anything envisaged in the latter. Similarly, the personal character of the Holy Spirit is not so apparent in the Synoptic Gospels and Acts, although the Spirit gives guidance and apparently speaks in the same way as the Lord or angels (e.g., Acts 5:32; 8:29; 10:19; 11:12; 13:2). Paul's clearer articulation of the personal nature of the Spirit is a natural development.

*The gospel—the need for salvation.* The Evangelists show Jesus condemning the sins of the Jewish religious leaders and humanity generally, although there is not a lot of stress on sin in general. In Acts, the Jews are assumed to be implicated in their rulers' sin in crucifying Jesus unless they repent and accept forgiveness; the Gentiles likewise are seen to be in need of the gospel because of their sin and failure to recognize the one God. Paul's understanding of human nature and sinfulness, with its basis in the relationship of the race to Adam and his sin, goes further: sinners are under the control of the flesh and in some sense dead in their sin. This radical language is not found in the Synoptic Gospels and Acts, although the wickedness (Mk 7:6, 21-23) and imperviousness of the heart to God's voice is taught (Is 6:10; Mt 13:15; Acts 28:27).

Paul's stress that human beings can do nothing to put themselves right with God brings out what is latent in the Gospels and Acts.

*The gospel—the means of salvation.* Paul and the leaders in Jerusalem agree on the essential contents of the gospel. Its content is centered on the death and resurrection of Jesus, understood as the means through which people can be delivered from their sins and God's judgment upon them. This understanding can be traced back to the teaching of Jesus as recorded in the Synoptic Gospels, where his death is understood as a ransom for many (Mk 10:45) and as having a sacrificial character (Mk 14:24). Admittedly the preaching in Acts assigns no particular saving significance to the death of Jesus, seeing it rather as the act of sinful opponents (though not outside the purpose of God), which was undone by the resurrection. However, sacrificial redemption language is not completely absent (Acts 20:28), and the identification of Jesus with the Suffering Servant is used by Luke (Lk 22:37; Acts 8:32-33); these points are capable of exposition in a Pauline direction, but for whatever reason, Luke has not done so. The importance of the resurrection for both Acts and Paul is self-evident. It is the exaltation of Jesus as Lord and Christ.

*The nature of salvation.* Paul has four key motifs for understanding the nature of the effects of Jesus' death and resurrection: *salvation, redemption, justification* and *reconciliation. Salvation* language is characteristic of Luke and is also found in Matthew and Mark. *Redemption* occurs in Luke-Acts but refers in a rather general way to God's action in delivering his people from their enemies and from their sins. *Justification* is very much a Pauline motif and is found on Paul's lips in Acts 13:38-39 (cf. Lk 18:14). The Pauline term *reconciliation* is not found in the Gospels and Acts, but what is the parable of the prodigal son about if it is not about forgiveness and reconciliation? Paul's theological vocabulary of salvation is in harmony with the Gospels and Acts but is much more articulate than they are.

*The reception of salvation.* For Paul, receiving salvation depends upon God's prior action in making the gospel known to those who do not yet believe. Paul and Acts agree on the necessity and sufficiency of faith as the human response to the gospel (e.g., Acts 10:43; 11:17; 16:31; 26:18). Although the contrast between faith and works, central to Paul's understanding of faith, is not found in Acts, Luke knows that justification is possible only through Jesus, not under the law of Moses (Acts 13:38-39). Gentiles are saved and receive the Spirit without having to keep the law and be circumcised (Acts 15:8; cf. Gal 3:1-4). The only requirements laid down concern foods offered to idols, sexual immorality and blood in meat. The first two of these requirements correspond with Paul's own teaching; the last may be simply a requirement not to offer unacceptable foods to

Jewish Christians in shared meals. There is no conflict with Paul at this point. As for Jewish Christians, Paul recognizes that they may continue to keep the law (Rom 14), and Acts presents him as doing the same, despite accusations brought against him (Acts 21:20-26).

*The ongoing work of God in the believer.* In Acts, the preaching is primarily evangelistic and thus has a different focus from Paul's letters to believers. Paul's language of being in Christ is absent. The concept of believers being united with Christ in his death and resurrection is likewise missing. Acts does not mention "the works of the flesh" (though it is well aware of human sin!), nor does it speak of "the fruit of the Spirit". Yet it shares with Paul the belief that the Spirit is given to all believers and is an essential element in their experience (Acts 2:38). In Acts, the Spirit is primarily associated with guiding and empowering individuals and the church for witness and mission. Nevertheless, the Spirit's presence is to be seen as a sign of salvation's reality and hence as the means of Christian assurance (Acts 2:38; 9:17) and reassurance (Acts 4:31); the Spirit is associated with encouragement (Acts 9:31) and joy (Acts 13:52). The gift of tongues is an evidence of conversion, and this is for the benefit of the recipients themselves, since it moves them to praise God, as well as a testimony to other people (Acts 10:44-46; 19:6). There is no difficulty in seeing the Spirit-inspired phenomena of 1 Corinthians 12 in the context of Luke's record in Acts. Further, Luke recognizes the importance of Christian character (Acts 9:36; 11:24).

Conversion leads to new patterns and standards of behavior. Paul bases the practice of Christian life as individuals and as community on the gospel. The instruction is sometimes given "in the Lord", acknowledging his authority to direct the life of his people. Occasionally Paul gives teaching of the earthly Jesus, referring to him in this context as "the Lord". The Mosaic law finds its fulfillment in the law of love and in the Spirit's working, producing the fruit of Christian character. All of this is in implicit agreement with the Gospels, where Jesus teaches the same law of love. A life lived "in the Lord", as Paul calls it, is one in which the teaching of Jesus provides the pattern for life. What is lacking in the Gospels and Acts is the developed teaching of Paul about the direction and enabling of the Holy Spirit for believers in their personal lives.

*The community of believers.* For both Luke and Paul, the church consists of Jewish and Gentile believers and stands in continuity with Israel, the historical people of God under the old covenant. A major theme of Acts is the way in which the church, originally composed of Jewish believers, realizes that it is called by God to be open to Gentile believers, who share equally with Jewish believers in forgiveness, the gift of the Spirit, and membership among God's people without the requirement of circumcision. This Pauline understanding is the one that prevails in the church at Jerusalem, according to both Luke and Paul.

Paul develops the thought of the church as Christ's body. There is some analogy with the usage in Matthew where Jesus speaks of "my church" (Mt 16:18), but the rich understanding of the church in Colossians and Ephesians goes well beyond anything in Acts. Baptism is the rite of initiation into the church. The association of baptism with forgiveness (Acts 22:16), the reception of the Holy Spirit, and entry into the body of Christ, the church—all these are common to Acts and Paul (1 Cor 6:11; 12:13; cf. Tit 3:5). Where Paul goes beyond the rest of the early church is in his understanding of baptism as being into Christ's death so as to share in his resurrection life here and now and his physical resurrection in the future. In Acts, baptism is done in (or into) the name of Jesus, but in Paul it is done into Christ (Rom 6:3; Gal 3:27). The personal relationship with the risen Jesus is less conspicuous in Acts.

We learn more about the internal life of the congregations from Paul, but Acts testifies to communal prayer and praise to God, the functions of prophets and others gifted by the Spirit, and the celebration of the Lord's Supper in a domestic setting. The accounts of breaking bread in Acts must be read in the light of the Emmaus story in Luke 24; the meals are the occasion of fellowship with the risen (but unseen) Lord. This element is present in Paul (1 Cor 10:14-22). As for remembrance of the death of Jesus (1 Cor 11:26), again Acts should be read in the light of the Gospel, where the link with the death of Jesus emerges in the Last Supper.

Paul and Luke have in common the recognition of the existence of the Twelve and other apostles. Both writers view mission as the work of traveling missionaries, with Paul working alongside one or more companions. The Twelve, headed by Peter, are concerned with mission to the Jews, whereas Paul and his companions are called to go to the Gentiles (though neither group goes exclusively to the one constituency). Luke and Paul envisage leaders being appointed in new congregations, using such terms as *elders* and *overseers* to refer to them. Inevitably there is more about this in Paul.

*The future of God and his people.* The Evangelists share with Paul the belief in Christ's future coming and both depict something of the course of future events. They all recognize Christ's place as judge and that he will gather his people to be with him. The resurrection of the dead is a belief shared by Jews (other than the Sadducees) and Christians but mocked by Greeks. Neither in Acts nor in Paul is there much emphasis on the kind of matters treated in the apocalyptic passages in the Gospels. Primarily Acts is concerned with the need for people to repent and accept the salvation offered by the risen Lord here and now, lest they come under his judgment. Acts recognizes the fact of ongoing persecution for believers but does not frame this as "signs of the end", which we find in the Gospels, and it is silent on the judgment to fall on Jerusalem, despite clear references to this in Luke 21. The kind of warnings Jesus gives regarding the coming judgment on Jerusalem find no place in the preaching of the apostles. Similarly, the apocalyptic manner of presenting the future is largely absent from Paul; when found in 1 Thessalonians 4—5 and in 1 Corinthians 15, it arises out of problems relating to the destiny of deceased believers, and in 2 Thessalonians it functions to give a different understanding of the events surrounding the End from that held by the readers. The material used by Paul is certainly related to traditions utilized in the Gospels, and it is clear that there was a place for such teaching in his instruction of believers, but it was not central to the gospel as he understood it. Paul's understanding of the believers' transformation at the second advent and their close relationship to Christ is of decisive importance; here he is once again developing theological motifs in an individual manner when compared with the Synoptic Gospels and Acts.

## CONCLUSION

Paul affirms that he and the first followers of Jesus preached one and the same gospel (1 Cor 15:3-11). There is a developed entity that may fairly be called Paulinism, but it is in harmony with the teaching inspired by Jesus' mission and continued in his followers' mission in the early church. The Paul who rejoices in the preaching of other believers, even if their motives are questionable in his eyes (Phil 1:15-18), would rejoice all the more in the gospel reflected in the Synoptic Gospels and Acts.

# 18

# THE GOSPEL OF JOHN

John gives his readers a somewhat different set of events and teachings of Jesus from the other Gospels. Although some of the events are the same, and others are of a basically similar character, the general way in which they are narrated and the character of the theological argumentation are distinctive. The historical traditions regarding Jesus have been given fresh expression in a different idiom.

## THE THEOLOGICAL STORY: THE PROLOGUE (JOHN 1:1-18)

John begins with a prologue that combines events and their theological explanation. One event is the coming of John (the Baptist) as a witness (Jn 1:6-7) and his identification of Jesus as the one who would come after him and surpass him (Jn 1:15). Between these statements is recorded the central historical event, the Word becoming a human being (Jn 1:14). These events are placed in the context of a theological statement by the author himself.

As far back as we can go in thought, there was a being with God (the Father) called the Word, who was himself God and was the creator of the universe. He was the source of life and light for humanity. But the light was not generally recognized in the world, although some did recognize and accept it by faith, and they became God's children through a spiritual birth brought about by him.

The Word entered the world by becoming "flesh"; he became a human being (but without ceasing to be divine). Grace and truth are fully revealed in him, in such a way that Jesus as the only One, himself God, reveals God.

This introduction has set out the basic "story" of salvation in brief fashion, anchoring what happens on the historical plane in a metanarrative. This account understands what is going on in terms of divine activity transcending the universe and before its creation. Above all, it explains who Jesus is and what he does, but it does so by starting with another figure, the Word, describing him and then identifying Jesus as the incarnation of this Word.

After the prologue, Jesus is no longer referred to as "the Word". Yet he continues to fulfill the functions of the Word in that he reveals and communicates life, light, and glory and makes the Father known, and he does this primarily through his words. Just as Jesus both dispenses the bread of life and is that bread, so too he speaks the words of God and thereby functions as the Word of God.

## THE THEOLOGICAL STORY: JESUS AND THE JEWS (JOHN 1:19—12:50)

*John's testimony to Jesus (Jn 1:19-51).* The story, already begun, now gets under way. John the Baptist himself confirms that he is not any recognizably messianic figure but only a witness (Jn 1:19-28). He points out Jesus as the one who fulfills his own prophecy of the one who is coming after him. Jesus is not only the Word who reveals God. He is also equally "the Lamb of God, who takes away the sin of the world!" (Jn 1:29, 36). *Lamb of God* is probably a messianic term, and *taking away sin* indicates that Jesus takes away the guilt and penalty that await sinners. Further, Jesus will baptize with the Holy Spirit (Jn 1:33). What John achieves by a rite involving a symbolic cleansing with water will be paralleled and achieved on a higher level, through an action carried out with the Holy Spirit. If baptism signifies cleansing from sin, then Jesus will carry out the spiritual side of that which John's baptism with water only symbolizes and will deliver people from sin. Thus the activities of Jesus as the Lamb and as the baptizer with the Spirit are complementary.

Some of the people who hear John's testimony find that Jesus already knows who they are (and what they can become), and they recognize that he is the Messiah, the coming one prophesied in Scripture, the Son of God, and the King of Israel. Through him, in his role as Son of Man, communication with the heavenly world is established (Jn 1:51).

*The old and the new (Jn 2:1-25).* Jesus' action at a wedding is the first of a series of "signs" or symbolical actions that point to what God can accomplish on a spiritual level. Wine is an image of God's kingdom as a banquet in which God's people eat and drink in his presence. There is the implication also that the old ways of Israel, exemplified by water as a means of outward cleansing from defilement, are being superseded. The so-called cleansing of the temple constitutes a condemnation of its misuse for trade instead of being a place where God the Father may be met. The saying about destroying and rebuilding it, typically misunderstood by his hearers to refer to physical destruction and miraculous reconstruction, implies that Jesus himself will replace the temple as the "place" where the Father is revealed (cf. Jn 1:18). There may be a reference to the group of disciples as the new temple in which this revelation through Jesus takes place.

Some people believe in Jesus because of the miraculous signs that he does. Such faith, however, is not sufficiently deep for him to commit him self to them. Signs are necessary in order to reveal God's glory, but the response to them may be amazement and not real conversion of the heart.

*The new birth and eternal life (Jn 3:1-36).* Nicodemus's positive but in-adequate response leads Jesus to enlarge upon new birth as a life-giving action by the Holy Spirit. There is a fundamental set of contrasts expressing a dualism between the world and the divine sphere (heaven), the sphere of darkness and that of light, the world of death and the world of life, the kingdom of evil and the kingdom of righteousness. Entry into God's kingdom is the same as coming to life, so that a believer, while continuing to exist physically in this evil world, is nevertheless now alive spiritually. Jesus is the divine messenger who came down from heaven and who was "lifted up" to die, so that those who believe in him might have eternal life. People who perish do so because they are committed to evil and therefore hate the light; although Jesus came as the light of the world, primarily to save people, he condemns those whose evil nature is revealed in their refusal to believe in him.

*The Savior of the world (Jn 4:1-54).* In the conversation with the woman at the well, Jesus is again depicted as the giver of life, in this case symbolized by water. Although he recognizes the superiority of Judaism to Samaritanism, both are superseded in a new way of approaching God, doing so in the realm of the spirit on the basis of the new, true revelation of him. Jesus is the promised Messiah of Judaism (and Samaritanism) and actually is the Savior of all people (although it is unclear whether or not the royal official whose son is healed is a Gentile).

*The Father and the Son (Jn 5:1-47).* Jesus' cure of a paralyzed man is criticized as breaking the Jewish sabbath commandment. Jesus claims that he is doing only what his Father, God, does on the sabbath. He further claims the exclusive divine prerogatives of judging and conferring life, while nevertheless being God's obedient Son. Yet he encourages people not to take his own word for it but to consider the testimonies of John, the Scriptures, and the mighty works that God grants him to perform.

*The bread of life (Jn 6:1-71).* The miraculous feeding leads some people to conclude that Jesus is the expected Prophet. Jesus moves the discussion to a higher level by interpreting the bread as a symbol of spiritual food. This spiritual bread is then identified with Jesus himself; ultimately salvation is a personal relationship with the giver of life rather than something that can be handed over by him and then he withdraws, his task completed. The mystery of why some respond to Jesus and others do not is ascribed to a drawing action by the Father. If anybody comes to Jesus and seeks salvation, they are welcome because the Father and the Son are united in loving purpose. Salvation results from God's initiative and deed and not from anything that people "do". The passage must be read in the context of God's love for the world (Jn 3:16) and the statement that "They will all be taught by God" (Jn 6:45).

Jesus further insists that people who want life must eat his flesh and drink his blood, a clear allusion to the symbolism of the Lord's Supper (although John's account of the Supper is silent about this motif). But there is a warning against assuming that physically eating the bread and drinking the cup confer life: what Jesus is talking about is once again the relationship of belief in him.

*Who is Jesus? (Jn 7:1—8:59).* At the Feast of Tabernacles, Jesus again deals with the divine origin of his teaching, the murderous intent of his opponents springing from his apparent breaking of the sabbath law, and his identity as the Messiah. His opponents, however, cannot take action against him because his "time", set by God, has not yet come (Jn 7:30). There is a divine timetable that is being followed, and human beings are powerless to change it.

The water that Jesus has earlier promised to give (Jn 4:10) is now identified with the Spirit, who will be given to believers after Jesus' glorification. Putting the different statements together, we have a number of symbols (bread, water) expressive of eternal life, and this life (or what produces it) is identified sometimes with Jesus himself and sometimes with the Holy Spirit.

Jesus then takes up the further symbol of light (cf. Jn 1:9) and applies it to himself, again making an exclusive spiritual claim that constitutes an invitation to believe. Those who come to belief, accepting his teaching, which is truth, will become truly free. The implication is that other people are slaves to sin and therefore will be excluded from God's family (where only sons and daughters are permanent members). Abraham is said to have rejoiced at the thought of seeing the day of Jesus. Jesus states that before Abraham was born, "I am". This phrase may echo the self-identification of God, "I am [he]" (Deut 32:39; Is 41:4; 43:10, 13; et al.), and be a claim to parity with him.

*Spiritual blindness (Jn 9:1-41).* Jesus has already been identified as the spiritual light of the world (Jn 8:12). Now we see him in action (cf. Jn 9:4-5) as a blind man gradually comes to recognize Jesus as a man of God, a prophet, and the Son of Man (Jn 9:11, 17, 35-36), whereas the Jewish authorities are blindly obsessed with the fact that the healing is done on the sabbath.

*True and false shepherds (Jn 10:1-42).* Jesus is also both the shepherd who truly cares for the sheep and the gate by which they enter the sheepfold, which typifies salvation and life. If the *sheep* stand for Jews, the *other sheep* who will come in and join the one flock must be Gentiles. The good shepherd goes to the uttermost in self-sacrifice to care for the sheep and to give them life. The people who do not believe that Jesus is the Christ, despite his mighty works, show that they are not his sheep. Jesus' sheep cannot be snatched out of the Father's hand; no matter how fierce the coming persecution against disciples (cf. Jn 12:10; 15:18—16:4), that ordeal is powerless to deprive them of their salvation.

*The raising of the dead (Jn 11:1-57).* Bringing a dead man back to life, a miracle remarkable in its own right and glorifying God, points to its spiritual counterpart, raising people to eternal life, which necessarily includes their ultimate and permanent resurrection. This final event turns the growing unbelief and hostility of the Jewish authorities into action against Jesus. They argue that, if Jesus gains many followers, there will be an uprising that the Romans will put down by force, and they themselves will be put out of office. It is cheaper for one man to be put out of the way by execution "for the sake of the people" than for the whole nation to suffer (Jn 11:50 Gk.). Jesus would indeed die for the people, but not in the sense that Caiaphas imagined.

*The end of the witness to the Jews (Jn 12:1-50).* The hour appointed by the Father has now come. Jesus must die, but his death will be like that of a seed, which leads to new life. He will bring about judgment upon the ruler of this world (the devil) and draw people to himself. John comments on the unbelief of those who are still unmoved by the signs. People can go so far in rejection of the light that eventually God judges them by making it impossible for them to respond to it.

## THE THEOLOGICAL STORY: JESUS AND HIS DISCIPLES (JN 13—17)

*The Last Supper (Jn 13:1-30).* At his last meal with his disciples, Jesus washes their feet as a symbol of his serving them and also as an example to encourage their humble service to one another. Jesus also identifies the disciple who will betray him despite having shared in the fellowship of the meal and the foot washing.

*Farewell teaching (Jn 13:31—17:26).* Jesus interprets his own impending death in terms of the Son of Man being glorified (Jn 13:31-32; cf. Jn

12:23). It is not a case of suffering followed by glorification, but of the Son of Man being "lifted up" and glorified on the cross, and thereby glorifying God. Thereafter Jesus will no longer be physically with the disciples. In his absence they will be marked by their love for one another. Obedience to his commands is the condition for being his friends and remaining in his love (Jn 15:10-17). Such obedience arises out of love, just as Jesus' love for the Father issues in obedience (Jn 14:31).

Jesus' departure is necessary because he is going ahead of the disciples to prepare their future abode with the Father. He himself is the way there, in that to know him is to know the Father. The thoughts of knowing and being with the Father spiritually on earth through Jesus and of going to be with the Father in heaven intermingle. Jesus can now speak plainly about his closeness to the Father: they are "in" each other. Consequently, the disciples will do even greater works than Jesus because the Father will answer their prayers offered in Jesus' name.

The Holy Spirit (Jn 7:37-39) will take on the task of Jesus as "another" *Paraclete* (cf. 1 Jn 2:1), a word that here means a "Helper" or "Counselor" to believers (Jn 14:16-17). Through this Helper's agency, Jesus makes himself present. The Paraclete will teach them and remind them of the teaching of Jesus (Jn 14:25-26). He will testify through the disciples (Jn 15:26-27), convicting the world by getting it to understand that (1) it is guilty of sin because it rejects Jesus; (2) Jesus is shown to be righteous by his going to the Father, who accepts him; and (3) judgment is certain because the evil ruler of this world already stands condemned (Jn 16:8-11). In all this, the Spirit glorifies Jesus by continuing his work and pointing people to him (Jn 16:13-15).

Meanwhile, left alone without Jesus, the disciples will be hated just as he was (Jn 15:18—16:4). They are encouraged to remain in close union with Jesus, who is likened to a vine supplying nourishment to its branches so that they will bear fruit. Branches that do not remain in union with the vine itself will be cut off and burned (Jn 15:1-11).

Finally, Jesus contemplates the victory that he has in effect already won over the world and its hostility (Jn 16:25-33). Then he turns to the Father in a lengthy prayer (Jn 17), which is partly concerned with himself and his imminent glorification, but mostly is about the disciples. He prays that

God will protect them from the hostile world and keep them pure from its sins. By observing how they live like Jesus and love one another, the world may come to believe that Jesus is indeed God's agent.

## THE THEOLOGICAL STORY: THE DEATH AND RESURRECTION OF JESUS (JN 18—21)

*Trial and crucifixion (Jn 18:1—19:42).* Jesus now faces the Father's "cup" (Jn 18:11; cf. Mk 10:38), suffering of the kind that God lays upon sinful peoples as a judgment upon their sin, but which now is borne by Jesus on their behalf. His trial centers on the two themes of kingship and truth. Pilate represents a world that does not understand what truth is or is perhaps unconcerned about it. Also, he certainly does not understand that he really has no imperial authority over Jesus unless God allows it to him. Nor, again, do he and the other participants realize that it is actually they who are implicitly on trial.

The account of the crucifixion emphasizes that what happens is not simply what human beings want to do with Jesus. The distribution of his clothes, his cry "I am thirsty", and the piercing of his side—all take place in fulfillment of scriptural patterns and prophecies concerning the Messiah.

*Empty tomb and resurrection appearances (Jn 20—21).* There is no public glorification of Jesus after his death and burial, but there is an empty tomb discovered by the disciples and a series of appearances. There is doubt and lack of recognition, but the disciples do believe. The promise of "peace" given by Jesus (Jn 14:27; 16:33) is fulfilled. The disciples are granted the Holy Spirit and the commission to forgive sins. Here is the Johannine equivalent of the Great Commission. The comment to Thomas does not disparage those who have seen Jesus and believed. Jesus is drawing a contrast between the time of his earthly mission and the time when he is physically absent and it will in a sense be more difficult for people to believe.

Finally John states that the aim of the Gospel is to bring people to a faith in Jesus, which will confer eternal life on them (Jn 20:30-31). His disciples have a commission to evangelism and care of the sheep. Even though they may suffer, they are still to remain faithful disciples and glorify God by their death, as by their life.

## THEOLOGICAL THEMES

The main theme of the Gospel is undoubtedly its presentation of Jesus as the Messiah and Son of God, who came into the world to bear witness to the truth and to give his life so that all people might have the opportunity of receiving eternal life through faith in him.

*Jesus, his role and status.* The verb *send* expresses the fundamental relationship between God and Jesus while he is the world. The Jewish concept of *the sent one* (Heb. *šaliaḥ*) who has the authority of the sender portrays Jesus as the authorized agent of God, to whom significant functions are delegated (Jn 3:17; 4:34; 5:23-24, 36; 6:29, 38-39; 9:4; 10:36; 11:42; 17:3; et al.). Similarly, the Holy Spirit is sent by the Father and Jesus (Jn 14:26; 15:26), and the disciples are sent by Jesus (Jn 13:20; 17:18; 20:21). Behind the sending is the will and purpose of God the Father to save the world, as has already been established in the Scriptures (Jn 6:45; 7:38, 42; 12:14-16; 20:9).

Thus the Gospel is about a missionary whom God sent into the world with the task of being the light and offering people eternal life. Jesus is thus *the founder of salvation*, the counterpart to Moses (cf. Jn 1:17): Jesus establishes the new community, bestows salvation on its members, and gives the new people its rule for life.

John is the only New Testament writer to use the Semitic term *Messiah* (Jn 1:41), which he straightaway translates as "Christ". The purpose of the Gospel is that people may come to believe, like Martha (Jn 11:27), that Jesus is the Christ (Jn 20:31; cf. Jn 17:3).

Side by side with this is the role of Jesus as *prophet*. He is actually seen not as just *a* prophet but as *the* final prophet (cf. Jn 1:21), who was expected to come to the world (Jn 6:14; 7:40), and when the people recognize him as such, they want to make him *king* (Jn 6:15). This is a major theme in the trial before Pilate, where Jesus' kingship is distinguished from human kingship and put on a higher plane. The concept of the *shepherd* is quite closely related to this, since the role of the king was understood to be the shepherd of his people (Jn 10; cf. Jn 21:15-17).

As *Son of Man*, Jesus is a figure who must be "lifted up" in crucifixion (Jn 3:14; 12:34), yet who will also take part in judgment (Jn 5:27). He has come down from heaven (to which he will return) and is the agent of revelation (Jn 1:51; 3:13; 6:62). Jesus is the giver of salvation (Jn 6:27) and is identified with salvation itself (Jn 6:53) in that he is the dispenser of the bread of life and people must eat his flesh in order to have life. The term "lifted up" seems to encompass resurrection and exaltation as well as crucifixion, and the events of the passion constitute a glorification of the Son of Man (Jn 3:14; 12:23, 34; 13:31).

Supremely, Jesus is to be understood as the *Son of God*, who was with the Father (Jn 1:18), was sent by him to the world from heaven and returns thither (Jn 3:17; cf. Jn 17:13). John contains one of the clearest New Testament statements of *incarnation*: the Word became human (lit., "flesh"; Jn 1:14) and has truly human experiences, including death. His personal relationship with God comes openly to the fore. The major term for God is *Father*, especially on the lips of Jesus, who refers repeatedly to "the Father" and "my Father". The Father loves the Son (Jn 5:20) and confers authority on him to exercise judgment and to give life. Yet at all times the Son follows and obeys the Father's will (Jn 5:19). There is no place for any other being occupying such a position in relation to the Father; he is the "only" Son (Jn 1:14, 18; 3:16, 18). Jesus is intimate with God's plans and as close to him as almost a "second self", so much so that to see and hear Jesus is equivalent to seeing and hearing the Father (Jn 14:9). As such, Jesus can be regarded as "God" (Jn 20:28). Yet this does not mean that there are two gods; Jesus himself refers to the Father as the only true God (Jn 17:3; cf. Jn 5:44).

The purpose of the Gospel is to bring readers to confess Jesus as the "Son of God" (Jn 1:49; 20:31), committing themselves in faith to him (Jn 3:18, 36; 6:40; 11:27) and honoring him (Jn 5:23). Nevertheless, Jesus opens up to human beings the possibility of becoming children of God (Jn 1:12), and the language of mutual indwelling that is used of the relation of Father and Son is extended to believers in relation to both God the Father and Jesus himself.

The term *the Word* may seem less personal than *Son*, but though *Son* in itself need imply nothing more than the relationship of Jesus to the Father, *Word* expresses his role as the means of divine communication with the world. He is the light through whom the invisible God and his grace are made known in the dark world (Jn 1:18; cf. Jn 5:37; 6:46). What God says is his Word, and in the last analysis this Word is Jesus.

In a number of statements Jesus uses the phrase "*I am [he]*" (Jn 4:26; 6:20). Although this may be nothing more than a self-identification ("Who's there?" "It's me!"), the phrase is used in the Old Testament by God to identify himself as God, and Jesus appears to echo this way, thus speaking in the place of God (Jn 8:24, 28; 13:19; 18:5-6).

*Humanity in its need.* Simply belonging to the Jewish people is not a means of salvation if that does not lead to acceptance of the Messiah (Jn 8:31-41). The people have generally failed to recognize Jesus as the Messiah despite the witness borne to him by the Scriptures (Jn 5:39), by John the Baptist (Jn 1:6-8, 19-36; 3:26-30; 5:33), by other people (Jn 4:39; 12:17; 19:35; cf. 21:24), and by his own mighty works (Jn 5:36; 10:25). Their conduct is typical for *the world*. The term refers both to the arena of human life and to the people in it. Though created by God, the world is characterized by sin, falsehood, bondage and darkness (Jn 1:5; 3:19; 8:34; 12:46). Its ruler is fundamentally opposed to God (Jn 12:31; 14:30). A dualism is expressed in various pairs of contrasts: light and darkness (Jn 1:4-5; 3:19-21; 8:12; 9:4-5; 11:9-10; 12:35-36, 46), truth and falsehood (Jn 8:44; cf. Jn 14:6), freedom and slavery (Jn 8:31-36), and life and death (Jn 5:24). The people in the world do not know God (Jn 1:10; 16:3; 17:25) and reject the light (Jn 3:19). They stand under judgment from God (Jn 5:24, 29; 12:48) and are already under sentence of death (Jn 3:18, 36; 8:24).

Sinners fail to glorify God (Jn 5:44; 12:43), by contrast with Jesus, who does not seek praise and honor for himself but acts so as to bring honor to God (Jn 7:18; 8:50, 54; 17:1). Jesus himself is glorified in that his self-sacrifice on the cross is the kind of action that demonstrates his character and is recognized and approved by God (Jn 7:39; 12:16, 23; 13:31). Although glory can refer to the splendor that the Son enjoyed with God before the world's creation (Jn 17:5), the more usual reference is to the kind of character and conduct shown by him that should lead people to praise God. Failure do so constitutes the sin of those who love darkness rather than light (Jn 3:19).

Nevertheless, the light of God shines in the darkness (Jn 8:12), bringing knowledge of him and salvation (Jn 1:1-9). Those who reject the revelation (Jn 3:19-21) come under judgment because the coming of the light has exposed and brought to expression their fundamental rejection of God (Jn 12:37-50).

*The Savior.* The task of Jesus is twofold. First, he is the Word of God, communicating the message of God to the world. His task is revelation. The content of the revelation is *truth*, a term that includes both trustworthiness and reliability (Jn 3:33) and also ultimate reality (Jn 6:55; 17:3). The world into which Jesus came was characterized by error and untruth (Jn 8:44), but whatever Jesus says is true (Jn 8:40), so that he himself can be said to be the truth (Jn 14:6) and to bear witness to the truth (Jn 18:37). Similarly, the Spirit of truth guides people into the truth (Jn 16:13).

Second, Jesus comes to die for the world and so remove its sin (Jn 1:29, 36; 11:50-52). He is the Lamb of God, and his death is a sacrifice (Jn 19:36). Bread symbolizes his flesh, which he gives for the world's life (Jn 6:51-58). He drinks the cup that the Father has given him (Jn 18:11). His lifting up on the cross becomes the means whereby he overcomes Satan (Jn 12:31) and draws all people to himself (Jn 12:32).

*Salvation.* The nature of salvation corresponds with the description of human need. *Life* or *eternal life* is a sharing in God's life (Jn 1:4). It is eternal: those who receive this life shall never perish (Jn 3:16; 6:27; 10:28). In Judaism, eternal life tended to be thought of as a future, otherworldly experience; here it is regarded as also a present possession (Jn 3:36; 5:24; 6:47; 11:25-26). It is sustained by Jesus, who offers the life-giving water (Jn 4:10-14; cf. Jn 7:38) and himself as the bread of life (Jn 6:27-36). The metaphor of birth from God (Jn 1:13; 3:3, 5) conveys the fact that people are without life until they receive the divine gift. Such life is defined as "knowing" God and Jesus Christ (Jn 17:3). It is thus a life in relationship with God, in which God's love for the world becomes a reality in human experience and there is a response of love to him. It is also an incorporation into the life of God. God the Father (Jn 14:23; 17:21), Jesus (Jn 14:20, 23; 17:21, 23, 26) and the Holy Spirit (Jn 7:39; 14:17) all come into believers, and believers are in God.

Salvation is entirely due to God's initiative. Nobody can come to Jesus unless the Father draws them (Jn 6:44; cf. Jn 6:37, 65; 8:47; 10:29; 15:16, 19; 17:2, 6). From start to finish, salvation is the gift of God. Yet people are not to sit and do nothing and wait until they feel constrained to come to Jesus.

On the contrary, Jesus appeals to them to come to him, and the offer of salvation is to all (Jn 3:16-17; 6:45; 12:32; cf. 1 Jn 2:2). And it is to those who believe that God gives the right to become his children (Jn 1:12-13), so that the new birth appears to be dependent upon faith (so also in Jn 7:38-39).

Alongside God's calling, then, there is the need for the human response to the gospel. The basic relationship with Jesus is belief or faith (Jn 3:16-18), which involves total commitment to him. Faith is not only believing what Jesus says (Jn 6:68-69; 8:24; 11:26-27, 42) but also making a commitment on the basis of his word (Jn 1:12; 2:11, 23; 3:16, 18, 36). There can be a level of faith that is no more than accepting that Jesus has come from God and falls short of commitment to him (Jn 2:23-25; 12:42-43). True faith is more than a single act but becomes a continuing holding on to Jesus and his teaching expressed by the term *remain* (Jn 6:56; 8:31; 15:4-10). The same term expresses how Jesus and his teaching remain in believers (Jn 5:38; 15:4-7); the Spirit also remains in them (Jn 14:17). Just as the Father is in the Son (Jn 14:11; 17:21, 23) and the Son is in the Father (Jn 14:11, 20; 17:21), so believers are in the Son (Jn 14:20; 17:21) and he is in them (Jn 14:20, 23; 17:23, 26); equally they are in the Father (Jn 17:21) and he is in them (Jn 14:23). There is the danger that believers may fall away under persecution (Jn 16:1), accompanied by the promise that Jesus will preserve his people and raise them up at the last day (Jn 6:39-40, 44, 54; 10:28-29; 17:11-12).

*The relationships of believers.* Just as the Father and the Son know each other (Jn 10:15), so believers know the Father (Jn 8:19; 14:7; 17:3) and the Son (Jn 10:14b) and are known by the Son (Jn 10:14a); eternal life can even be defined as knowing the Father and the Son (Jn 17:3).

Similarly, believers receive and know the Spirit (Jn 7:37-38; 14:17). The term *Paraclete* (Jn 14:16, 26; 15:26; 16:7) brings out the personal nature of the Spirit. John provides a solid basis for the understanding of God as a Trinity of divine persons in communion with one another and all related to believers; yet the personhood of the Spirit is much more inferential than is the case with the Father and the Son, whose names primarily express the existence of relationships.

"Love" describes the mutual relationships between God and Jesus (Jn 3:35; 5:20; 17:23-26) and between God and Jesus and believers

(Jn 13:1, 34; 14:21; 15:9; 21:15-17) and between believers and one another (Jn 13:34-35; 15:12, 17). Love for Jesus is expressed in keeping his commandments (Jn 14:15, 21; 15:10) and in disciples loving one another, and this will be the sign to the world that they are disciples (Jn 13:34-35; 15:12-13). There is also a one-directional relationship in which God loves the sinful world (Jn 3:16), and both Jesus and his followers are sent out in mission to the world (Jn 20:21-23). Their task is to bear fruit, an activity that probably includes the winning of converts. Jesus prays for those who will believe through their activity (Jn 17:9, 20).

Mutual love indicates an organic unity binding believers to God and to one another. They are members of God's flock under the good Shepherd, imagery indicating not merely that they belong together but also that they belong to the Israel of God, whether or not they are Jews by birth (Jn 10:16; 11:52; 12:20-22). They are branches of the vine, which is also a symbol for Israel (Jn 15:1-8). As God's people, they are *sanctified*, a term that refers to being set apart and dedicated to God's service (cf. Jn 10:36; 17:19 of Jesus); it also includes moral transformation even while they remain in the sinful world, in which the evil one is operative (Jn 17:15-19).

Pastoral care and teaching are indicated in the command to Peter to feed the flock (Jn 21:15-17). The outward practices of baptism and the Lord's Supper are implied. The language of eating and drinking is employed in John 6:51-58 in a way that most probably indicates the spiritual significance of what happens in the church meeting. The true worship of God (Jn 4:21-24) is not confined to the traditional holy places of the Jews and the Samaritans but is possible anywhere.

*History and the future.* John is aware of the past history of Israel and its possession of the Scriptures. Jesus and salvation are seen as the fulfillment of the Old Testament promises (Jn 1:45; 5:39, 46-47; 6:45). Rejection of him and his passion and crucifixion are also seen as fulfillment of prophecy (Jn 2:17, 22; 12:14-16, 37-41; 13:18; 15:25; 17:12; 19:24, 28, 36-37; 20:9).

The future "history" of the church—its mission and suffering—is anticipated in the teaching of Jesus. His future coming is a horizon to human history. He will come to take his people to himself (Jn 14:3; cf. Jn 17:24), and there will be a "last day" with a resurrection of all to face judgment, issuing in life for believers and condemnation for others (Jn 5:25-29; 6:39-40, 44, 54; 11:24; 12:48). Yet this future hope is not the content of salvation to the exclusion of present experience. Jesus already comes to his disciples through the Holy Spirit (Jn 14:18, 23). The formula "the hour is coming and now is" brings out the "already/not yet" tension that is characteristic of New Testament Christianity (Jn 4:23; 5:25; 16:32).

## CONCLUSION

In the Gospel of John, the framework of thought is decisively shaped by the same Old Testament and Jewish background that we found in the other Gospels, but there is also a sharp dualism between God and the world, light and darkness, and truth and error, righteousness and sin.

The main theme of the Gospel is to present Jesus as the Messiah and Son of God, who came into the world to reveal the truth and to die so that all people might have the opportunity to receive life through believing in him.

Various significant themes are developed in detail:

1. The situation of the world, including the Jewish people, is characterized by darkness and the absence of eternal life, despite the fact that the Scriptures bear witness to the Messiah as the source of life.

2. Jesus comes to reveal the truth, by knowledge of which people are set free from bondage to sin. Even more than in the other Gospels, Jesus depicts the character of God as Father.

3. Jesus is the incarnate Word, through whom God created the world and communicates with it. Jesus is the Son, who was with the Father before he came into the world and will return to him. He acts as God's messenger, and his mission establishes the possibility of salvation. In so doing, he brings glory to God.

4. Jesus gathers disciples, but the language of believing in him is used more than in the other Gospels. He is both the giver of salvation and the gift itself; eternal life is not an abstract thing but a living relationship with Jesus himself. The relationship between believers and himself

is expressed as a mutual indwelling, similar to that between the Father and the Son and between the Father and believers. The Holy Spirit, or Paraclete, creates and sustain disciples. The new community thus created will be characterized by mutual love.

5. The Gospel looks forward to the bringing in of other sheep, typified by the response of the Samaritan converts and some Greeks. Jesus himself is the one way to life.

6. There is great stress on the new commandment of love and the need for believers to live together in love so that the world may believe. Although love for people in the world by the disciples is not stressed, the fact that God loves the world is doubtlessly intended to be exemplary to them.

7. Although Jesus' whole life reveals God and knowledge of the truth brings freedom, his death, which takes away the sin of the world, is the key element; far more is said about faith than about knowledge as the way to eternal life.

8. The fact of future judgment carried out by the Son of Man sets the need to respond to the gospel and receive eternal life in its context.

# 19

# The Letters of John

## THE THEOLOGICAL STORY: THIRD JOHN

Third John is a personal letter from the unnamed "elder" (either the author of the Gospel of John or somebody closely associated with its composition) to his friend Gaius, commending him for his hospitality to traveling teachers and evangelists. It also warns against following the example of the inhospitable Diotrephes.

Although Christ himself is not mentioned, Christian missionaries are said to travel "on behalf of the Name", which must be his name. The writer is very concerned about "the truth" (3 Jn 1, 3a, 3b, 4, 8, 12), his term for the Christian message, as he understands it, and about love (3 Jn 6). He believes that his version of the faith is authentic over against other versions, which may be corrupt in one way or another. He wants Christians to persevere in loyalty to the truth contained in the gospel and in the practice of love to one another, and he makes a sharp distinction between those who do so and those who do not. The latter are said not to have seen God.

## THE THEOLOGICAL STORY: SECOND JOHN

Similar thoughts reappear in 2 John, which is a general, pastoral letter with the same two concerns.

Truth is again emphasized (2 Jn 1a, 1b, 2, 3, 4). A significant new item is the identification of the error; people holding to it show that they are not in a right relationship with God. They do not confess Jesus Christ as coming in the flesh; this probably refers to the reality of his earthly human life (the incarnation) rather than to his future coming (cf. 1 Jn below). Precisely what they believe instead is not clear. They are condemned in the strongest terms as deceivers and being "antichrists". Only those who hold to this teaching "have" a positive, personal and permanent relationship with God and Jesus. Those who are enticed away from it are actually denying that Jesus is the one way to God and eternal life.

There must be love between those who know the truth. From the beginning, God's command has been one of mutual love; there is nothing novel about Christians insisting on it. God's command (singular) is to love (2 Jn 5, 6b; cf. 1 Jn 2:7-8; 3:23; 4:21), and loving involves carrying out his commands (plural; 2 Jn 6a; cf. 1 Jn 2:3-4; 3:22, 24).

## THE THEOLOGICAL STORY: FIRST JOHN

In 1 John, these two basic themes are developed at much greater length, even repetitiously. Its writer and his colleagues have had personal experience of the incarnate Word that conveys eternal life (cf. Jn 1:1-18). He proclaims this life so that the readers may share in their fellowship with God the Father and with the Son. Although this could be an evangelistic aim, the letter is actually addressed to Christian believers, to help them to persist and develop in their faith and avoid being led astray by wrong teachings and a subchristian way of life (1 Jn 1:1-4).

The fellowship that the writer longs for is threatened by sin and the failure to seek forgiveness for it. A distinction between light and darkness runs through the letter. Light symbolizes truth, purity, goodness and revelation, whereas darkness indicates ignorance and evil. Sinners are in the darkness, even if they claim to be in the light and in fellowship with God. Certainly all the readers are sinners (therefore in the darkness), but by confession of sin they can be forgiven and purified and thereby come into or remain in the realm of light and avoid sinning. The paradox is that they are living in the light, although apparently they go on sinning and are continually in need of cleansing. Forgiveness is through "the blood of Jesus"; his death is a means of canceling out sins without limit, and on that basis he is like a counsel for the defense, pleading successfully with his Father to forgive (1 Jn 1:5—2:2).

Sin is failure to keep God's commands. Those who know God keep his commands (his "word") and live in the same way as Jesus did. Since the content of the commands is love, obedience to them means that God's love is expressed perfectly in obedient people. Although the command is an old one, it is now being fulfilled in a new way as the darkness is dissipated through the shining light of God's revelation in Jesus (1 Jn 2:3-11).

Believers have God's Word in them, bringing knowledge and power that help them in their effort to conquer evil (1 Jn 2:12-14). They are warned against loving the world and its ways instead of loving God (1 Jn 2:15-17).

As the world draws near to its end, evil is becoming particularly rampant; many people really opposed to Christ and the truth have left the church itself. Sharp lines are drawn between the readers who know the truth because God has anointed them and the liars who deny that Jesus is the Christ and the Son of God and thereby deny God also. Believers have the spiritual resources to enable them to resist this temptation, although this apparently is not an automatic guarantee of success (1 Jn 2:18-27).

So the readers have to be positively encouraged to stay "in him". At his future coming they can look forward to standing before him without fear. They are again reminded of the need to do what is righteous. When he appears, they will resemble him in their righteousness. All of this causes the writer to burst out into praise of the greatness of God's love (1 Jn 2:28—3:3).

Sin is now defined as "lawlessness" (with the sense of "rebellion"). Those who remain "in him" do not sin. This could simply mean that claiming oneself to be in him and yet continuing to sin are incompatible (cf. 1 Jn 2:4). But the writer also states the inverse: if anybody sins, they have not seen or known him. He actually goes on to say that people who are born of God and have God's seed in them cannot sin (1 Jn 3:4-10).

The practical expressions of doing righteousness and unrighteousness (or sin) are explained as love and hatred respectively. Love between Christians must be sincere and shown in action; such love has been paradigmatically demonstrated in Jesus' death for them (1 Jn 3:11-24).

A fresh section deals with spiritual messages, likely purported revelations by prophets. These must be tested as to whether they express the true doctrine about Jesus Christ. The readers have God's Spirit and can recognize the truth, whereas false prophets draw their inspiration from the world and the spirit of falsehood (1 Jn 4:1-6).

Again we have the need for love as the outward expression and evidence of a positive relationship with God; the paradigm of love is God's own love. The God who is light is also love. Loving God and keeping his commandments is the way to have confidence before him. In principle his commands can be fulfilled because we have been born of God and have faith in him (1 Jn 4:7—5:5).

But once more it is emphasized that this faith must incorporate right belief about Jesus, who "came by water and blood" (1 Jn 5:6-12).

Finally, the writer sums up his aim to build up his readers' confidence that they have eternal life and can be sure that God will answer their prayers. God's children do not belong to the world, which is under the control of the evil one. They must keep themselves from idols, here in the broad sense of whatever people turn to when they turn away from Jesus, who is the true God (1 Jn 5:13-21).

## THEOLOGICAL THEMES

The central theme of these letters is encouragement to persist in truth and love on the basis of spiritual union with God. Such persistence will be expressed in freedom from sin, although the writer rejects specific claims actually to be free from sin.

*Truth.* The term *truth* can be used nontechnically to signify the opposite of lies and deceit (1 Jn 1:6), but it also refers concretely to the divine reality that finds expression in the Christian message and in Christian conduct. When the writer talks about the truth being "in" people, he means that there is a divine entity that exercises control over them, just as he can speak of God's love or even God himself or Christ or the Spirit being in them. "The truth", then, is an expression for God himself as the ultimate reality. The imagery of light expresses the pure character of this God, stressing his inapproachability and his condemnation of darkness, but it also conveys the idea of the revelation of truth, which dissipates the darkness of ignorance and evil. The dark world is illuminated from outside by the light shining from God, so that a new "space" or "area" is constituted within it, like the area on which a spotlight is shining. People can move out of darkness into light and vice versa. So the thought is really of two conditions that people can be in rather than simply two spheres to which they may belong.

*Righteousness* is an obvious characteristic of the sphere of light. It is seen to perfection in Jesus, and those who live in the light are accordingly to be like him. If people are not righteous, they are not from God. In this context there is a stress on commandments, meaning the basic command to believe and to love one another, but also a plurality of commands given by God that must be obeyed.

*Love.* Love stands out in the author's vocabulary; one-fifth of all the occurrences in the New Testament are in 1-3 John. For all the emphasis on right doctrine, the author's main concern is with his readers' Christian behavior. He encourages them not to set their hearts on the things in the world, and he contrasts that kind of love with love for God (1 Jn 2:15).

God himself is so loving that he can actually be said to be love. His love is shown to humankind in the death of Jesus, his Son, which is a sacrifice for sins carried out for their benefit. In response to God's love for us, we should love him. Those who so love thereby demonstrate that they are born of God.

Their love for God must be expressed in obedience to his commandment to love one another. Such love is real only when it is expressed in action as well as words. So integral is such mutual love to a right relationship with God that John can argue from its presence to our belonging to God as well as from its absence to a lack of love for God.

*The importance of right belief about Jesus.* Since Jesus, the Son of God, laid down his life for us and shed his blood in a way that made him an atoning sacrifice for sins, and since he will reappear in accordance with Christian hope, it is essential to believe in him and so be drawn into a spiritual relationship with him. Consequently, salvation is jeopardized if there is false belief about Jesus. Denying that Jesus is the Christ and the Son of God means denying that there is a Savior and also denying that a relationship with God is possible. Little is said about those who turn to unbelief coming (back) to the truth. There is the possibility of prayer for sinners to be saved, but not if theirs is a sin that leads to death. The sin referred to is probably that of deliberate and persistent apostasy; the rejection of Christ as Savior may go so far as to put a person virtually beyond the reach of prayer.

In what sense can people in the church deny that Jesus is the Messiah? John says that Jesus Christ "did not come not by water only, but by water and blood" (1 Jn 5:6). One possible explanation of this cryptic statement (among many) is that some people held that the heavenly Christ descended on Jesus at his baptism, thus saying that Jesus Christ came by water; yet they also hold that this "Christ" departed from him before his crucifixion, so that Jesus Christ did not come by blood. Such a view rejects a real and lasting incarnation of the Son of God in Jesus, possibly because of assuming that a divine being could not have suffered crucifixion and death.

The important fact for John is that Jesus did come in the flesh, in a real incarnation, so that he is the Christ, the Son of God, in the flesh. As for the puzzling three witnesses to him, the Spirit and the water and the blood, probably the Spirit witnesses through the baptism or the birth of Jesus and through his death (1 Jn 5:7-8).

Some people may also have been majoring on their experiences of the Spirit and developing a form of Christianity in which the significance of Jesus was downplayed and the importance of charismatic activities was played up. As in 1 Corinthians, the congregation needs to "test the spirits" (i.e., spiritual messages), since the mode of their delivery is no guarantee of their origin. John proposes the test of orthodox belief regarding Jesus on the part of those who deliver such messages (1 Jn 4:1-3).

*The problem of sinlessness.* Alongside doctrine and love, the other major problem in 1 John is sinlessness. John insists that believers are not free from sin and therefore need to confess their sins and be forgiven. His encouragement to them not to sin makes sense only if they do sin (1 Jn 2:1). But then he also states that people who remain in Christ do not and cannot sin because they have been born of God (1 Jn 3:4-10). The first affirmation can well be directed against people who claim that they are free from sin. Yet the second affirmation can be seen as supporting those who make such claims.

Some think that John is referring to a limited group of "super-Christians", or that he is referring to freedom from the one specific and fatal sin of apostasy (1 Jn 5:16-17). The TNIV boldly translates by the present continuous forms "keeps on sinning" and "continues to sin" (1 Jn 3:6, 9), but this is dubious syntactically. Others suggest that an ideal rather than a reality is being described, or that the statements really function as exhortations and imperatives: John is describing what will be true in the new age but is not yet complete in the time "between the ages". Since, however, God's Spirit is "in" the believer, there is genuine potential for actualizing God's ideal here and now. Consequently, John is not speaking simply about an ideal that the church ought to pursue and expressing it as if it were already a fact, but he is speaking about the character of the new life, which is already being increasingly realized in the lives of believers.

## THE LETTERS AND THE GOSPEL

We should not expect to find the same theological emphases in the letters as in the Gospel since they have different aims and belong to different genres of composition. They share a common theological vocabulary and idiom, but the Gospel is richer in its theology because of its wealth of imagery and the breadth of the issues discussed.

First John is more narrowly concerned with things that can go wrong in the church, and so it concentrates essentially on the issues of denial of Christ, claims to sinlessness, lack of brotherly love, and dubious spiritual revelations. But arising from these concerns, it sets out a positive theology and way of life for its readers. It can certainly be seen as applying the kind of theology found in the Gospel to specific problems and developing it accordingly.

Thus the opening statement echoes the prologue to the Gospel, establishing the reality of the revelation of the Word of life. The Christian life is understood as a life of fellowship with God and with Christ, characterized positively by obedience to Christ's commands. The tone is one of encouragement not to sin, coupled with the positive promise that sin in the lives of believers is forgiven by God in response to Christ's intercession. This picture coheres with that in the Gospel, where the Christian life is spelled out in terms of a spiritual relationship of mutual indwelling, and where disciples are expected to follow the commands of Jesus (Jn 13:34; 14:15, 21; 15:10-12). The specific command at issue is that of love for other believers, as in John 13:34-35 (cf. Jn 17:21-23).

The teaching about the world ties in with the Gospel, where the world is the sphere of human life characterized by darkness and sin; yet it is still the object of God's loving concern. Both the Gospel and 1 John are familiar with the activity of the devil as the ruler of this world, but only 1 John has the concept of antichrists who deny Jesus Christ (1 Jn 2:18). Those who reject Jesus as the Son of God are thereby rejecting the Father as well (as in Jn 5:23). In the Gospel the identity of Jesus as Messiah is closely tied to his divine sonship (cf. Jn 1:49; 10:24, 36; 11:27; 20:31); essentially the same kind of understanding is found in 1 John. Both the Gospel and 1 John are prepared to use the designation "God" of Jesus (Jn 1:1; 20:28; 1 Jn 5:20).

First John lays more stress than the Gospel on the sacrificial character of Jesus' death (1 Jn 2:2; 4:10), but like the Gospel it teaches that Jesus' death is an expression of divine love (1 Jn 4:10), that Jesus bears sin (1 Jn 3:5), and that he laid down his life on behalf of us (1 Jn 3:16). First John does not mention Jesus' resurrection, although it assumes that he is in heaven and has access to the Father (1 Jn 2:1) and that believers can have a spiritual relationship with him.

Statements about anointing with the Spirit express the Gospel teaching about the Spirit being given to believers (Jn 7:39; 20:22) by using a new metaphor (1 Jn 2:20, 27). The motif of believers' sanctification (Jn 17:17; 1 Jn 3:3) is present but not developed in the Gospel or 1 John. In 1 John, the discussion of believers' sin is a clear case of development to deal with a contingent situation. The future hope that believers will be like Christ (1 Jn 3:2) is new, but it could be deduced from statements in John 17, where Jesus speaks of the disciples being with him, seeing his glory, and receiving the glory that the Father has given him (Jn 17:20-24). The fact that God keeps and protects believers is common to both writings (Jn 10:28-29; 1 Jn 5:18).

In all of this, the writer of 1 John maintains the theological idiom of the Gospel and develops an appropriately contingent application of the same basic "Johannine" theology.

## CONCLUSION

The author's main aim is to encourage the believers, and the whole letter is one of positive encouragement. We may summarize the significant elements in 1-3 John as follows:

1. The ideal of a sinless life is seen as the only appropriate way of life for God's children, who claim to be in the light. This is expressed paradoxically by saying that believers do sin and can be forgiven and purified by confessing their sins, and also that people who live in God do not sin.

2. The reality of a spiritual union with God is expressed in terms of living "in God" and his word or anointing being in believers.

3. The love of God needs to be expressed in love for one another within the community of faith, and this love is to be a matter of action and not simply of words.

4. The hearers need to avoid false belief, especially about Jesus having come in the flesh, and therefore need to test the statements of people who claim the Spirit's inspiration for their prophecies.

5. Believers can be confident that God will answer their prayers.

6. Believers are kept from harm by Christ and yet paradoxically they must ensure that they remain "in him".

# 20

# THE REVELATION OF JOHN

Revelation is an apocalypse, an account of a visionary experience by a writer in which he is permitted to see inside heaven and to be given a prophecy of what will happen in the future. God knows what his enemies are capable of doing, and he will act in such a way as to ensure their final defeat. The author's purpose is to prepare and encourage a group of congregations that on the whole are spiritually ill-equipped to face a future in which faith will be tried to the limit.

I take the view that John presents a richly symbolical account of the ongoing conflict between God and the evil forces opposed to him. The book is heavily dependent upon the Old Testament for much of its language and content. There is abundant use of the imagery of cosmic events, which may refer to judgments in history rather than in nature.

## THE THEOLOGICAL STORY

*Prologue and greeting; Jesus and his message (Rev 1).* The prologue establishes that what we have is the account of a revelation that Jesus Christ gives to the author. As a prophecy, it contains both commands and promises for the readers to receive and act upon, and also an account of the future that is intended to prepare them for what is to happen and also to encourage them by assuring them of God's victory and of the ultimate peace in which they will live with God.

The opening greeting conveys blessings from God. The reference to "seven spirits" probably refers to the varied functions and powers of the one Spirit (Rev 1:4 TNIV note), and the description of Jesus Christ indicates his immense significance in the accomplishment of God's purposes for the world and for his people.

Jesus is the faithful witness *(martys)*, and therefore the pattern for his followers; as he has risen from the dead, so also will they if they are faithful to death. Readers are to praise him because he loved the readers and set them free from their sins by his blood. His redeemed followers have a new status as a kingdom and as priests to God. The latter phrase indicates that they are now God's servants, with the privileges of access to him (cf. Exod 19:6) and of finally reigning with him (Rev 22:5). His future coming will be as the judge before whom his opponents will appear (Rev 1:7).

John has received a message for the churches from Jesus Christ himself (Rev 1:9-20). The description of Jesus combines elements of the Son of Man (Dan 7), possibly the high priest, and God himself. The sword proceeding from his mouth refers to his powerful words. For the future the readers are thus encouraged by the picture of God and Christ's superior power and assured of the authority of the revelation they are receiving.

*Seven congregations (Rev 2—3).* The individual messages to the seven congregations have much the same basic structure and message. From the outside the readers are opposed by the state with its emperor worship, yet also by opposing religious groups. Despite commendable elements of witness and love, there is spiritual and moral weakness, representing some drop from earlier zeal. The congregations are in a poor state to cope with the hard times ahead; let them recognize the voice of Christ calling them to repentance before it is too late. Individual believers are called to "conquer": they are to stand firm in the battle against temptation and persecution. Their future reward is richly described as the tree of life, deliverance from the second death, the crown of life, sharing the authority of Christ and so on. These are all ways of expressing eternal salvation, not special rewards for first-class Christians, but the promised reward for every believer who remains faithful.

*The scene in heaven (Rev 4—5).* Revelation is concerned with a conflict taking place in both heaven and earth, in which superhuman powers of good and evil are involved. Now John describes the heavenly scene; it is one of glory and power. Against a background of perpetual worship of God for his eternal being in holiness and his creation of everything, there is some action! God holds up a sealed book that nobody is able to open, because nobody is worthy to do so. Except for one person! The Messiah is able to act because he has triumphed by being willing to die (Rev 3:21). Now he is pictured as a Lamb bearing the marks of slaughter; his death, therefore, is interpreted as a sacrifice by which he has redeemed God's people from the peoples of the world, with the ultimate aim that they will be kings and priests for God.

*A series of judgments (Rev 6).* As the first four seals are broken, four riders appear to cause mayhem in the world. The limited nature of the judgments indicates that they are warnings to make people aware that God's wrath is about to fall completely on the world (cf. Rev 6:16) and to encourage them to repentance (cf. Rev 9:20-21; 16:9). The fifth seal reveals a group of martyrs for the gospel and for their witness to Christ; they call out to God to hasten the time of his final judgment, but they are told that this will not happen until the full number of martyrs is complete. Further cosmic disasters indicate that the day of the Lord's wrath has come and judgment is about to strike; nevertheless, there is no indication of readiness to repent. And instead of proceeding to the denouement, the writer describes further sets of visions that give parallel accounts of the future from different aspects.

*Sealing, prayer and further judgments (Rev 7—10).* But first there is an interlude during which God places a seal on his people to make it clear that they belong to him and so to preserve them from the effect of judgments to come (Rev 9:4). The description of them as people who belong to the twelve tribes of Israel cannot be meant literally, since the tribe of Dan is omitted and the tribe of Manasseh (Rev 7:6) was a subgroup of the tribe of Joseph (Rev 7:8). Then we see an innumerable crowd in the presence of God. This is a proleptic vision of their future reward, placed here to encourage those on earth who must undergo tribulation. They owe their position to the salvation bestowed by God and the Lamb through the Lamb's death. There is general agreement that the symbolical 144,000 and the great multitude are the same people before and after their deaths. God has set his mark on his people, and they will receive their reward, no matter what the opposition arrayed against them.

The opening of the final seal does not bring about the end but rather opens up to reveal a further set of judgments heralded by trumpets. The enormous disasters described are again partial in their effects; they warn people that these judgments are because of their sin and thus urge them to repent, lest worse befall them (Rev 9:20-21).

*The two witnesses (Rev 11).* After an announcement that there will be no further delay in the execution of God's plans (Rev 10:6-7), there is a vision of two witnesses, who have divine protection until they complete their act of testimony. They are slain by God's archenemy from the abyss and then are visibly caught up to heaven. The imagery, based on the figures of Moses and Elijah and Jesus, symbolizes the church in its witness. So the nature of the church is to bear witness during this period of persecution and judgment.

At last comes the sound of the seventh trumpet, announcing the final victory of God. This must be an anticipatory vision of the end-time event.

*The woman and child; the dragon; angelic messages (Rev 12—14).* Before the end is described, yet another parallel account follows in chapter 12 with the imagery of a woman who brings forth a child (clearly identified as Christ). There is opposition from a dragon; it is unable to harm the child, who is caught up to God. The dragon is defeated (cf. Lk 10:18; Jn 12:31) and cast down to the world, where it attacks the woman and the rest of her offspring. She personifies Israel, both the godly people in the old Israel, from which came the Messiah, and then the new Israel, consisting of Jesus' followers.

The casting down of the dragon may seem to be an odd way of describing the coming of God's salvation and kingdom, but the point is that the accuser of God's people has been cast out of heaven and can no longer prosecute them there. But there is a price to be paid for the victory.

The dragon's agents on earth take over and impose a totalitarian regime in which the followers of the Lamb are attacked and overcome, while everybody else follows and worships the anti-Christian beast. Since what is to happen is so fearsome for believers, another vision of the 144,000 is given, this time showing that they have safely arrived in heaven.

Angelic messages indicate that there is still opportunity for people to hear the gospel and to repent; nevertheless, when the seven last plagues come, there will be a melancholy refrain that people did not repent (Rev 16:9, 11). There are further warnings of eternal judgment and a vision of people actually being gathered for judgment by the Son of Man.

*Seven final plagues; Babylon and its fate (Rev 15—18).* The seven final plagues are much more severe than previous ones, but are not yet the final judgment. Although they are intended to lead people to repentance, they fail to do so. They culminate with the surviving people gathering to war against God for the last time. A final judgment falls upon "Babylon", a symbol of both Jerusalem and Rome and indeed of the whole sinful earth.

*The victory of God (Rev 19—20).* Chapter 19 celebrates both the victory of God over this evil system and also the reward of God's people in terms of their taking part in a banquet where the guests also figure as the bride of the Lamb.

The judgment itself is described as total defeat for God's enemies. Yet no battle is described, and all that we hear is the announcement of victory and defeat, and the death of all the enemy participants.

Chapter 20 describes an imprisonment of the dragon (Satan) to prevent him from deceiving the nations for a thousand years (but did they not all die in Rev 19?). Meanwhile, the martyrs come to life and reign with Christ. Then Satan is released and deceives the nations again, and a further battle and judgment follows, including the dead, who are now resurrected to face judgment. A literal interpretation of this millennium seems to be ruled out both because of the problems of determining where the nations come from and also because a temporary kingdom of Christ seems pointless. One solution is that John takes us back again to the beginning: the binding of Satan achieved by the death and exaltation of Christ, the millennium is the present age, and there is a final fling of evil leading to its defeat (the battle in Rev 19 and the destruction of evil in Rev

20:9-10 are the same event). Alternatively, the millennium is a proleptic image for the new earth, which will be described in remarkably similar terms in Revelation 21—22. No solution is free from problems.

*The new Jerusalem (Rev 21—22)*. Finally, John depicts the new Jerusalem, where God dwells with his people. His plastic use of imagery allows the city to be identified with the bride of the Lamb. God's people no longer need a physical temple, because God is with them. They do not need physical light, because God is their light. In Rev 22:14-15 it seems that there are still sinful people outside the city. This may be another image for their exclusion from God's new world (a milder image than the fires of hell, but can anything be worse than to be cut off from God's blessings?), or it may contrast the saints and sinners now on earth, as part of the appeal for people to come and receive the water of life and so to qualify for entrance into the heavenly city.

## THEOLOGICAL THEMES

*Framework: The "geography" of Revelation*. For John, there is a three-level universe. God is in heaven, surrounded by his servants who worship him, and God decides what is to happen upon the earth. The earth itself is the arena of conflict between the followers of Jesus and the world. Supernatural powers of evil can come down or be cast down from heaven to earth. Underneath the earth is the abyss, which is a place of captivity and punishment for these powers and those who yield to them.

*Main theme*. Revelation is a powerful statement of hope, based upon the sovereignty of the God who has revealed himself in Jesus. It prepares God's people for the difficult future that lies ahead of them and issues an evangelistic appeal to those who have not yet responded to their witness. The writer calls his readers to overcome their weaknesses as they face persecution and opposition. He presents them with a series of visions showing how God will work in the world. Despite martyrdom, God will vindicate his people by judging their opponents, acting so as to warn them to repent and also bringing final condemnation upon those who refuse to repent. The future of believers is bound up with Christ, who will bring his people to the heavenly city.

*God and his power*. God's mighty power dominates the book. Revelation presents God like a superhuman champion, thus indicating his power and authority to overcome his powerful enemies. This imagery may make God seem to be distant and removed from his people, but nevertheless he is to them "our God" (Rev 7:12). He wipes away tears from eyes, like a caring mother or nurse (Rev 21:4). Similarly the picture of the Lion of Judah is matched by the picture of the Lamb acting as a caring shepherd for his people (Rev 5:5-6; 7:17). In the context of the oppression experienced and feared by the church, the stress on divine omnipotence and ultimate control of history is both natural and essential.

The appropriate response to such a God (and to the Lamb) is worship. What takes place continually in his presence in heaven is intended as a pattern for believers on earth, over against the temptation to worship the rulers of this world.

*Jesus Christ, Messiah and witness.* Equally central alongside God is Christ, depicted preeminently as a Lamb who has been slain. The metaphor is messianic, but the fact that the Lamb has been slain (Rev 5:6, 12; 13:8; cf. Rev 12:11) evokes a powerful image of sacrifice. Raised from the dead and exalted, Jesus still bears the marks of death: the efficacy of his sacrifice persists eternally. Language used of God, such as "first and last", is also used of Jesus Christ. He is not only the highest being under God, qualified to open the scroll that sets God's future plan into operation; he is also on a level with God, to whom he refers as "my Father" (Rev 2:28; 3:5, 21; cf. Rev 1:6; 14:1). Christ as the Lamb is praised and worshiped in the same way as God; they share the same throne (Rev 22:1, 3), and often the two of them are bracketed together (Rev 5:13; cf. Rev 12:10).

Jesus is also described as the faithful witness, who has set the example of faithfulness unto death. He himself does not practice violence. Despite the warlike imagery (Rev 19:11-16), there is no account of him actually engaging in conflict.

*The Holy Spirit; the angels.* The role of the Spirit is much less central. The unusual reference to the seven spirits (Rev 1:4; 3:1; 4:5; 5:6) apparently refers to the functions of the one Spirit of God; it seems that the imagery of the angels who surround God and go out to do his bidding has been transferred to the Spirit. The Spirit speaks to the seven congregations and conveys the promises of God to them but otherwise plays no part in the action. Angels, however, are very important. They dominate the book, acting as messengers conveying revelation to human beings, as heralds of the successive series of judgments, and generally as God's agents. The role of the seven angels of the congregations, who receive the messages to the churches, is obscure.

*The forces of evil.* The beastology of Revelation is as complicated as the angelology. The principal evil force is the dragon, alias the devil and Satan (Rev 12:9 and 20:2), who is the instigator of action against God. In heaven, Satan is involved in conflict with Michael, is defeated, and is hurled down to earth, so that he ceases to accuse the people of God before God himself, but now is able to persecute the church on earth. His allies are two wild animals, who are satanically inspired to mimic Christ's power and the role of the prophets; together the two beasts exercise totalitarian power over the world through supernatural agents. Yet their power is limited by God (Rev 6:2, 4, 8, 11). The resulting setup is strongly condemned for its way of life, described in Revelation 18, where the world is characterized like ancient Babylon as a city that has grown wealthy not only on its trade but also on its violence and godlessness and especially its attacks on God's people.

*The church.* Human beings are sharply divided into two groups, those who follow the Lamb and those who yield to the enticements and temptations of the satanic forces. There are calls to the latter to repent, and also warnings to the former not to succumb to apostasy. Yet the followers of the Lamb are sealed by God before the judgments take place, and their names are written in the book of life (Rev 13:8; 17:8). We have the familiar New Testament tension between calls to persevere and assurances of divine protection, which should not be blandly smoothed out in favor of guaranteed perseverance or timid uncertainty. The all-important thing is that believers should "conquer" or prevail, in the sense that they stand up to temptation and persecution and successfully resist it. For John, it is necessary not only to be a believer but also to overcome the temptations to unbelief, and thus to be faithful, like Jesus (Rev 1:5; 2:10, 13; 3:14; 17:14; 19:11).

The various congregations in different localities have a primary missionary task of witness to Jesus (Rev 11:18; 16:6; 18:24). Within them, prophets are active, John himself being the outstanding example (Rev 1:3; cf. Rev 22:9), but there can be false prophets alongside the true (Rev 2:20).

There are also apostles (cf. the false ones in Rev 2:2), who are linked with the saints and prophets (Rev 18:20). These should be differentiated from the twelve apostles (Rev 21:14). There are echoes of the language of baptism and the Lord's Supper, but no direct references (Rev 3:20; 7:14; 22:14).

*The action.* The godless world goes about its own business with no thought of God, rejecting the witness of believers to the gospel and killing them. The world is open to evil influences and taken over by them. But the major action is that of God, who brings various judgments upon the world for its evil in the form of awful and unimaginable disaster; the boundary between what is meant literally and what can only be symbolical is hard to draw. However, we hear little, if anything, of the disasters being successful in bringing people to repentance. The nature of the final judgment on the evil forces and those who succumbed to them is portrayed with various different kinds of imagery. Mostly the imagery is of destruction and death; at one point there is a lake of fire, in which the devil and his accomplices are tormented day and night forever (Rev 20:10), and those whose names are not in the book of life are also thrown in there (Rev 20:15). Since literal death and everlasting torment are incompatible, it is debatable whether everlasting torment is the dominating image, or whether, as seems more probable, the images of death and destruction control the discourse.

The final destiny of God's people also combines images. God's people are invited to the marriage banquet of the Lamb, but the bride and the guests are the same people. There is a holy city, which is likened to a bride and appears to be identified with the bride (Rev 21:2, 9-10). The city is on a new earth rather than in heaven, and since God and the Lamb are in the city, it would seem that earth and heaven merge. Within the city is a garden with the tree of life, whose fruit is now there for the picking. The city apparently has gates through which God's people may enter, but sinners are excluded: is this yet another image for the final fate of the sinners, or is John thinking of the possibilities of entry and exclusion here and now?

For John, the action that he describes is to take place soon (Rev 1:1; 22:6-7); his last words emphasize that Jesus is coming soon (Rev 22:20).

The book thus shares the general New Testament belief that the end is not far distant. What was certainly not far distant is the development of the kind of godless human society described in the book, in whose history may be seen sin and its judgments, the witness of the church and the attacks upon it, and the failures of the church and attempts to reform it. God's final triumph is certain, even if the length of the period leading up to it remains hidden from us.

## REVELATION AND THE GOSPEL AND LETTERS OF JOHN

Revelation stands apart from the Gospel of John and 1-3 John by reason of its genre. Its prophetic, apocalyptic character sharply distinguishes it from the Gospel and the letters. It is obviously Christian, despite the suggestion sometimes made that its depictions of judgment are subchristian. But is it specifically Johannine rather than anything else?

So far as its understanding of Jesus Christ is concerned, its dominant title "the Lamb" *(arnion)* echoes the title "Lamb" *(amnos) of God* (Jn 1:29, 36). In both cases the imagery is that of a sacrificial animal, but the usage in the Gospel is hardly central, and the importance and positive significance of the term in Revelation are quite distinctive. The unique use of the title *the Word of God* (Rev 19:13) reminds us of John 1:1-14 and 1 John 1:1-4, but it is not clear whether the rich background of these two texts is needed to understand the usage in Revelation. Another possible link is the use of "I am" sayings (Rev 1:17; 2:23; 21:6; 22:13, 16), but the predicates in Revelation are different from those in the Gospel. However, the use of "I am [he]" in the Gospel, which appears to be a divine self-affirmation, is paralleled in Revelation with the use of "I am the Alpha and the Omega, the First and the Last, the Beginning and the End" by Christ (Rev 22:13), which echoes God's self-affirmation (Rev 1:8; 22:12).

The terminology used to express salvation also has links with Johannine usage. The term *life* is widely used in both books, but this term is too well-attested throughout the New Testament to be regarded as distinctively Johannine. The metaphorical use of *water* for salvation is found in both the Gospel and Revelation, thematically in the former (Jn 4; 7:38) and occasionally in the latter (Rev 7:17; 21:6; 22:1, 17), but is not found elsewhere; the related metaphorical term *thirst* is common to both books

(Jn 4:13-15; 6:35; 7:37; Rev 7:16; 21:6; 22:17). Revelation does not use *bread*, but it does have the imagery of manna (Rev 2:17; cf. Jn 6:31, 49). Both books are conspicuous for their use of a range of imagery in describing salvation and the blessings given to God's people, but they go their own ways in doing so. The imagery of Christ coming in through the door and having table fellowship with the believer (Rev 3:20) is not unlike the imagery of indwelling used in the Gospel (Jn 14:23).

But there are also differences. The use of *Father* to refer to God is of central importance in the Gospel but infrequent in Revelation and then always qualified as the Father of Christ (Rev 1:6; 2:28; 3:5, 21; 14:1). The adjective "almighty" *(pantokratōr)* is characteristic (elsewhere in the New Testament only in 2 Cor 6:18). The overwhelming picture of God is of a mighty potentate seated on his throne (another characteristic concept), a picture determined by the book's visionary nature and the need to stress God's sovereignty over the forces of evil.

The Holy Spirit acts primarily as the conveyor of divine messages in Revelation (Rev 2:7; 14:13; 22:17), and there is also the unusual reference to "the seven spirits", which are held by Christ (Rev 1:4; 3:1; 4:5; 5:6), but the relationship of the Spirit to individual believers is absent.

In both the Gospel and Revelation there is a consciousness of persecution threatening the church and possibly leading to death (Jn 15:18—16:4), but the theme is almost incidental in the Gospel as compared with its centrality in Revelation. The term *world* plays no significant role as a theological entity in Revelation, and the detailed development of God's judgments upon rebellious and unbelieving society has no parallel in the Gospel, which speaks simply of judgment. The Gospel does not have the apocalyptic descriptions of what is to happen in the future (this also distinguishes the Gospel of John from the Synoptic Gospels).

These points are sufficient to show that there are features of the underlying Johannine theology in Revelation, but they are used in a book that has a quite differently expressed set of interests.

## REVELATION AND THE REST OF THE NEW TESTAMENT

The most conspicuous feature of the book is its use of the apparatus of apocalyptic. The situation of the congregations is understood in terms of a clash with the satanically inspired forces of the world, engaged in persecution of the followers of the Lamb; the forces arrayed against the church are worldwide and cosmic, and there is no human hope of survival. The threat of suffering and martyrdom looms large and fills the horizon. So part of the book's message is to warn against the temptation to apostasy and to encourage steadfastness even to the point of death by assuring the threatened believers that God is on their side and they are assured of a heavenly reward, provided that they continue to be faithful. At the same time the book makes it clear that God will judge the forces arrayed against them and ultimately totally destroy them. The judgment of the oppressors is something that is a necessary part of God's victory and his people's vindication. Great stress is laid on the recalcitrance of the oppressors, who refuse to repent despite every painful warning. The implication is that God is more powerful than the oppressors, and therefore the believers can be assured of ultimate victory. This understanding of the contemporary situation in apocalyptic categories may have been the only viable option for a church that felt overwhelmed and threatened.

A similar stress on the future and understanding of it is found elsewhere in the New Testament (see 1 and 2 Thessalonians; 1 Cor 15; 2 Peter; Jude). This is particularly so in the first three Gospels, with their awareness of the appalling horrors of the Jewish war with Rome and the hard times to follow. They prophesy the destruction of the temple and the end of the world. There will be attacks on Christians; nevertheless, they must continue to preach the gospel. They are in danger of being deceived by false claimants to be prophets and messiahs. They are counseled to stand firm. Jesus gives specific warnings about getting away from Jerusalem when it is attacked. Finally, the Son of Man will come and gather together his elect, and they must remain spiritually vigilant in anticipation of that event. A final judgment involving the Son of Man will separate people, depending on their attitude to him and his brothers and sisters.

Although there are similarities in the basic account of what will happen, Revelation goes well beyond the Gospel material in extent and content. Whereas the Gospels deal almost entirely with events in this world, Revelation also describes concurrent events in heaven, from which the judgments come. At some length, Revelation also describes the actual final judgment and the new world that follows it. It goes into much detail about the temporal judgments of God on the sinful world. The city imagery speaks of Rome as well as of Jerusalem and has become symbolical of the unbelieving world as a whole. Above all, coming to the fore is the concept of the devil and his allies in an evil trinity, opposed to God and his people in a final showdown. The danger of believers being forced to conform to false worship is strong, but the concept of divine protection for God's people is also emphasized. In all of this the book apparently aims to prepare the church to face persecution that lies ahead; it issues a call for preparedness for martyrdom and it assures believers of God's ultimate triumph and of the new world into which they will be resurrected.

When we look at the theological motifs expressed within this framework, we find that the picture of God concentrates in a vivid way on his sheer power. Although his sovereignty and power are taken for granted elsewhere in the New Testament, Revelation makes much of them, partly because the author is adopting an apocalyptic style, with its striking imagery, and partly because he sees the immensity of the threats to the church and needs to reassure his readers that God is in ultimate control.

The picture of Jesus is a combination of typical messianic features and of an exalted figure closely related to God and sharing his status. The specific concentration on the imagery of the Lamb is unusual and again may be due to the apocalyptic background; it aids the author in presenting a crucified Messiah and indicating the sacrificial character of his death. The understanding of his death as redemptive fits in with the use of this motif elsewhere.

Revelation is unique in portraying the seven spirits of God as divine messengers and in the prominent place given to angels as divine agents. Certainly the New Testament uses plastic imagery in depicting heavenly and supernatural agents, both good and evil, and the language used may well be rhetorical rather than realistic. Revelation offers a much more distinctive presentation here, which again fits in with its apocalyptic genre. The same is true as it describes the sinful world and the evil forces that control it. Here we have a pictorial, imaginative presentation of what is expressed in more sober and abstract terms elsewhere.

In calling sinners and opponents of God to repent rather than to believe, the phrasing is not surprising in view of the way in which their sin is seen as rebellion and enmity. It is also entirely fitting that the call to God's people is to avoid contamination with sin and to resist like an army fighting a battle and making every effort to win. Elsewhere in the New Testament, we can readily find appeals to separation from sin and to perseverance in resisting temptation, especially the temptation to yield to persecution, appeals that say the same thing in less-vivid ways.

Revelation goes beyond the other New Testament writings in its rather detailed account of the new Jerusalem. Here is a rich variety of scriptural allusions and pictorial imagery, which creates an attractive prospect. Yet this imagery does not detract from the fact that the central feature of the age to come is God and the Lamb's presence with the saints, so that their chief delight is in him and the Lamb.

## CONCLUSION

Revelation is a book on its own in the New Testament, but in its broad features, its theology does not significantly differ from that of the other books. Its main concern is to assure believers of God's victory over the evil forces arrayed against them, reiterating his judgments upon evildoers, calling God's people to persevere even to the point of martyrdom, assuring them of God's protection, and encouraging them with the vision of God's final triumph over the evil powers and of his eternal kingdom of peace and salvation being set up. Significant features include these:

1. Cosmic imagery is concentrated to express the course of history.

2. The framework of the action is set by the dualism and conflict between the devil and God.

3. God is the all-powerful judge of the world, superior in power to the devil and his agents.

4. Jesus Christ is the slain Lamb and faithful witness, who conquered by submission to death.

5. God's people are called to overcome their enemies by steadfastness to death.

6. The vision of the new Jerusalem encourages the saints to endure.

# 21

# JOHN, THE SYNOPTIC GOSPELS AND PAUL

In our discussion of the so-called Johannine literature we have seen that the Gospel and the letters stand close to one another in style and content, although they are different in genre and intended to deal with different situations in the church; the book of Revelation stands more to one side, yet its theology fits into the early church's background. The two big points of discussion that remain concern the relationship of Johannine theology, particularly in the Gospel, to the picture of Jesus in the Synoptic Gospels, and this Gospel's relationship to the theology of the Pauline letters. In both cases our purpose is limited simply to establishing whether there is a common core of belief rather than trying to account for how the different presentations developed. In short, the question is simply this: Is there a reasonable unity to be seen despite all the diversity?

## THE GOSPEL OF JOHN AND THE SYNOPTIC GOSPELS

*The kingdom of God.* In the Gospels of Matthew, Mark and Luke, Jesus' main theme is the coming of the kingdom or reign of God. This reign brings God's blessings to human beings, both now and in the form of entry into God's heavenly kingdom in the future. But what is the relationship of Jesus himself to the kingdom? Does he merely announce its coming, or does he somehow bring it about? The identity of Jesus as God's agent is a central issue, even if Jesus himself is reticent about the matter. Especially in Matthew and Mark, the story can be seen as falling into two parts, concerned first with whether Jesus is the Messiah, and then with what kind of Messiah he is. The proclamation of the kingdom challenges the hearers to respond positively to the message, and this involves being disciples of Jesus and total commitment to him. Discipleship imposes a way of life upon those who enter the kingdom, with Matthew especially systematizing Jesus' teaching on how people should live.

In John, the language of God's kingdom has all but disappeared (Jn 3:3, 5), although the concept of Jesus as *king* (Jn 18:36) is powerfully present. In effect it is replaced by the concept of (eternal) life, rather like Luke's use of the concept of salvation. The question of Jesus' identity becomes a matter that is openly discussed. Jesus remains reticent about revealing who he is to those who are set on unbelief, but in John there is much more debate about who he is.

*The identity of Jesus.* In the Synoptic Gospels, the essential question about Jesus is whether he is the Messiah of Jewish expectation and how his suffering and death fit in with this. The same question figures in John, and we have the same combination of terms to describe him but with a shift in emphasis. The Synoptic Gospels use the designation *Son (of God)* for Jesus, and it is clearly important for the Evangelists. But it does not become the object of Jesus' public teaching and controversy with his opponents. *Son* is only rarely linked to teaching about a close personal relationship between Jesus and his Father and about preexistence in the way that it is in John.

It is a moot point whether the picture of Jesus given by the Synoptic Evangelists includes the concept of his preexistence. For Matthew and Luke (it could be argued), Jesus comes into being through the operation of the Holy Spirit on Mary rather than, as in John, through the preexistent Word or Son of God coming into the world. For John, there need be no tension with the birth stories; there has to be some means by which the preexistent Son comes into the human world, and conception via the Spirit and the virgin birth can be the means. John has no problem with Jesus having a human mother and siblings. For Matthew and Luke, however, the birth stories in themselves do not necessarily imply preexistence. However, elsewhere in the Synoptic Gospels are sayings about Jesus coming from or being sent by God, which may point in this direction. One should also mention the possibility that the Son of Man is understood to be a preexistent figure who comes from God.

The difference, therefore, lies more in the way in which the preexistence of the Logos (Word) or Son of God is thematic and central in John. The Synoptic Gospels reflect what was actually said in Jesus' lifetime; John rather is bringing out issues that emerged with the passage of time and fuller and deeper reflection on Jesus' identity.

As far as Jesus' role is concerned, recognition of him as a prophet is common to all the Gospels. The concept of Jesus as *the prophet* emerges much more clearly in John (1:21; 6:14; 7:40) and chimes in with the presentation of Jesus in Acts 3:22-23, where the prophet is equated with the Messiah. Messiahship is understood in much the same way in the Synoptic Gospels and John. In John 4 the revelation that Jesus is the Messiah leads to the broader confession that he is the "Savior of the world" (Jn 4:29, 42).

The usage of *Son of Man* goes far beyond what we found in the Synoptic Gospels. The close link between the Son of Man and the passion and resurrection of Jesus persists, but his role as the judge or counsel at the last judgment (Jn 5:27) is not stressed. The Son of Man is identified as having come down from heaven and being the agent of revelation and salvation.

The concept of Jesus as the Son is much more prominent in John and is used in discussion with the crowds and Jesus' opponents in an open way. As such, he is God's agent, sent into the world to bring salvation, and he has full authority to act on behalf of God. The term *Logos* is used in much the same way.

*Response to the message.* In John, God's love extends to the whole world, and salvation is offered to all who believe; those who are drawn by the Father can come to the Son and believe and will be raised up at the last day. The Synoptic Gospels do not stress these points. Occasionally the offer of the universality of salvation emerges explicitly (Mt 11:28-30), but it is always implicit: a call such as that in Mark 1:14-15 is manifestly intended for all who hear it. Some of the pericopes on discipleship are so framed that the initiative lies with Jesus, who calls people to be his disciples (Mk 1:16-20; 2:13-17), although cases of people coming to him are also recorded (Lk 9:57-62).

In John faith/belief as the essential response of people to the Christian message and the means of appropriating salvation comes to the fore. The verb is used in the Synoptic Gospels in connection with the mighty works, but the thought of accepting Jesus as the Messiah is also present. Now in John faith becomes the crucial mark of the followers of Jesus. *Faith* means believing what a person says to be true and accepting their statements (e.g., Jn 6:69; 8:24; 11:26-27, 42; 14:10; 16:27; 20:31). It also includes self-commitment to the person whose teaching has been accepted intellectually (e.g., Jn 1:12; 2:11, 23; 3:16; 6:29; 7:31). There is also the element of faithfulness in a continuing relationship, uniquely expressed in Johannine vocabulary by the term *remain* (Jn 6:56; 8:31; 15:4-10).

This understanding of response to Jesus' message corresponds to what we find in the Synoptic Gospels. There the essential element of commitment to Jesus is expressed in terms of following him, and there are demands for self-denial. This element persists in John (Jn 12:25-26); moreover, just as the call to self-denial and bearing the cross comes in the context of references to Jesus' own way to the cross in the Synoptic Gospels (Mk 8:31-38), so also here (Jn 12:23-24). Similarly, the opposition that disciples will face is associated with the fate of Jesus himself (Jn 15:20-21). The thought of continuing faithfulness to Jesus is expressed in the Synoptic Gospels by the imagery of bearing the cross.

*Salvation and eternal life.* The proclamation of Jesus regarding the kingdom of God is already understood in terms of salvation in the Synoptic Gospels, especially Luke (but cf. Mk 10:26, 52 Gk.; Mt 1:21; 19:25). This tendency is carried further in John. Kingship and the kingdom are not absent, particularly in the trial and crucifixion narrative (Jn 18:33-39; 19:3-21), where the question whether Jesus is a king assumes central importance, and also in the conversation with Nicodemus, where entry into salvation is understood as entry into God's kingdom (Jn 3:3, 5). For John, the purpose of Jesus is saving the world (Jn 3:17; 4:42; 12:47). Much more common is the theme of *eternal life*. This concept is used in the Synoptic Gospels for the life of the world to come (Mt 7:14; Mk 9:43, 45; 10:17, 30; Lk 10:25) and also on occasion for a present experience of life (cf. Mt 4:4; 9:18; Mk 5:23; cf. Lk 15:24, 32). By contrast, the usage of *life* and *live* assumes massive proportions in John. The gift of life resides in Jesus himself (Jn 1:4; cf. Jn 6:35, 48; 11:25; 14:6) or is identified with him, and his teaching leads to life (Jn 6:68). Such life is closely associated with resurrection (Jn 5:29; 11:25), but it is equally understood as a present experience (Jn 3:36; 5:24; 6:47), so that physical death does not interrupt it. It is God's gift to those who believe in him or in Jesus (Jn 3:16, 36; 5:24). The life of the world to come becomes a reality here and now for believers.

*Union with Christ.* In John Jesus is a spiritual figure who is in the disciples, and they are in him, just as they are in the Father and the Father is in them. Jesus speaks in the future tense of what will happen after he has gone, when the Father will send the Counselor (Jn 14—16). He also uses the present tense to describe spiritual relationships that exist after his resurrection; yet he speaks as if these relationships are already possible during his earthly life, as indeed in some sense they are. Thus, for example, he offers living water to the Samaritan woman there and then, and he tells the crowds that they must eat his flesh and drink his blood and that if they do so, they will remain in him and he in them (Jn 6:53-57). A similar motif of spiritual union with Christ is found in Paul, who speaks of Christ living in him (Gal 2:20), of being "in Christ", of knowing Christ (Phil 3:10), and of somehow dying and rising with Christ.

The nearest that we come to this in the Synoptic Gospels is in Matthew 18:20 and perhaps at the Last Supper, where Jesus identifies the bread with his body (or flesh) and the wine with his blood and invites the disciples to eat and drink. In Luke, the risen Christ is present with the disciples at the breaking of bread. Here is the symbolism of feeding on Christ and receiving the benefits of his death, and this is understood in terms of a spiritual relationship between the believer and Christ.

Similarly, teaching about the Holy Spirit that is elemental in the Synoptic Gospels is taken much further in John. John's teaching is much more akin to the Pauline understanding, with his understanding of the

Spirit as the inward source of eternal life and spiritual guidance.

*The way of life.* The way of life expected of disciples in the kingdom of God as it is presented in the Synoptic Gospels can be summed up as follows: Negatively, there are warnings against following the practices and teachings of other people, specifically the hypocrisy of the Pharisees, which includes self-seeking and outward observance of certain aspects of the law while ignoring the core values of righteousness and mercy. By contrast, Jesus gives teaching about the right attitude in giving alms, praying and fasting. Positively, there are the commandments to love God and one's neighbor, stretched to include love of enemies. There is specific instruction regarding marriage and divorce. Jesus teaches his disciples about the hard times that will come in the future, before the coming of the Son of Man, and urges them to be watchful and ready. He warns against the dangers associated with wealth and calls at least some disciples to give away their wealth. Jesus inculcates trust in God to provide for their needs and bases this on the character of God as Father. He also promises the Holy Spirit's help in times of special need. Jesus instructs his disciples on how to pray and encourages them to pray. Some disciples are sent out on mission, with specific instructions regarding their conduct, particularly in terms of material conditions. There is some teaching related to establishing a community of disciples and how they are to live together.

In John, warnings against the Pharisaic way of life are largely absent; the questions that arise in discussion with the Pharisees have more to do with who Jesus is. They are castigated for their love of human praise, and this may well reflect the same criticism that we find in the Synoptic Gospels, but here the accusation is made more because they refuse to believe in Christ (Jn 12:42-43).

The centrality of *love* in John is self-evident, although love for enemies is not explicitly mentioned. The issue of marriage and divorce does not arise (except in Jn 4:16-18). There are specific warnings against persecution, but no detailed apocalyptic forecasts. The issue of wealth does not arise (except indirectly in Jn 12:6). Trust in God and the promise of help from the Spirit are expounded at length. The role of the Spirit is considerably enlarged. There is strong encouragement to pray (lit., "ask") in the name of Jesus. The mission of the disciples is a conspicuous feature (Jn 4:38; 17:18; 20:21). Through the use of such imagery as that of the *flock* and the *vine*, the disciples are addressed as if they are a community.

This comparison shows a basic agreement between the Synoptic Gospels and John on the nature of the disciples' way of life.

*The future and believers.* Although the Synoptic Gospels are primarily concerned with the new situation brought about by Jesus' proclamation and activity, they also contain teaching about the future. The negative reaction of the Jewish authorities to Jesus will continue, directed now against his followers; Jesus himself has foreseen that this will happen. The Evangelists are conscious that the kind of cosmic and human events that Jesus associated with the approaching end of the world were already happening. Imposters will appear, claiming to be the Messiah or Jesus himself, with the danger that followers of Jesus may be misled. Therefore, there are detailed warnings to prepare the readers for these events, accompanied by assurances that, despite the dreadful things that are going to happen, the Son of Man will intervene to rescue his people and bring about the final judgment. All the Synoptic Gospels devote major sections to these matters and use cosmic imagery, typical of apocalyptic writings, to describe what will happen.

John's Gospel similarly takes account of the future of the disciples and the world. Two sections in the Johannine literature correspond to the so-called apocalyptic discourses in the Synoptic Gospels. One is the main story line in Revelation, which likewise traces the course of future events. The other is in the Gospel itself, where Jesus deals at length with the situation of believers after his departure (Jn 14—17). The dangers arising from opposition and persecution are made clear; there is a warning against the possibility that believers may fall away. The disciples are promised the Spirit's help in a much broader way than is found in the Synoptic Gospels, and they are allowed to overhear the prayer of Jesus in which he seeks divine resources for them to protect them. But otherwise there is little resemblance. The shadow of the Jewish war is not evident. The coming of Jesus for his disciples is muted (Jn 14:3). The end of the world is scarcely in view.

The core teaching can thus be presented in two different idioms. John 14—17 prepares the disciples for the future without Jesus' physical presence, forewarning them of hostility and persecution and urging them to stand firm, relying on the Holy Spirit's help. This passage implicitly rather than explicitly indicates that the time of trial is limited, since Jesus will return. As he has returned to the Father after being sent into the world to bear witness, so they too will be with Jesus in the end. Elsewhere in the Gospel are promises that the disciples will be raised at the last day (Jn 6:39-52; cf. Jn 11:24; 21:22), and the hope of being with Christ when he comes is repeated in 1 John 2:28; 3:2. What is said here in a mood of didactic encouragement is in essence what is said much more graphically in a different idiom in the Synoptic Gospels (as also in Revelation), but there the teaching about the Spirit's help is much less developed, and the material is interwoven with the other theme of the fall of Jerusalem and the temple, coupled with the danger of misreading this event as a sign of the imminence of the last day.

*Conclusion.* John has a distinctive framework of thought formed by his dualism, with its clear distinction between the spheres symbolized by light and darkness. The world is in darkness, but the light can shine in it, and there can be people who belong to the light within it (Jn 12:35-36). The language is not so very different from that found occasionally in the Synoptic Gospels (Mt 4:16 [Is 9:2]; Mt 5:14-16), but now it expresses the basic structure of John's thought.

Despite such developments, we can discern that the same essential message is being conveyed by the Synoptic Gospels and John. The former are probably much closer to the actual words (the ipsissima verba) of Jesus, whereas John evidences a much more developed theology, which more fully reflects the early Christians' insights in the period after the resurrection. But we can see that the same underlying theological apprehension of what God was doing in Jesus' coming appears in both sets of sources.

## JOHN AND PAUL

Paul's theology developed in part through the debate with Judaizers and with proponents of a way of thinking that was more indebted to Hellenistic ways of thinking, emphasizing wisdom, knowledge and human status. The later Pauline writings exhibit a strong consciousness of the threat from supernatural powers, which are worrying believers. Throughout Paul's letters we see much engagement with general problems and issues that arise within the congregations as they struggle with the growing pains of learning to live as Christians in fellowship. But in the Gospel of John the focus is on the Jewish authorities, who reject Jesus as the Messiah, and the more specific issues of life within the church are not a primary concern. We shall therefore expect that the general shape and manner of expression may be rather different.

*God and Jesus Christ.* Clearly the understanding of God is the same for both writers. For Paul, as for John, there is one God, whose character is summed up in the title of *Father.* He is the God of Israel, active throughout the history of that people.

For Paul, Jesus Christ is the one Lord and is regularly placed alongside God the Father with regard not only to creation but also to the spiritual blessings given to believers. He is pre-existent, associated with God in creation. Jesus is the Son of God, sent from God to the world to redeem humanity. In so doing, he laid aside his equality with God and took the role of a servant in becoming human. He was raised from the dead and exalted to sit at the right hand of God, where he presently reigns, and he will return at the end of history to gather his people, to raise the dead, and to execute judgment.

John presents the same picture. Jesus is the eternal Word, who was with God in the beginning and shared in the task of creation. The Word became flesh and shared human life. The humanity of Jesus is real in John; the term *incarnation* means nothing less than that. John describes Jesus as the Son of God, sent into the world. Originally sharing a glorious state with the Father, he came into the world, where his glory was visible to his disciples, although in a different form, and he returns to God and to the position that he formerly had. Where Paul stresses more his exaltation to the right hand of God (cf. Ps 110), John emphasizes his close relation to God as Son. Where Paul makes some limited use of the concept of wisdom, John's prologue makes full use of the concept of the Word (which is closely linked to wisdom).

*The Holy Spirit.* For Paul, the Holy Spirit is beginning to be understood as a personal being who can be named along with the Father and the Son. In John, the Spirit is identified as the Paraclete, who acts as a person and is not simply a form of divine power.

*The Scriptures.* Both Paul and John accept the authority of the Scriptures as divine revelation (Rom 1:2; cf. 2 Tim 3:16; Jn 7:19; 8:17; 10:34). They recount an ongoing history of God's dealings with his people in judging and saving them. Moses and the prophets bear witness to the coming of the Messiah and to the way of salvation through him (Rom 3:21; Jn 1:45). Paul has a lot to say about the law of Moses because it was an issue with the Judaizers. This is evidently not the case for John; his reference to the law in John 1:17 is not pejorative. Similarly, the issue of works of the law is marginal in John (Jn 6:28-29), presumably because the matter of Gentiles being required to keep the law is not a problem for his readers.

*Humanity and its need.* For both writers the main concern is with the fact of human sin and the divine response. Paul paints a picture of humanity in which the concepts of *sin* and the *flesh* are central tools for his exposition. Sin is the alien power that overcomes human beings and renders them liable to death. The flesh is human nature, captivated by sin and incapable of doing what is good and right. John works with the same concept of sin but does not have the same concept of the flesh; instead, he operates with various expressions of a dualism in which the world of human beings is in darkness, conceived as a sphere in which evil reigns, a realm "below" and distinct from the divine realm. Either way, human beings are in the grip of sin and under the threat of death. They stand under divine judgment. Where Paul speaks of God's wrath already being revealed from heaven (Rom 1:18), John talks of a divine judgment that people have already brought upon themselves (Jn 3:18); for both authors the future judgment is a recognition of the existing state of humanity, and the issue is death (cf. 1 Jn 5:16-17).

*Jesus and his role.* For John, Jesus appears much more in the role of a teacher simply because he has expressed his theology in the form of a Gospel. Nevertheless, this earthly role becomes one of revelation that through the Spirit is ongoing after the departure of Jesus. The human life of Jesus plays an almost negligible role in Paul; it is important that he was a man, born of a woman and born under the law, and there is the occasional reference to his authoritative teaching. Like the Apostles' Creed, Paul moves straight from the incarnation to the cross, and the cross-resurrection is the saving event. For John, the life and teaching of

Jesus constitute the heart of the story, but in the Johannine letters they disappear almost completely from view in the same way as in Paul. Nevertheless, the way in which the role of Jesus as the Lamb of God is stressed at the outset of the Gospel and the way in which this Gospel devotes an even greater proportion of its space than the Synoptic Gospels do to the final visit of Jesus to Jerusalem—these features show that "his hour" is indeed the climax of the story, for which the rest is preparation.

In Paul, the death of Jesus is understood as his becoming one with sinners in order that through him they may become righteous. The concept of justification is the most fully developed of the images used by Paul, probably because of the need to interact with Judaizers. This language is unknown to John. But he knows that Jesus takes away sins, that he dies on behalf of human beings, and that the cross and resurrection constitute the point where Satan is driven out. And in 1 John as in Paul, the same understanding of the cross as an atoning sacrifice for the sins of the world is clearly present. Even without the evidence of 1 John, the testimony of the Gospel, where the Lamb of God takes away sin, is quite sufficient to make the point.

*God's initiative in salvation.* Both authors unequivocally indicate that God sent his Son to provide all people with a means of salvation from sin. Paul stresses that this purpose includes Gentiles alongside Jews. This point is equally firmly made in John (Jn 12:20-33; cf. Jn 10:16). Both recognize that not everybody who hears responds to the offer with faith. Equally, both authors indicate that salvation results entirely from God's initiative, both in sending Christ and in sending out his followers to proclaim the good news; human beings can contribute nothing to their own salvation, and the only "work" that is required of them is not a work but is faith.

In the case of some people, their continuing refusal to believe is because of a divine hardening of their hearts, apparently as a judgment upon them for an earlier refusal to believe. The question of those who never have the opportunity to hear the gospel is not raised. Paul appears to believe that all Israelites have heard the message through the messengers whom God sends, and he urges the importance of evangelists taking the good news into the world (Rom 10:14-21).

*New life in union with Christ.* Paul and John agree in their profound understanding of the spiritual relationship between Christ and believers, both corporately and individually. In Paul, this is primarily conveyed by the *in Christ* phraseology, which establishes the way in which the lives of believers are determined by their relationship to Christ. The reciprocal thought that Christ is in believers is extremely rare by comparison (Gal 2:20; cf. Eph 3:17; Col 1:27). The same closeness of relationship to God is expressed by the way in which the Holy Spirit is closely linked to believers. Corporately, the church is the body and bride of Christ, and the later letters express this in terms of a divine fullness that flows from Christ to the church. Through the relationship with Christ, believers are understood to have died with Christ and to have been raised to newness of life, which will culminate when they are raised with spiritual bodies or are caught up to be with Christ (1 Thess 4:17). John speaks of mutual indwelling between Christ and believers, and between the Father and believers; all this is closely linked to the thought of the Spirit coming or being given to believers. John does not have the concept of dying and rising with Christ (but he comes close to the concept of dying with Christ in Jn 12:24-26). John develops the imagery of the vine and its branches to describe the relationship of believers collectively to Christ, and Paul has something similar in his brief allusion to the olive tree and its branches (Rom 11:16-24). John also states that the essential content of eternal life is to know God and Christ (Jn 17:3), a thought that surfaces briefly in Paul (Phil 3:8; cf. Eph 3:19). In both sets of writings there is frequent reference to prayer as the natural expression of the relationship between believers and God.

*Life in community.* John's Gospel implicitly understands the disciples of Jesus as forming a community. The images of the flock and the vine bring out this fact that disciples are not isolated individuals but belong together. The imagery of the vine is immediately followed by Jesus' teaching about love and specifically that the disciples are to love one another as he has loved them (Jn 15:1-17). This teaching is then reinforced in 1 John, where the recipients are related to one another as brothers and sisters; they must love one another in action and not just in words (1 Jn 3:11-18, 23; 4:11-12; 4:20—5:2; 2 Jn 5), and also pray for one another (1 Jn 5:16).

Paul shares this understanding of the church and develops it in much greater detail. The exercise of the varied gifts of the Spirit is prominent, not just in 1 Corinthians 12 and Romans 12 but also briefly in 2 Corinthians 12:12; Galatians 3:5; and 1 Thessalonians 5:19-21 (cf. Eph 4:7-13). John is also aware of the Spirit's activity in the disciples' work. The Spirit gifts the disciples for mission (Jn 20:21-23). Indeed, the Spirit's activity in witnessing to the world about sin, righteousness and judgment (Jn 16:7-11) is carried out through the disciples. The Spirit teaches within the Christian group (Jn 14:25-26; 16:12-15); we should not understand this simply as the guidance of individual believers but also as the gift of teaching to benefit the disciples generally. In 1 John, the readers are said to have received an anointing that conveys teaching to them, and it is recognized that the existence of prophets in the congregation makes it necessary somehow to test them, to see whether they are truly inspired by the Spirit, since unfortunately in every age there is the danger of false prophets leading God's people astray (1 Jn 2:26-27; 4:1-6). Here we have a remarkably close parallel to Paul's teaching about the need for testing prophecies (1 Thess 5:21). From 2 and 3 John we learn of the existence of traveling teachers and the development of local leadership (not without some problems, as reflected in 3 John) in a way that is not dissimilar from what we find in Paul. Whatever the differences in detail, we can see the charismatic nature of congregational life coupled with the development of local leadership across early Christianity.

*Mission.* The missionary nature of the church is immediately apparent in Paul's letters. He introduces himself as an apostle or missionary, writing to the congregations that he has founded and planted. Paul is obligated to an ongoing mission and has a sense of geographical goals to be reached. Although he says surprisingly little about the responsibility of congregations to engage in mission where they are, he expects them to participate in the mission that has been entrusted to his colleagues and himself by their support in prayer and by the provision of helpers.

In John, Jesus has a mission: the goal is to save the world, and he entrusts his mission to his followers (Jn 4:38; 17:18; 20:21). The catch of 153 fish after the resurrection appears to symbolize the harvest to be gathered. The disciples are to confer forgiveness (or to withhold it, presumably from people who refuse to believe), and they are given the Spirit to enable them for their task. The Pauline and Johannine pictures agree on the fundamental fact that the followers of Christ are called to a mission that brings salvation to those who accept their message.

*The coming of Christ and the resurrection.* Paul's teaching about the ultimate future centers on the coming of Christ and the resurrection of the dead. History moves toward a climax at which the effective dominion of Christ is extended over all things; he will return as a glorious figure to gather his people who are still alive, raise those who have died, and transform them to be like himself for their future life with him. The rest of the dead are raised (but not transformed) to face God's wrath at the judgment, which is carried out by Christ. Paul knows of a final outbreak of powerful evil before the end comes.

For John, there is the same hope of eternal life for those who belong to Christ. All the dead will hear the voice of the Son of Man and be raised to life or to condemnation and wrath (Jn 5:28-29). As in Paul, Christ is the one to whom the task of judgment is delegated. The hope of Christ's return is still in view, but there is less stress on it in this Gospel. The basic structure of expectation that we have in Paul is thus also present in John, but the accents are differently placed, with rather more stress on eternal life. This would not be surprising for an author writing somewhat later, at a point when far more believers have already died. The other Johannine literature includes the full-scale drama concerning the activity of evil in the last days, the judgment upon all people in Revelation, and the need to recognize the activities of antichrists here and now, wherever the (first) coming of Jesus as the Christ is denied (1 Jn 2:22; 2 Jn 7).

*Conclusion.* In Paul and John we have two presentations of early Christian theology that have essentially the same basic structures and agree to a very considerable extent in their detailed content. At the same time they do differ in their conceptualizations and styles. We have two different artists (or schools of artists) who see the same subject in different ways, yet it is the same subject, and we need both pictures to bring out the richness of the common theme.

# 22

# THE LETTER TO THE HEBREWS

Hebrews is a written sermon addressed to readers who were being tempted to fall away from their Christian faith, possibly relapsing into the Judaism from which they had turned to Christianity. Arguing from the Old Testament Scriptures the unknown author demonstrates to them the impossibility of salvation apart from Christ and calls them to be prepared for the long haul of faith and the tribulations associated with it. His mood alternates between sections that are more doctrinal and those that are more paraenetical (for the latter see Heb 2:1-4; 3:1—4:14; 5:11—6:12; 10:19-39; 12:1-13; 12:14—13:25).

## THE THEOLOGICAL STORY

*The revelation of God through his Son (Heb 1:1—2:18).* The writer begins with the high position of Jesus, who is superior to the prophets and the angels by virtue of his status as the one who shares the being of God and is enthroned beside him. In Scripture, God has made assertions about Jesus that are superior to anything that is ever said about angels (Heb 1:1-14). The practical consequence is that since the lesser message (the law) spoken by angels incurred penalties for disobedience, people are all the more culpable if they neglect the salvation provided by Jesus. The description of the announcement of salvation resembles the way in which Acts describes the preaching of the gospel with accompanying signs and the gifts of the Spirit (Heb 2:1-4). Jesus' suffering and death might appear to be an argument against his superiority to the angels, but Psalm 8 is used to show how he was briefly made lower than the angels so as to die and thus defeat the devil and make atonement for human sins (Heb 2:5-18).

*The Son as high priest (Heb 3:1—5:10).* Before focusing on Jesus as high priest, the writer compares Jesus with Moses. In contrast to faithful Moses the Israelites were persistently unbelieving, and those who have heard the gospel may equally fail to believe and so be excluded from the "rest" or salvation spoken of in Psalm 95. The implicit exhortation to persevere in belief is buttressed: negatively by a warning that the state of the human heart is visible to God; and positively by an intimation that with Jesus as their high priest, the readers can come with confidence before this God and expect to find mercy (Heb 3:1—4:13). Humanity needs a sympathetic high priest appointed by God to his office. Jesus fulfills this role, particularly through his suffering, which "perfected" him for his role as Savior (Heb 5:1-10).

*The high priestly office of the Son (Heb 5:11—10:39).* The readers are warned that they are in danger of being spiritually unprepared: if they turn their backs on salvation and the Savior, there is no hope for them. However, the writer has observed the signs of salvation in them and urges them to continue in faith so that they will inherit what God has promised. They have an unseen hope on which they can rely in the heavenly sanctuary, where Jesus is their high priest (Heb 5:11—6:20).

The right of Jesus to be high priest, although he did not belong to the priestly tribe of Levi, is justified by comparison with the intriguing figure of Melchizedek, who functioned as an independent priest of God in the time of Abraham. Similarly, appointed by God, Jesus is able to continue in office, uninterrupted by death, by contrast with the earthly Levitical priests. He has made a once-for-all sacrifice and is able to exercise an uninterrupted ministry of intercession. A contrast is drawn between the earthly character of the Levitical priesthood and the heavenly character of Jesus' priesthood. There is a heavenly tabernacle to which the earthly one corresponds, as a shadowy outline of the real thing (Exod 25:40). Another contrast is between the first, or "old", covenant made with Moses and the promise of a "new" covenant made to Jeremiah and now inaugurated by the death of Jesus.

The old and new systems have the same general structure of a tabernacle with an altar and a system of sacrificial offerings, whose blood cleanses from sin. But the heavenly tabernacle is not material: Christ has offered himself and not an animal, he has made one offering of himself once for all, and there is no need for repetition of the one offering. However, the contrast is not between two efficacious ways of dealing with sin. In fact the Levitical sacrifices could not of themselves take away sin: how could the blood of animals possibly do so? These sacrifices, therefore, were simply shadows or reflections of the real thing. The sacrifice of Christ inaugurates a new covenant under which people can be truly cleansed from sin (Heb 7:1—10:18).

Christian believers can confidently approach God in prayer, free from the guilt of sin. They must remember that if they go on sinning, there is no other way of forgiveness. Let them persist in their faith, for it cannot be that long until Jesus returns (Heb 10:19-39).

*The need for faith and endurance (Heb 11:1—12:13).* The word *faith* creates the bridge to the letter's final teaching section, which develops the notion of the faith of those who trust in God where they cannot see and persist in belief despite every disincentive to do so. Under the old covenant faithful believers persisted in faith, although they could not yet see the realization of God's promises and walked by faith rather than by sight. So it also is with those who live under the new covenant; they are equally strangers and pilgrims, gripped by the firm hope that God will fulfill his promises. There is every encouragement from the believers of the past and Jesus himself to persist and persevere. Let the readers see the pressures to abandon faith positively as tests to strengthen faith; God is using this painful means of discipline to make them stronger.

*The Christian life in a hostile world (Heb 12:14—13:25).* Finally, there are warnings against sexual immorality and material greed. There is encouragement built on a contrast between the fearsomeness of Mount Sinai, where the law was given, and Mount Zion, where there is a vast company to welcome the readers. The letter sees the Christian situation as privilege but also as disgrace and social exclusion. Christians depend upon their prayers for one another and the inward working of God's power to aid them in their pilgrimage (Heb 13:21).

## THEOLOGICAL THEMES

*The old and the new.* The letter's conceptualization is provided in large measure by the category of priesthood and sacrifice. The argument is structured in terms of a basic general contrast between "the past" and "these last days". In the past God interacted with his people through his messengers, the prophets; through the agency of Moses, who ranked highly as the servant in charge of God's house; through the angels and the law that they mediated; through the promises of God; specifically through the sacrificial system; and through their faith, by which they gained genuine blessings. But this setup is no longer valid, however much it once was. The new covenant has succeeded the old, but the way of faith is still the same.

The old setup provides the pattern for interpreting what is going on now. We learn what a covenant is from the old covenant. Understanding Jesus' work as sacrificial depends upon drawing analogies from the Old Testament system to apply to Jesus' work. In fact, however, what Christ did in the heavenly sanctuary is the pattern that was followed by the old system of tabernacle and sacrifices, which thus can be regarded as shadows of the real thing (Heb 8:5; 9:23-24). And although the law laid down God's requirements, which had to be carried out (Heb 10:8), the old setup could not take away sins and hence was not efficacious (Heb 9:9; 10:11). Its effects were purely external (Heb 9:13). The old covenant had something wrong with it, or else it would not have needed to be replaced (Heb 8:7).

It was only a shadow or reflection of the true system (Heb 10:1). Since the letter says that people who sinned under the first covenant are granted redemption through the death of Jesus (Heb 9:15), the sacrifices under the old system may have achieved an outward cleansing, which symbolized the spiritual cleansing achieved by Christ's sacrifice, to which they pointed. Those old sacrifices were not able to "perfect" the worshipers as far as their consciences were concerned, but only to cleanse them externally

(Heb 9:9) and temporally (Heb 10:1). By contrast, Christ is able to make perfect those who are being made holy (Heb 10:14) and so make them fit to enter into God's presence without fear (Heb 12:23). Yet this prospect is held out as a reality for people of faith under the old covenant as well as the new (Heb 11:40).

Accordingly, the relationship between the old and the new systems is not simply one of contrast. There is also a strong element of continuity. This is provided by the concept of faith. Faith was characteristic of God's true people right through the Old Testament period (Heb 11), despite the lack of faith in others (Heb 3:19; 4:2, 11).

*The Christian life as a journey.* A further important structural element in the theology of Hebrews is the concept of the journey in space and time. Abraham left his own country to go wherever God would direct him. His hoped-for goal was a city, a place of security built by God (Heb 11:16). But he spent his life in a tent, waiting for the fulfillment of the promise. Evidently the city is heavenly, and to some extent the promised land of Canaan may be seen as a shadow or foretaste of the ultimate goal, the heavenly Jerusalem (Heb 12:22; 13:14; cf. Gal 4:26). God's people are strangers and aliens in this world, looking forward to a better country. At the same time the writer can tell his readers that they have come to the heavenly city, so that there is the characteristic Christian blend of the "already" and the "not yet". For the writer, this seems to be a difference between the believers under the old covenant, who merely looked forward, and new-covenant believers, who already enjoy that to which they look forward.

There is a related contrast between the two mountains to which people may come. The first generation of Israelites in the desert literally came to Sinai, which was a fearsome place. But the readers have come to Mount Zion, understood spiritually as the city of God, populated by God and his people, and to a sacrifice that is efficacious. Again this is the goal, but it is also the place with which they are in spiritual contact through their faith. The imagery stresses that, if failure to listen to the God of Sinai carried such serious consequences, how much more will failure to listen to the God of the new covenant.

The same pattern is established with the concept of "rest". On a literal reading the rest promised by God was the goal of the journey through the wilderness to Canaan; his angry response to the rebellion of Israel was to condemn them to forty years of wanderings and deprive them of entry (Heb 3:7-11, citing Ps 95:7-11). Unbelief leads to exclusion from God's blessings. But the promise of rest is still there for the readers; Psalm 95 challenges the readers not to behave like the wilderness generation and so cut themselves off from God's rest.

A further image used by the writer is that of the race, in which the readers are moving toward a goal where Jesus stands to inspire them with his example. The runners must keep going to the end and bear with the tough demands of the course (Heb 12:1-3).

The use of "journey" language was not seen by the author as incompatible with the hope of Christ's appearing at the end of the age, bringing salvation to those awaiting him (Heb 9:28). Travelers can also be people living in hope of a taxi drawing up alongside them to take them the rest of the way!

*The nature of faith.* Faith is "being sure of what we hope for and certain of what we do not see" (Heb 11:1). In this phrase are the two elements of futurity and invisibility. There is a realm that we cannot at present see nor enter, but one day we shall both see the unseen and enter the inaccessible. So faith is concerned both with belief in the invisible God (e.g., Heb 11:6) and with conviction that what is prophesied for the future will happen (e.g., Heb 11:7). It was characteristic of the old covenant as well as of the new, as typified by Abel, Abraham, who was willing to offer Isaac in sacrifice (Heb 11:17), and Moses. Such faith involves commitment, shown by a willingness to live a tough life here, trust in God that he will fulfill his promises, and perseverance in the face of opposition and every temptation to fall back into a more-comfortable way of living (Heb 12:4-13). To some extent, the writer is stressing the need for perseverance and hope for the future, rather than for the personal relationship with God and Christ, since this is the kind of faith needed in their situation, pressing on forward and not drifting backward (Heb 2:1).

*Salvation, future and present.* The writer of the letter is addressing a group of people who have received a message concerning salvation, which has been powerfully attested to them in various ways (Heb 2:1-4). The accent is probably on the future in Hebrews 5:9, where Christ is the source of eternal salvation for all who obey him, and also in Hebrews 9:28, where Christ will appear the second time to bring salvation to those awaiting him. There is a clear concept of a heavenly sphere into which believers will one day enter. This might suggest that believers do not yet "have" salvation but live in a hostile world, experiencing pain and hardship, falling far short of God's purpose for their lives, being not yet mature and always liable to fall away, and thinking of salvation as the perfected life of heaven, to be reached after a long and arduous journey.

However, in Hebrews 2:1-4 the possible danger is to ignore an announced salvation rather than an announcement of salvation. Salvation itself, not just a message about future salvation, has been brought to the readers. The readers have been freed from the fear of death (Heb 2:15) and are already God's sons and daughters, destined for glory through Jesus as the author of their salvation (Heb 2:10; cf. Heb 5:9). They already share in Christ (Heb 3:14). Believers can enter into rest—which may combine elements of the present and the future (Heb 4:1-11). They receive mercy and grace as divine power, motivated by love, which strengthens believers facing temptation and hostility (Heb 4:16). The readers are able to come to God in prayer, even though they cannot see him (Heb 4:16). Christ is able to save completely and for all time those who come to God through him (Heb 7:25). They have been made holy (Heb 10:10).

Believers thus look forward to a salvation yet to be revealed (cf. 1 Pet 1:5), but at the same time they experience a real and comprehensive set of divine blessings, including entry into God's presence with complete confidence (cf. Rom 5:1).

*Falling away.* Yet there are warnings that people may experience all these divine gifts and then fall away from their faith (Heb 2:1-4; 3:7—4:13; 5:11—6:20; 10:19-39; 12:12—13:19). These passages seem to allow that a person who has been a believer and enjoyed the blessings of salvation may lapse into a state of unbelief. It is said to be impossible to bring them back to repentance, and all that awaits them is judgment (cf. Esau). This means that people who reject the way of salvation and the Savior cannot be saved so long as they do so. The warnings are addressed to those who are tempted to reject Christ and to persist in doing so. There may be a point, known only to God, at which repentance becomes impossible; it is dangerous to flirt with apostasy. However, while the tone is indeed one of warning against a possible danger, it is coupled with strong statements of encouragement: "We are confident of better things in your case" (Heb 6:9 NRSV). Nobody is unequivocally identified here as having crossed over the fatal line.

*God as judge and Father.* God—the glorious and omnipotent ruler of the universe, who speaks through the prophets and his Son and is aware of all that goes on in the whole of his creation—is presented in solemn terms as the judge (Heb 12:23) who acts to punish those who transgress the commands given through Moses and reject the salvation offered through his Son. At the same time he is the gracious Father to the children who constitute his family (Heb 2:10; 12:5-8). His discipline may seem harsh but is intended for the good of the children (Heb 12:4-11). Believers have access to him through the efficacy of Christ's sacrifice (Heb 10:19-22) and are able to serve him like priests (Heb 9:14; 12:28).

*Son and high priest.* The sonship of Jesus forms the basis for his high priesthood. It is striking that the simple term *Jesus* is found no less than ten times. It may point to his real human existence, made in all respects like his human brothers and sisters (Heb 2:17), both in learning obedience to God and in suffering a human death (Heb 2:14-18; 5:7-9). His kinship and sympathy with humankind constituted the indispensable qualification for acting as a high priest, both in his intercession for them and in his dying for them.

The same term "perfecting" is used with reference to Jesus as with believers. As the author or originator of salvation, he had to be made perfect through suffering (Heb 2:10; cf. Heb 5:9; 7:28). He did not simply make a costly self-sacrifice but fully entered into the situation of humanity and is able to sympathize with them, so that his sacrifice is a genuine appeal by the representative of humanity to God.

Hebrews expresses Jesus' exalted status by describing the Son in terms used elsewhere of Wisdom as sharing in the glorious image of God and being his close companion and helper (Heb 1:1-4; cf. Wis 7:25-26). This implies the preexistence of the Son before creation. An unusual feature is the introduction of the figure of Melchizedek. Melchizedek had a priesthood distinct from that of the tribe of Levi but yet perfectly legitimate in its function and in a sense superior to that of Levi. The priesthood of

Christ, who came from Judah and not from Levi, can be seen as falling into the same category. The writer has read Psalm 110 and understands verse 1 as referring to Christ (Heb 1:13); he then develops this motif in the light of Genesis 14 and its picture of a priest whose origin was unknown and who therefore had, so far as Scripture is concerned, no genealogical qualifications for his task. Further, the biblical language about being "a priest forever after the order of Melchizedek" (Heb 5:6 ESV; Ps 110:4) can be taken to imply that Melchizedek himself, whose death is not reported in Scripture, held an eternal priesthood.

The task of Christ is to bring salvation (Heb 2:3; 7:25). This goal is variously described as glory (Heb 2:10), God's original aim for humanity (Ps 8), and as rest; it may be fanciful to see an implied contrast between the Joshua, who did not give rest, and the "new" Joshua (Jesus), who can do so (Heb 4:8). Christ also delivers people from the fear of death (Heb 2:15). This is achieved (at least in part) by rendering the devil powerless since he has the power of death.

But the main aim is to make people holy (Heb 2:11) or to cleanse them (Heb 9:14). Christ offers a sacrifice and provides forgiveness (Heb 8:12). Aspects of the Old Testament sacrificial system provide the imagery. The principal one is the annual Day of Atonement, on which the high priest entered the innermost part of the tabernacle, carrying the blood of a sacrificed animal; he sprinkled it on the cover of the ark of the covenant with that blood to expiate the people's sins (Lev 16). The death of Jesus on the cross constituted the sacrifice. His exaltation to heaven and entry into the presence of God constituted the offering to God. Unlike the Levitical priests (Heb 7:27; 9:12, 26, 28; 10:10, 14; cf. 1 Pet 3:18), Jesus made his offering once and for all, and then he sat down (Heb 10:12). His intercession for sinners continues (Heb 7:25)—a motif that must not be misunderstood to mean that God the judge has to be persuaded by an external agent to forgive sinners: the grace of God himself actually led to the whole action of salvation (Heb 2:10).

Alongside the offering of the sacrifice to God, another aspect of sacrifice is sprinkling the sinful worshipers with blood (Heb 9:13). This symbolism, associated particularly with inaugurating the old covenant, signifies both the cleansing of the people and their consecration to God.

The effect of sacrifice is that people can come into God's presence without fear (Heb 10:19). Whereas under the old covenant only the high priest could enter right into the innermost part of the tabernacle, which symbolized God's presence, Christian believers now have a positive relationship with God, which can be described in terms of coming into his presence—a present anticipation of the future consummation.

*The people of God.* Hebrews says little about the common life of Christian believers. It assumes that they meet together as a congregation and warns against slipping away from the church meetings—and so from Christian profession (Heb 10:25). It encourages believers to express their faith in praise to God and doing good to others; these activities provide the opportunity for something equivalent to sacrifice in the Christian life (Heb 13:15-16).

## HEBREWS AND THE NEW TESTAMENT

*Missionary theology.* The theology of Hebrews is distinctive in many ways, but it nevertheless rests firmly upon the basic beliefs of early Christianity. Admittedly the missionary character of the theology is not obvious at first sight. This letter is concerned more with the danger of Christian believers falling away from their faith than with the winning of new converts. The author appeals to his readers to hold fast to their faith and to persevere. In doing so, he reminds them how they came to faith. They heard the message that was first spoken by the Lord, then confirmed to the readers by those who heard the Lord, while God supported these testifiers and backed up their message with signs and wonders and gifts of the Holy Spirit (Heb 2:3-4). There are echoes here both of 1 Corinthians 12, with the reference to the Spirit giving gifts as God wills (1 Cor 12:11), and also of Luke-Acts; it has been claimed that Hebrews 2:3-4 is an admirable summary of Luke-Acts, capturing precisely its structure and atmosphere.

*Covenant and journey.* Hebrews develops the contrast between the two covenants, the old and the new, to show how the Christian faith can be understood as the fulfillment of the Jewish religion, so that it does not make sense to go back to the old. This motif of *covenant* is not all that widespread in the New Testament. The cup saying at the Last Supper indicates that the death of Jesus is to be understood as the sacrifice inaugurating the new covenant, and this is also reflected in 1 Peter 1:2. The concept of the new covenant is then taken up by Paul both in Galatians (Gal 4:24) and 2 Corinthians 3. Nowhere, however, is the motif so fully and distinctively developed as it is in Hebrews.

The notion of the Christian life as a journey through the wilderness is also part of early Christian paraenesis. Luke uses it with reference to the life of Jesus and also to the Christian movement. Peter portrays believers as strangers in this world, although his motif is more that of believers living in a world to which they do not belong rather than of travelers making their way through it (1 Pet 2:11). The metaphor of the Christian life as a race to be run in Philippians 3 is not dissimilar. Hebrews goes furthest in elaborating the concept of the traveling people of God. The Christian life is a journey like that of the Israelites through the wilderness, in which they must maintain a steadfast faith in God; already they are experiencing the life of the world to come, but they must press on until they reach perfection. Great emphasis is given to the element of continuing in faith, as expressed in the cognate English term *faithfulness*. This is not a different understanding of faith from that elsewhere in the New Testament, but it accentuates an element in faith that is most needed in this situation.

*Priesthood and sacrifice.* Priestly language is used elsewhere of Jesus to a limited extent; it is more usual to think of him as the sacrifice. We find the rudiments of it in the statements that he gave himself up for us, and then in the statement that he gave himself for us as an offering and sacrifice to God (Eph 5:2). But the theme is more widespread. The understanding of Jesus' death as sacrificial is an underlying motif, which surfaces regularly without being thematized at length. Paul sees the death of Jesus in terms of the Passover sacrifice and the sin offering, alongside his probable understanding of Jesus' role as scapegoat (Gal 3:10-14; cf. Lev 16:20-22). Sacrificial ideas are also present in John, 1 John, 1 Peter and Revelation.

Hebrews uses the device of typology, whereby God is seen to act in certain ways in people and institutions in Old Testament times, ways embodying patterns according to which he acts later in a superlative and final matter. Jesus is the new Moses and the new Aaron. The former embodiments of these roles have now run their course and gone into retirement. The sacrifices prescribed in the Old Testament had a limited effectiveness in their time because the blood of bulls and goats could not really take away sin, and the cleansing produced was external. They are now replaced by the fully effective sacrifice of Christ, which is able to bring "perfection" to the worshipers.

The author goes into considerable detail to show how the sacrifice on the Day of Atonement is the model for understanding the sacrifice of Christ. He takes up the pattern of slaying the animal on the altar and then taking its blood into the innermost part of the tabernacle to make atonement for sin. The writer compares all this with the way in which Christ could be said to shed his blood on the cross and then to go into heaven to offer his sacrifice to God, to make full and final atonement for human sin. He provides us with the rationale of how the sacrifice made on the cross takes effect, indicating how Christ's exaltation, or rather his entry into heaven, is an essential part of the saving event.

*The problem of falling away.* It is commonly thought that elsewhere in the New Testament the nature of salvation is such that, once a person has become a Christian believer, there is no possibility of their falling away and losing their salvation. Believers are chosen by God for salvation, called by God, and drawn to Christ in faith through God's action. They have been born or regenerated by God's Spirit and have an indelible status and character conferred upon them. Jesus has promised that they will be kept by God's power. Nothing can separate them from God's love. They may sin grievously, but their sins will never be great enough to cause God to reject them, for he will so work in their lives as to preserve them from falling away. This does not mean that they may presume on their security and sin to their heart's content. In some cases the presence of a sinning tendency may indicate that they were never truly saved after all. In other cases, true believers who fall into sin will suffer other penalties or chastisements short of final separation from God.

Nevertheless, Hebrews warns against the danger of believers falling away from Christ and coming under divine judgment. Some claim that the description of those in danger of falling away is of people who were never truly believers and had no real or full Christian experience. Alternatively, it is argued that the cases described are hypothetical, for God will always intervene to prevent people from reaching the point of danger and apostatizing; the warnings are there as God's way of ensuring that his people do persevere. To others, the warnings appear to be genuine and not hypothetical; they point to a danger that is real, even if remote.

The New Testament writers lay stress on God's faithfulness in caring for his people and preserving them from falling (Jude 24) while at the same time encouraging them to continue having faith in this God and not to fall away from him. Their security rests on the faithful love of God. Nevertheless, alongside this motif there are the warnings against the danger of falling away, warnings that are not to be emptied of their force. These writers urge people to put their faith in the Lord and to accept his promises. There is a paradox here akin to that of the relationship between divine empowering and human effort in achieving holiness. The warnings would lose their effectiveness in preventing believers from falling if they knew that there is actually no danger of falling.

*The nature of the Christian life.* There is rather less in this letter about the work of the Holy Spirit or about spiritual union with God and Christ than in Paul or John. Nevertheless, the Spirit is closely related to the lives of believers (Heb 6:4; cf. Heb 10:29), and the power of God is present in them to enable them to do God's will (Heb 13:21; cf. Phil 2:12-13). God's people are upheld by hope, like an anchor rope holding them absolutely firmly; inverting the metaphor, we might perhaps think of a lifeline connecting a diver to a ship and conveying the life-sustaining oxygen. In this respect, Hebrews may be thought to be more akin to Acts, where there is certainly spiritual succor for believers in various kinds of ways, but the concept of a personal relationship with Christ and the inward working of the Spirit (other than in empowering for mission) is considerably muted.

Moreover, through prayer believers have access to God in his heavenly dwelling, thanks to Christ's priestly mediation, and thus participate in the life of heaven. Here we have an expression of the nature of the new spiritual life to which believers are admitted, an expression bearing some resemblance to concepts of the Jerusalem above (Gal 4:26), the heavenly places in which believers now exist (Eph 1:3), and the realm above to which they have been raised with Christ (Col 3:1). There is thus a spiritual life for believers in which they are in the heavenly presence of God, while still on earth (cf. Rom 5:1), as well as the future hope of Christ's coming (Heb 9:28; 10:37). Being in the heavenly presence of God here and now, with the privilege of prayer to him, seems to correspond with the concept of present union with Christ, which is so prominent in Paul and John. With all its individual theological developments, Hebrews clearly has strong connections with the other main expressions of early Christian theology.

## CONCLUSION

Hebrews uses the continuity and contrasts between the old and new covenants to expound the superiority of the new in its own time. Linked to this contrast is that between the earthly tabernacle and the heavenly temple. A typological understanding of the Old Testament is developed. The obsolescence of the old covenant and its replacement by the new make it inconceivable that Christians should want to abandon their pilgrimage of faith.

Significant elements in the theology are the following:

1. Hebrews understands Jesus as the Son of God and thus superior to Moses as the mediator of the new covenant.

2. The concept of Jesus Christ's priesthood is central.

3. The self-sacrifice of Jesus in his death is followed by his entry into the heavenly temple, to make a once-for-all offering for sin.

4. Forgiveness is impossible other than by Christ's offering, and forgiveness is impossible for those who turn away from Christ and persist on that track.

5. Hebrews understands the Christian life as a pilgrimage or journey in faith.

# 23

# THE LETTER OF JAMES

## THE THEOLOGICAL STORY

The letter of James is implicitly addressed to Christians as (the new) Israel, using the Jewish term *Diaspora*, or *Dispersion* (the name used for Jews living outside Judea). Their situation is one of testing and oppression. They are threatened by pressure from outside, apparently from rich people who oppress the poor Christians and attack their religion (Jas 2:6-7). There is also internal bickering associated with slander, envy and ambition (Jas 3:16; 4:1, 11). James does not refer to false theological teaching. His aim is pastoral, to strengthen and encourage the believers but equally to exhort them to Christian behavior as they progress toward maturity of faith. Rather than going through the letter in order, it will be more helpful to trace its five recurring main themes.

*Temptation and maturity (Jas 1:2-8, 12-18).* The readers are constantly subjected to temptations. These can be seen positively as circumstances in which God is testing and developing their faith, or negatively as situations in which they are being enticed to do what is evil and become trapped into a process that culminates in death (cf. Jas 5:20). Temptation works by stimulating evil desires, which are part of a person's own nature. There can therefore be no excuse for sin by claiming that it was the result of an overpowering outside impulse (Jas 1:13-15). Believers face the continual temptation to follow worldly "wisdom" (Jas 4:4), with its emphasis on success and consequent boasting (Jas 3:14). They are called to be patient and persevering in the face of suffering (Jas 5:7-11).

Testing leads to the goal of maturity or perfection (Jas 1:4). Believers must move forward to a faith that is perfect, working in harmony with complementary deeds (Jas 2:22). One evidence of perfection is the absence of sins committed by the tongue (Jas 3:2).

*Wealth and poverty (Jas 1:9-11; 2:1-13; 4:8-10, 13-16; 5:1-6).* The church includes both rich and poor, with a temptation for those in the middle to show partiality toward the rich and to discriminate against the poor. The rich tend to complacency and oppression of the poor. The author sides with the poor who trust in God and warns of the judgments awaiting the rich and the immoral.

*Faith and actions (Jas 1:19-25; 2:14-26; 3:13-18; 4:1-7, 17).* Faith is extremely important as the essential characteristic of the Christian (Jas 2:5), but there is the danger of assuming that faith is sufficient without demonstrating its reality through appropriate action. The lack of suitable action is seen in the bad relationships within the congregations, the partiality shown to the rich, and the absence of concern for the needy.

*Sins of speech (Jas 1:26-27; 3:1-12; 4:11-12; 5:12).* There is a considerable body of traditional teaching on the sins of speech. The tongue can be an uncontrollable source of evil, especially in the slanderous and angry things it says about other people, particularly fellow believers.

*Patience and prayer (Jas 5:7-11, 13-20).* The closing section of the letter stresses the importance of patience and of intercessory prayer for the members of the church.

## THEOLOGICAL THEMES

James emphasizes elements in New Testament theology and ethics that are less prominent elsewhere, and he has an important corrective to offer to some mistaken ideas about faith and action. He is more "theological" than is sometimes thought. For example, respect for other people rests on a doctrine of the image of God (Jas 3:9). Again, he is concerned with the crucial questions of how people are saved (Jas 1:21; 2:14; 4:12) and justified (Jas 2:21-25).

*Jesus Christ.* Jesus is mentioned or alluded to only four times in the body of the letter, but James frequently echoes his teaching. The readers are instructed to be patient until the Lord's coming (Jas 5:7-8). Here the Old Testament hope of God's future coming as judge (Jas 4:12) is expressed in terms of the coming of the Lord Jesus as judge. He is thus not simply a human teacher or a human Messiah, but the Father's supreme agent, "our glorious Lord Jesus Christ" (Jas 2:1). "The excellent name that was invoked over you" (Jas 2:7 NRSV) is surely an allusion to baptism in the name of Jesus as Lord and Savior. Those who are ill are to be anointed in the name of the Lord, who will forgive any sins that they have committed (Jas 5:14-15).

*God as giver and judge.* Against the possible misconceptions that God is not good and willing to answer prayer and that he is the author of temptation, James reassures his readers that he is gracious (Jas 4:6; 5:11) and generous (Jas 1:5, 17). God chooses the poor for his kingdom (Jas 2:5) and condemns the favoritism and injustice that fail to give the poor their rights (Jas 5:4); his people must follow his example. He desires a righteous people, following Old Testament morality, concerned for the needy and free from worldly sinfulness (Jas 1:20, 25). God is the impartial judge before whom all will eventually stand (Jas 2:12-13; 4:12). There is a fearsome judgment in store for the wicked and unjust (Jas 5:1, 3, 6, 9, 12). God will ultimately uphold the poor, not necessarily the poor in general but the poor who believe in him and commit themselves to him, just as Jesus did (Jas 1:12; 5:10-11). In all this, James stands in the tradition of wisdom teaching, which some of Jesus' teaching earlier carried on.

*The life of the believer.* In terms of God's action, Christians are people who have been given birth through "the word of truth" (Jas 1:18; cf. 1 Pet 1:23), but in terms of human action, they are people who profess faith in Jesus Christ (Jas 2:1). They are under the law that sets people free (Jas 1:25; cf. Jas 2:8). James makes no mention of the Holy Spirit in relation to the life of the believer. In James, wisdom functions like the Holy Spirit elsewhere: wisdom is a gift given by God (Jas 1:5; 3:15), leading to humility (Jas 3:13) and other qualities (Jas 3:17-18) that are remarkably similar to the fruit of the Spirit (Gal 5:22-23).

*Faith and actions.* The Christian life can be summed up in terms of faith (Jas 1:3; 2:1, 5); faith is essential to our ongoing relationship with God and is expressed in prayer (Jas 1:6; 5:15). A false view of faith sees it as little more than orthodox belief, which does not change a person's lifestyle. Faith is not genuine without being expressed in actions (e.g., Jas 2:1-4) and is useless without them (Jas 2:14-26); mere words without loving actions are useless (Jas 2:15-16). Listening to the Word must be accompanied by obedience to what it says (Jas 1:22). Faith not accompanied by works is dead (Jas 2:14, 17). All this is backed up by biblical examples of faith in action, such as being prepared to offer one's son to God (Jas 2:21) or welcoming spies and protecting them from capture (Jas 2:25).

*The life of the congregation.* The reference to the "Dispersion" (Jas 1:1 NRSV) probably indicates that believers regard themselves as successors of God's people of the Old Testament, claiming Abraham as their father (Jas 2:21). They are "strangers and pilgrims" (1 Pet 2:11 KJV), living in the midst of an environment that at best is uninterested and at worst inimical to their faith. Their gatherings are called by the Jewish name of "synagogue" (Jas 2:1-4 Gk.). They are led by elders (Jas 5:14), whose pastoral care extends to visiting the sick, anointing them, and praying for them. There appears to be a wider circle of people who give teaching or have a recognized role as teachers. Teaching is regarded as a desirable occupation even by people who are not well-suited to it (Jas 3:1-2). The teaching is described as "the word" (Jas 1:22-25), and it can include the "perfect law" as well as specifically Christian instruction. Congregational activities include prayer and singing of praise (Jas 3:9) as well as mutual confession of sins and prayers for healing (Jas 5:13-18). The "name" in James 2:7 has been plausibly connected with baptism.

## JAMES IN THE NEW TESTAMENT

Despite the undoubtedly Christian character of James, there are astonishing silences. James says nothing on the incarnation, death and resurrection of Jesus. There is no reference to the Holy Spirit. The letter has none of the deeply theological teaching on the nature of the spiritual life that we find especially in Paul and John. We lack here any development of spiritual communion with God or of a life in Christ, in which believers are identified with him in his death and resurrection. In a down-to-earth manner, James is primarily concerned with how people behave in the world, how they may suffer, and whether they pray.

Nevertheless, there is a much more considerable theological substratum to James than is often realized. James is essentially concerned with living the Christian life amid temptation. It stands in the tradition of Jewish wisdom and has its own characteristic way of expressing its teaching. James is primarily concerned with practical problems in the church; his letter resembles what Ephesians or Colossians would have been like if we only had the second halves of these letters. He reminds people who attach great weight to the significance of Jesus as Lord not to neglect his down-to-earth teaching out of an overconcern with mouthing the right confessions concerning him.

At numerous points, James reflects the common theology of the early church. His understanding of God as one—as lawgiver and judge, and as the gracious giver of gifts, who hears the prayers of his people—is fully in line with the central understanding of God. His concern for the poor reflects the teaching of Jesus. Although little is said about Jesus, his exalted, glorious position is assumed, and his future coming is awaited. James is concerned with how Christians behave, particularly stressing the need to honor and care for the poor, pray for one another, and exercise pastoral care, especially for those in danger of falling away from their faith. He affirms the reality of divine healing of illness in response to prayer. All of this clearly ties in with teaching elsewhere in the New Testament.

For James, the Christian life begins with a new birth and is a continuing life of faith. He offers his own analysis of the nature of temptation and sin and is a realist in recognizing the temptations and trials that come to believers. James assumes that to be a Christian is to be a believer, but he corrects any misapprehension that belief is a mere matter of the head and does not affect behavior. Although James has often been thought to take up a different, indeed an opposing, position to Paul on the issue of faith and works, their positions are harmonious.

The main issue here is that of faith and works (Jas 2:14-26), where it is often thought that James is attacking the Pauline understanding of justification by faith and not by works. More probably James and Paul stand back to back, defending the gospel against different misunderstandings. Paul is contesting the misunderstanding that obedience to the Jewish law, especially circumcision and its ritual aspects, is necessary in order to be justified here and now; James is contesting the misunderstanding that if one has faith in God, this need not express itself in the love that Paul also sees as the indispensable expression of faith (Gal 5:6). For Paul, justification is primarily what makes a person a Christian. Thus Romans 5:1 Greek strikingly says: *"Having been* justified"! For James, the focus may be more on justification as God's action at the last judgment, when the reality of faith is to be assessed; that scene corresponds to future salvation in Paul's thinking, as illustrated in Romans 5:9: *"Having been* justified now by his blood, we *shall be* saved from the wrath through him [Christ]" (author's translation).

Further, James does not place works in antithesis to faith, which is the view that Paul combats so fiercely in Galatians and Romans. What Paul condemns is the view that *works of the law* are required instead of or in addition to faith in order to be justified. But James is concerned with the kind of good works that indicate the change of character needed to accompany Christian conversion. It is entirely possible that some of Paul's hearers took his insistence on "faith alone" as an excuse for lack of effort to do good actions.

## CONCLUSION

The main theme of James is the development of Christian perfection, seen in a life of active faith that successfully copes with the temptations arising from the love of money and the abuse of the tongue. The significant elements he stresses are the following:

1. All people must answer to God's judgment through Christ, whose coming is near.

2. The provision of God's word and divine wisdom enables believers to develop maturity.

3. Faith needs to be expressed in action.

4. Life lived according to God's law means loving one's neighbor and avoiding partiality.

5. Life is to be lived in dependence on God through prayer.

# 24

# THE FIRST LETTER OF PETER

The first letter of Peter is set in the context of attacks on Christians that constitute a "fiery ordeal" (1 Pet 4:12). Their sufferings are mostly insults and harsh treatment from other people (1 Pet 2:18-20) rather than any kind of official state action. Peter is concerned with the way in which Christian believers are to live in the world despite its hostility. He interweaves theology with exhortation and encouragement.

## THE THEOLOGICAL STORY

*Greeting and blessing (1 Pet 1:1-12).* The readers are scattered abroad as the Christian "Dispersion" (1 Pet 1:1 NRSV; cf. Jas 1:1) of God's elect people. God has taken the initiative in bringing the church into being; by his Spirit, he is molding his people so that they may be obedient and consecrated to him (1 Pet 1:1-2).

An extended expression of praise to God reminds the readers of the nature of their salvation (1 Pet 1:3-12). Although they may be suffering now in all kinds of ways, they can confidently look forward to a promised future in heaven. God allows their present trials as a means of testing and strengthening their faith. For the moment they live by faith rather than by sight of Jesus Christ.

Yet there is a strong element of present salvation. The readers have already experienced a new birth (1 Pet 1:3, 23). Although they look forward to Christ's coming (1 Pet 1:7; 5:4), their present experience causes intense emotions of joy (1 Pet 1:8). Already they are receiving salvation and have tasted that the Lord is good (1 Pet 1:9; 2:3).

Peter is concerned with how believers live in this interim period. He stresses the certainty of their hope being fulfilled. It is rooted in the resurrection of Jesus as an event. The prophets who foresaw the sufferings of Christ and the glories to follow were told by God that their message was for the benefit of the future generation to which the readers belong (1 Pet 1:10-12).

*The basic characteristics of Christian living (1 Pet 1:13—2:10).* Despite their present trials, the readers are to set their sights on the future. They are to seek to be holy, like their God (Lev 11:44-45). He is their Father, but a Father can also be a judge (1 Pet 1:17; cf. 1 Pet 2:23; 4:5). They have been delivered from their old, futile way of life by the shedding of Jesus' blood. Here redemption is not simply from the consequences of sin but also from a sinful way of life. So precious a gift is not to be treated lightly by continuing to live useless lives. Gratitude should be a powerful motive to sustain them in their pilgrimage.

Further statements of their new status use the metaphors of rebirth through the word of God to eternal life, sustained by spiritual "milk", and of a spiritual building, with Christ as the reliable cornerstone; the building is specifically a temple, and the readers are both the building stones and the priests who function within it. They are the new Israel, a priestly nation whose task is to praise God.

*The social conduct of believers (1 Pet 2:11—3:12).* Conduct generally acceptable in the world as good is here motivated and taken to a higher level by theological backing. For the Lord's sake, believers are to be submissive to the rulers and to honor people in general. Slaves are to obey their masters, no matter whether the latter are good or faulty. Undeserved suffering brings credit with God, as with Jesus, here described as the Suffering Servant (Is 53), who bore the sins of the readers and healed them.

Wives are to be submissive to their husbands, an attitude that will help to commend the gospel to non-Christian partners. For their part, husbands are to show due consideration to their wives; their equality as inheritors of God's salvation is emphasized. All believers must show mutual love and refrain from answering evil with evil (Ps 34).

*The attitude of believers to hostility (1 Pet 3:13—5:11).* Suffering will inevitably come to God's people but cannot really harm them. Therefore, they should not be frightened of the opposition but be prepared to bear witness to their faith. It is no credit to anybody to put up with punishment because it is deserved, but if a person bears undeserved suffering, then this is creditworthy. Jesus, the innocent sufferer, was brought back to life and preached to the spirits in prison who had been disobedient in Noah's time. God, who acted to save Noah, is now acting to save believers through "baptism". The victory of Jesus thus encourages believers in their witness; they know that the forces arrayed against them are ultimately powerless. Their sufferings will turn out for their good. They are to lead lives that are different from their former pattern, knowing that even if they are abused for it, they will ultimately be vindicated. The Christian alternative lifestyle is one of sobriety, prayer, mutual love and mutual service, using God-given gifts to glorify him.

Persecution can be understood as a means that God uses to purify the church, by separating out the faithful from the unfaithful. Sufferings can thus be regarded as a kind of purgative judgment by God (1 Pet 4:17). In this situation the church needs caring leaders and members who are humble toward one another and God. The church is under attack from the devil, but God will strengthen his people and bring them to glory just as he exalted Christ after his sufferings.

## THEOLOGICAL THEMES

*The general character of the theology.* The Christian life is expressed in praise, worship and thanksgiving to God; it is lived in opposition to Satan and evil; and it derives its strength from God's gift of salvation. The effect of Peter's rehearsing the great deeds of God is to bring about spontaneous expressions of thanksgiving to God for his twofold working in the world. God's victory over the forces of evil leads to their defeat. After his death, Christ issued his triumphant message to the spirits in prison and was enthroned alongside God as supreme over angels, authorities and powers

(1 Pet 3:19, 22). Christ saves people from sin to bring them to God and to the promise of their future inheritance (1 Pet 1:18-19).

*The influence of the Old Testament.* The written and spoken word of God is the means whereby God saves and strengthens his people (1 Pet 1:23-25; 3:1). The Old Testament prophetically explains who Jesus is and what he does (1 Pet 1:10-12). He is preeminently the Suffering Servant, who bore the sins of humanity so that they might die to sin and live to righteousness, following his example (1 Pet 2:21-25). Jesus is like a sacrificial lamb, whose blood was shed to redeem or deliver people from their old, sinful way of life and its consequences.

This phraseology is part of a general application of the idea of a new exodus. The opening description of the readers as God's chosen people—made holy by his Spirit and destined for obedience to God and being sprinkled with the blood of Christ (1 Pet 1:2)—shows how Peter regards the church as the counterpart of Israel at Sinai (Ex 24). Christian living must show a new holiness (1 Pet 1:15-16, based on Lev 11:44-45; 19:2; 20:7).

*The significance of Jesus Christ.* Although 1 Peter often echoes Jesus' teaching, the main focus is his death and resurrection and their significance for the readers' lives. Jesus is the one whom God chose before the creation of the world and now in these last times has revealed for the sake of the readers (1 Pet 1:20). This emphasizes that God takes the initiative in salvation and carries out his plan in due course. Probably Peter is thinking of a preexistent being whom God appointed for his task even before creation and then revealed him to the world.

Jesus was put to death "in flesh" but brought to life "in spirit" (1 Pet 3:18 Gk.). He died physically, but regarding the spiritual sphere of existence, he was made alive in a life that is not simply physical but indeed spiritual and eternal. He made a journey to the prison where the spirits are and preached to them. These spirits are best understood as the evil, supernatural powers that God keeps imprisoned until the judgment day (2 Pet 2:4; Jude 6; however, 1 Pet 4:6 refers to believers who eventually died and are destined for life with God). The "imprisoned spirits" are identified with the evil beings whose sin and rebellion led to the flood. The term "preached" (1 Pet 3:19 KJV) in itself does not tell us what Christ's message was; likely it was a "proclamation" of his victory (TNIV, NRSV). Just as

God saved Noah and his family then, despite the flood, so now too God saves the people who submit to the water of baptism; he saves them from perishing with God's opponents. The powers that threaten believers have been vanquished, and Christ is supreme over them. The purpose of the passage, therefore, is to encourage believers facing hostility by reassuring them of their salvation and the defeat of their enemies.

Christ is the source of all the blessings of salvation, and this is expressed by the use of the characteristically Pauline phrase "in Christ". God addresses his call to people in and through Christ (1 Pet 5:10). The readers who are "in Christ" (1 Pet 5:14) are joined to him so closely by their faith that he determines their way of life "in Christ" (1 Pet 3:16). Thanks to his death, they can die to sins and live to righteousness (1 Pet 2:24).

*The Holy Spirit.* The Spirit is the inspirer of the prophets and Christian preachers (1 Pet 1:11-12; cf. 1 Pet 4:10) and the sanctifier of believers (1 Pet 1:2). Also, he rests on believers when they are persecuted (1 Pet 4:14; cf. Mk 13:11).

*The church as God's people.* Believers are God's *flock*, and their leaders are subshepherds under the Chief Shepherd (1 Pet 5:2-4). They also form the *house* of God (1 Pet 4:17); this word can refer either to a "household" or to the place where God is present, his temple (cf. 1 Pet 2:4-5; Ezek 9:6; Mal 3:1). Language formerly used to describe the privileged position of the Jews as God's people is now deliberately applied to the readers. They are both temple and priesthood, charged to offer spiritual sacrifices of praise to God in both words and deeds (1 Pet 2:4-10).

The members of this community are to be lovingly hospitable to one another. They pray communally and privately (1 Pet 3:7; 4:7) and teach one another. There is oversight and pastoral care by elders (1 Pet 5:1), but the tasks of ministry are carried out by any members of the congregation who are appropriately gifted by God (1 Pet 4:10-11).

The outward mark of entry to the church is baptism (1 Pet 3:21), which is said to "save" the readers. It is the sign of acceptance into the church and above all a *pledge* to live a new life or a *prayer* to God to enable this to happen.

*The characteristics of believers.* Hope (1 Pet 1:3, 13, 21; 3:5, 15) and faith (1 Pet 1:5, 7, 8, 9, 21; 2:6-7; 5:9, 12; cf. 1 Pet 4:19) are the appropriate attitudes for people who are "strangers and exiles" (cf. 1 Pet 1:1; 2:11). They live in the world as temporary residents and do not really belong to it. Indeed, the world thinks them very strange people because its pleasures are not their pleasures, even though they once enjoyed them (1 Pet 4:1-4). They look forward and trust in the unseen Creator (1 Pet 4:19) and Christ (1 Pet 1:8). The strong stress on their being the people of God gives them a status and a self-respect that strongly contrasts with their situation vis-à-vis the world.

Alongside faith and hope, love for God and Christ (1 Pet 1:8) and for one another (1 Pet 1:22; 2:17; 4:8-9; 5:14) and holiness (1 Pet 1:2, 15-16; 2:5, 9; 3:5) are characteristics that Christians must show, mirroring the life of God. Rather than referring to the love shown by God, however, Peter speaks repeatedly of his *grace*, using this term to sum up the entire series of events and spiritual gifts through which life was brought to the world (1 Pet 1:2, 10, 13; 3:7; 4:10; 5:5, 10, 12; cf. the use of *mercy:* 1 Pet 1:3).

*Life in the world.* Peter stresses "doing good" (1 Pet 2:15, 20; 3:6, 17), an outgoing, positive attitude toward life in society, however much Christians are objects of hostility. He also calls for "submission" (1 Pet 2:13, 18; 3:1; 5:5) as the appropriate attitude toward people placed over the readers (1 Pet 2:13-17, 18-25; 3:1-7; 5:5). Ancient society took this attitude for granted, and so Christians show the effects of their obedience to the Lord by living according to the norms of ordered society.

Yet Christian husbands must show consideration to their wives as joint heirs of the gift of life (1 Pet 3:7), and all believers, including elders, must show humility toward one another (1 Pet 5:5b; cf. 1 Pet 3:8-12). Believers are fundamentally equal in the Lord.

Once some of Peter's audience lived like the rest of pagan society, but he expects that they will now live sober lives (1 Pet 4:3). They can expect abuse from other people, yet they can also reflect that there is no credit in suffering punishment or abuse for doing wrong; if they are doing what is right and suffer for it, this is praiseworthy in God's eyes (1 Pet 2:19-20; 4:13-16). They are not to withdraw from the world but to do good in it. The hope is that through their good deeds, Christians will lead non-Christians to glorify God (1 Pet 2:12); this ties in with the way in which Christians are also to be prepared to respond to people who question them about their faith (1 Pet 3:15-16).

## FIRST PETER AND THE LETTERS OF PAUL

There is considerable use of early Christian material in 1 Peter. As in the case of James, we find significant echoes of Jesus' teachings. There is a remarkably high amount of quotation from and allusion to passages from the Old Testament. Some of these passages are used independently by other New Testament authors, suggesting that a common pool of material was known to early Christians. Analysis of the doctrinal and practical teaching also reveals significant contacts in both form and content with other New Testament writings, demonstrating that 1 Peter stands in close contact with the common teaching of the church. In particular, the theology of the letter is close to that of the Pauline letters.

Thus Peter shares with Paul the common New Testament understanding of God as the gracious and faithful Father of Jesus Christ (1 Pet 1:3; 2 Cor 1:3) and of believers, who is also the sovereign and impartial judge of humankind (1 Pet 1:17; Rom 2:11; 14:11-12). His statements about God's foreknowledge of his people (1 Pet 1:2) place him alongside Paul, who uses similar language to indicate that the creation of God's people, to which the readers belong, rests on God's own purpose and initiative (Rom 8:28-30; Eph 1:3-6); the church is not a humanly created society of like-minded individuals.

Jesus Christ is the Son of the Father, and language is used that at least points in the direction of his preexistence. God's purpose of salvation through Jesus was conceived before the creation of the world, but only now revealed to the world (1 Pet 1:20; cf. Eph 1:4; Col 1:26). The Old Testament designation of Lord is applied to Jesus (1 Pet 2:3, 13; 3:15; 1 Cor 10:26). He fulfills the role of the Suffering Servant of Yahweh (1 Pet 2:21-25; Rom 4:25).

The Holy Spirit is active both in the inspiration of the prophets (1 Pet 1:11; cf. 2 Tim 3:16) and in the empowering of preachers (1 Pet 1:12; 1 Cor 2:10; 1 Thess 1:5). He is also at work in the sanctification of believers (1 Pet 1:2; 1 Thess 4:8) and is present with them in their sufferings (1 Pet 4:14; cf. Rom 8:26-27).

Peter's understanding of salvation is likewise close to that of Paul. The death, resurrection and exaltation of Jesus constitute the saving event, but Peter is alone in developing the significance of the period after his death, when Jesus visited the spirits in prison. The death is understood as sacrificial (1 Pet 1:2, 19; Rom 3:25; Eph 5:2), the means of redemption (1 Pet 1:18; Rom 3:24; Gal 3:13), the bearing of sin (1 Pet 2:24; cf. 2 Cor 5:21), and the means of reconciliation whereby sinners are brought back to God (1 Pet 2:25; 3:18; Rom 5:10). The hostile forces arrayed against them are subjugated to the exalted Lord (1 Pet 3:22; 1 Cor 15:25-27). Christians are people characterized by faith, hope and love directed to Jesus (1 Pet 1:3-9; 1 Thess 1:3). They have died to sin and live to righteousness (1 Pet 2:24; Rom 6:1-11), and their new life is "in Christ" (1 Pet 3:16; 5:10, 14; 1 Thess 2:14; 4:1). Corporately they constitute the people of God, in continuity with Israel, to which they now belong (Gal 6:16), and are a royal priesthood and temple (1 Pet 2:4-10; 2 Cor 6:16). They are God's flock and household (1 Pet 2:25; 4:17; 5:2; cf. 1 Cor 3:9; Eph 2:21). They are endowed with spiritual gifts to speak and serve in the congregation (1 Pet 4:10-11; Rom 12:6-8; 1 Cor 12). Though they are afflicted by opposition and persecution, they put their trust in God to keep them and will finally attain to sharing in God's glory, to which they have been called (1 Pet 1:5-9; Rom 8:31-39; 2 Cor 4:16-18; 2 Thess 2:14).

## CONCLUSION

The main theme in the theology of 1 Peter is the nature of the Christian life in a time of testing; believers, called to a living hope, are to live holy lives in the fear of God and mutual love, respecting the society in which they are placed, but avoiding its temptations and standing firm in the face of persecution. Significant themes worthy of note are these:

1. The theology of 1 Peter is expressed in strong dependence upon the Old Testament and in the consciousness that believers now form the people of God.

2. The accent falls on the hopeful aspect of faith as belief in the God who raises the dead and guards his people.

3. Jesus Christ is understood in terms of stone and servant imagery.

4. There is a unique reference to Christ's preaching to the spirits in prison.

5. First Peter recognizes persecution as an opportunity for witness and urges readers to take a positive attitude toward living out the Christian life in the world, despite its sinfulness and opposition.

# 25

# THE LETTER OF JUDE

Jude's letter is pastoral rather than polemical, warning the readers against the danger caused by infiltrators, exhorting them to remain faithful, and encouraging them to win back those gripped by error or in danger of succumbing to it. The heart of the letter is Jude 20-23; the theme is summed up in Jude 3, where the readers are encouraged to contend for the faith; and the danger is spelled out in Jude 4-19.

## THE THEOLOGICAL STORY

*Opening greeting and closing doxology (Jude 1-2, 24-25).* The opening greeting describes the readers as the objects of God's love, who are "kept for Jesus Christ", probably at his final coming (Jude 1). The closing doxology reminds them that God is able to keep them from falling (Jude 24), yet they must keep themselves in God's love (Jude 21).

*The danger caused by false teaching (Jude 3-16).* Some intruders in the congregations do not share the apostolic gospel and way of life. They may be wandering prophets with unorthodox teaching and questionable morality. They think that because they are saved by grace, they therefore are free to indulge in sin without fear of any consequences. Their denial of Jesus as Lord is a refusal to obey his commands. It is coupled with a lack of respect for any other spiritual authority. They do not possess the Spirit (Jude 19) and so are not truly Christian believers, despite whatever profession they make. The effect is a split in the church, and presumably the danger of orthodox Christians joining the immoral group.

*Responding to the false teachers (Jude 17-19, 22-23).* From the time of Cain onward, there have been sinners who have behaved similarly. Examples from Old Testament times show that such people will not escape divine judgment. Future judgment is also prophesied in *1 Enoch* 1:9 (picking up on Zech 14:5). The main concern is with those misled by the intruders or in danger from them. Jude 22-23 probably distinguishes between (1) believers who are being enticed by the false teachers and must be urgently rescued before they come under judgment; and (2) the false teachers themselves, to whom the offer of mercy must be extended, taking care not to be infected by their sin.

*Persevering in the faith (Jude 20-21).* The faithful must "contend for the faith" that was handed down to them (Jude 3-4). Personally they must build themselves up on the basis of their faith, pray as they are led by the Holy Spirit, keep themselves in the love that God has for them, and await Christ's mercy (at his future advent), which leads to eternal life (Jude 20-21).

## THEOLOGICAL THEMES

*God as loving and merciful.* Jude opens with references to God as the Father and to Jesus Christ; they are named in parallel as the spiritual agents through whom believers are loved and guarded. Thus the love and mercy of God are paramount (cf. Jude 21-22). The closing doxology characterizes God as Savior but also describes his "glory, majesty, power and authority". He is nevertheless the stern judge who destroyed those who did not believe and who is to be feared (Jude 23).

*Jesus Christ as Lord.* The descriptions of God the Father and of Christ are almost interchangeable (cf. Jude 5, where "the Lord" may be either of them). Both protect believers (Jude 1, 24) and show mercy or love to them (Jude 1, 21). Both have lordly authority, and Christ is the one who will come in judgment, according to Jude's likely interpretation of Enoch's prophecy. Thus Jesus is on an equal footing with God, although the closing doxology is addressed to God "through Jesus Christ".

*Possession of the Holy Spirit.* Believers "have" the Spirit (Jude 19) and sinners do not. The latter "follow mere natural instincts" *(psychikoi)*, pursuing life on a purely natural level. By contrast, believers are able to pray "in the Spirit" (Jude 20).

*Sin and judgment.* People are either ungodly sinners (Jude 4, 15) or saints (Jude 4). What happened to Sodom and Gomorrah is a vivid picture of what will finally happen to the sinners. The language of fire (Jude 23) is traditional for destruction, and it need not convey the sense of an unending torment. Nevertheless, the last word in the letter before the doxology is one of pastoral care for sinners. Faithful believers must show mercy to such people and thus try to rescue them from their danger. The sinners are depicted as victims to be pitied, but also as responsible persons who need to repent.

*Salvation.* The essential possession of the saints is salvation from sinful ways and judgment (Jude 3; cf. Jude 23, 25). Their characteristic quality is *faith*. This term can be used as a summing up of the Christian religion in terms of a body of saving truth handed over to God's people once and for all (Jude 3); any later alterations to it are ipso facto lacking in divine authority. Jude emphasizes faith as the content of the Christian message that is to be believed rather than faith as the activity of belief and commitment, but the use of the word *faith* for the gospel demonstrates that the activity of believing is integral to Christianity.

The goal of believers is to stand before God without any stains, an experience that will produce intense joy (Jude 24). Although the coming of the Lord is described in terms of judgment upon sinners, this is not its character for believers. This future hope, which will bring vindication for God's faithful people, remains living and real. For Jude, the readers are already living in the last days, and prophecy is being fulfilled (Jude 17-18).

*Scripture and other sources.* Jude rests his thought partly on what has been prophesied in the past and therefore is sure to happen. Such prophecies include the one cited from *1 Enoch* 1:9. Opinions differ on whether this means that Jude regards the pseudepigraphical *1 Enoch* as part of Scripture, and whether he ascribes the prophecy to a literal seventh-generation descendant from Adam. Earlier in the letter, Jude also describes the contention between Michael and the devil over the body of Moses (Jude 9), an account thought to be from the pseudepigraphical *Assumption of Moses.* Jude need be doing no more than citing what was generally believed, and at this time the dividing line between Scripture and what were presumably believed to be antique writings by inspired prophets was still fluid; a closed canon of Scripture was still in process of formation.

*The congregation and its life.* The church stands in continuity with God's people in the Old Testament. It meets together for what is here called a love feast (Jude 12), doubtless another name for the meal at which the Lord's Supper was celebrated. The responsibility for restoring sinners rests on the congregation as a whole.

## JUDE AND THE NEW TESTAMENT

Jude concentrates on the activity of pseudo-Christians, false teachers who live immoral lives and propound false doctrines. His concern is not just to expose and condemn them but also to preserve believers from their bad influence and enable them to persevere in their faith. He makes use of Jewish literature and traditions to characterize the heretics and to prophesy their fate.

The brevity of the letter curtails the amount of evidence provided for Jude's theology. What he has to say about God, Christ and the Spirit is in line with other early Christian writings. If the aspect of judgment emerges strongly, this is traditional language for the fate of rebels against God. The picture of God in relation to believers is of a merciful and loving being. Christ is described as functioning in the same ways as the Father and thus as being equal with him. Salvation depends upon God's calling, and perseverance is related to both his love and mercy and also to believers' faith and prayer.

The description of the readers as "called" (Jude 1) is a designation also used by Paul; it can stand as a name for Christians by virtue of an essential characteristic: they have been summoned by God to be his people and have responded to the summons (Rom 1:6-7; 8:28; 1 Cor 1:2, 24; cf. Rev 17:14). When the congregational members are urged to build themselves up in their faith (Jude 20), this most naturally refers to a mutual activity, similar to what Paul describes in 1 Corinthians 12 and 14.

The goal of appearing blameless before God is precisely what we find in Paul; believers will be able to stand before God without fear of blame since they will be made holy by him (1 Cor 1:8-9; Phil 1:9-11; 1 Thess 3:13; 5:23). The motif of intense joy is reminiscent of 1 Peter 1:8. The use of the doxology, in which these motifs appear (Jude 24-25), probably mirrors the practice of the church in its prayer language, and the closeness of the language to that of Romans 16:25-27 indicates Jude's relationship to mainstream Pauline Christianity.

## CONCLUSION

The main theme of Jude is the call for Christians to persevere in the faith under the protection of God, despite false teachers being among them, intruders whom God will judge, just as he has judged notorious sinners of the past. Significant elements include the following:

1. Jude correlates God's judgment upon immoral sinners and his mercy for those who repent.

2. God and Christ are juxtaposed in judgment and salvation.

3. Jude makes use of the apocalyptic strand in Judaism.

4. The congregation has an important role in pastoral care for sinners and in restoring those in danger of being led astray by the false teachers.

# 26

# THE SECOND LETTER OF PETER

Like Jude, 2 Peter warns its readers not to be attracted to false teachers, but here this warning is part of a much broader set of instructions and exhortations. The letter also has to deal with skepticism regarding the promises of Jesus' future coming since with the passage of time, it looks as if these promises are not going to be fulfilled.

## THE THEOLOGICAL STORY

*The spiritual progress of the readers (2 Pet 1:1-11).* The readers are described as people who have "obtained" faith "in [through] the righteousness of our God and Savior Jesus Christ" (2 Pet 1:1 Gk.). Faith is a gift that one can receive, and it is precious, doubtless because of the salvation that it brings. Believers may reach the twofold goal of escaping from the corruption that is in the world and participating in the nature of God himself. With this incentive before them, they are urged to develop a set of qualities that are closely akin to the fruit of the Spirit. Those who pursue this road will find that they increase in knowledge of God. In this way they will confirm that God has called them and made them part of his people, and they will enter his eternal kingdom.

*Apostolic testimony and the voice of prophecy (2 Pet 1:12-21).* Peter's main concern is to rehabilitate the expectation of Jesus' future coming. First, he emphasizes the importance and the reliability of his teaching. Even after Peter is gone, people will still be able to remember what he has said, presumably by having it in written form. The transfiguration of Jesus, witnessed by Peter himself and his companions, gave confirmation of the glorious status of Jesus. Like people in darkness who rely on a lantern until the day dawns, so believers—in this world's darkness and until the full light is revealed—should hold on to the words spoken by the prophets, as the Spirit moved them.

*Condemnation of false teachers (2 Pet 2:1-22).* Second, Peter states that the coming of false teachers is nothing new. They lack respect for authority and have a sensual, animal nature. These characters had escaped from the corruption of the world through their knowledge of Christ, but now they are in a worse position than previously; if their former sins may be regarded as sins of ignorance, their present sins are deliberate and thus are more culpable (2 Pet 2:20-21). So they are destined to certain judgment, like the fallen angels and the people of Sodom and Gomorrah. God can deliver his people from the false teachers' enticements, just as he rescued Noah and his family and Lot.

*Rebuttal of the false teaching (2 Pet 3:1-18).* Finally, Peter engages directly with the arguments of the false teachers and rebuts them. There is an antidote in the words of the prophets and of the apostles (2 Pet 3:1-10), who prophesied the coming of such people in the last days. These "scoffers" deny that there will be a future coming of the Lord, for life appears to go on unchanged. But they have forgotten the story of the flood! God will keep his promise to destroy the universe by fire. His timescale is not ours, and he is giving people every chance to repent before it is too late. Then God will create a new heaven and a new earth characterized by righteousness for those who are holy and godly. This hope should spur the readers on to live righteous lives and continue to grow in grace and knowledge (2 Pet 3:11-18).

## THEOLOGICAL THEMES

*Jesus as Savior.* When Peter refers to "the righteousness of our God and Savior Jesus Christ" (2 Pet 1:1), is he referring to two persons, "Our God and the Savior Jesus Christ"? Or to one figure, Jesus Christ, said to be both God and Savior? Both views are possible. In the next verse the rather similar-sounding wording clearly refers to two persons, but syntactically the opening phrase most naturally refers to one person, to Jesus as God. Elsewhere Jesus Christ is called "our Lord Jesus" and "Savior" (2 Pet 1:11; 2:20; 3:18).

Peter refers to Christ's "righteousness", through which people receive the gift of faith (2 Pet 1:1). This use of "righteousness" *(dikaiosynē)* may well refer to Christ's act that brings about justification (cf. Paul's reference to Christ's "righteous act" *[dikaiōma]* through which people receive justification; Rom 5:18). Jesus is also the Lord who "bought" his people (2 Pet 2:1); elsewhere this verb is used with specific mention of the price that was paid or of the blood of Christ (1 Cor 6:20; 7:23; Rev 5:9; 14:3-4). There is, therefore, probably an implicit reference to the death of Jesus in these two passages.

The supreme status given to Jesus as Savior, Lord and God indicates that he is regarded as the exalted Lord. Somewhat surprisingly the transfiguration is mentioned as a conferral of honor and glory by the Father.

*Faith.* The antidote to the false teaching that threatens the church is spiritual growth, both in knowledge of Christ and in the qualities characteristic of Christian community life. Faith is God's gift (2 Pet 1:1), the foundation on which believers are to build goodness and other qualities (2 Pet 1:5-7). The structure of the list is rhetorical and not meant to suggest that one acquires the characteristics in the order given. The fact that the readers are told to make every effort to gain such qualities may seem to stand in tension with teaching elsewhere that describes them as the fruit of the Spirit (Gal 5:22-23), but the same tension can be found in Paul himself (Gal 5:25).

*Knowledge.* All that we need for life and godliness and the continuing experience of God's grace and peace comes through our knowledge of God and Christ (2 Pet 1:2-3); it is the means by which salvation is gained (2 Pet 2:20). Such knowledge is of the way of righteousness and no doubt involves obedience to the "holy command", mentioned in the same context (2 Pet 2:21 NRSV).

*Partaking of the divine nature.* The phrase "partakers of the divine nature" (2 Pet 1:4 ESV) resembles Pauline statements that give believers a share in divine glory and Johannine statements that envisage believers being joined to God or Christ, just as the Father and the Son are joined to each other. This status is to be conferred in the future, doubtlessly when believers appear before God and Christ and are found blameless and at peace before him. The negative side of conversion is escaping from the corruption that is in the world, caused by evil desires (2 Pet 1:4) and culminating in destruction and death (2 Pet 2:12, 19). Peter apparently envisages the destruction of the world by fire as coinciding with the destruction of the evil at the final judgment.

*Salvation.* Salvation involves "cleansing" from the defiling character of sin (2 Pet 1:9 NRSV). It depends upon the call and choice of God (2 Pet 1:10), which are effective only insofar as they are confirmed by people's positive response to them. Those who do so respond attain a position of stability (2 Pet 1:10, 12; cf. 2 Pet 2:9) but need to be continually reminded of the danger of succumbing to the influence of the unstable false teachers (2 Pet 3:16). The Christian life thus calls for effort (2 Pet 3:14) and watchfulness (2 Pet 3:17). Although 2 Peter does not speak of the influence of the Holy Spirit in the lives of believers, he does mention the divine power that equips believers for the Christian life (2 Pet 1:3) and refers to growth in grace (2 Pet 3:18).

Salvation includes a future life in the eternal kingdom of our Lord and Savior Jesus Christ. This dimension of hope consequently imparts an urgency to the effort to be holy and blameless when the Lord comes (2 Pet 1:11).

## 2 PETER AND THE NEW TESTAMENT

Second Peter has much the same concerns as Jude. Its theology is similar to that in the Pauline tradition. Jesus Christ ranks alongside God the Father and is probably named as God (2 Pet 1:1) in a manner that is found elsewhere in the New Testament (Jn 20:28). Christ's function is summed up as that of *Savior*, a term whose currency is seen particularly in the letters to Timothy and Titus yet also in Luke-Acts. His saving activity consists in *redemption* (2 Pet 2:1), a term that probably carries a reference to his death, and there may be a reference to his righteous act that brings release from sin (2 Pet 1:1). We recognized the quite similar use of this motif by Paul and Revelation (1 Cor 6:20; 7:23; Rev 5:9; 14:3-4).

The reference to Jesus' transfiguration rather than his resurrection is unusual; Peter may have wished to appeal to the majestic appearance of the transfigured Christ, which does not figure in the resurrection appearance stories in the Gospels. The resurrection is certainly implicit in the references to Christ's present existence alongside God the Father.

The readers are characterized by faith, stated to be a gift of God (as in Eph 2:8), and the Christian life is regarded as one of growth in grace and knowledge; all this has close links to Pauline teaching on the fruit of the Spirit. *Knowledge* increasingly came to be used for a personal relationship with God and hence of shared insight into his purposes; the term does not indicate an intellectualization of Christian faith but something more personal (cf. Phil 3:10).

The language of sharing in the divine nature is unique to this letter, but the substance of the idea is expressed by both Paul and John. Believers are fellow heirs of the glory that is Christ's and sharers in his resurrection, receiving glorious bodies like his (Rom 8:17, 30; 2 Cor 3:18; Phil 3:21; cf. Eph 3:19). The relationships between believers and the Father and the Son are described in the same way as those between the Son and the Father (Jn 17:21).

The replacement of the perishable world by a new heaven and earth is most closely paralleled in Revelation (Rev 21:1), and this is confirmed by Romans 8:21, where the creation is liberated from decay and shares the glory of God's children.

Although the letter is concerned with inward problems in the church, the dominant motif in the picture of God and Christ is that of a God who does not want anybody to perish but rather that all people should come to repentance (2 Pet 3:9).

## CONCLUSION

The main theme of the theological message is the perseverance and spiritual growth of the readers in their faith in Christ. They are urged to avoid the dangers of false teaching, which have led some to immorality and skepticism about the Christian hope of Christ's second advent. Significant elements include the following:

1. Second Peter's unusual stress on Jesus' transfiguration points to his exaltation as Savior, Lord and God.

2. Faith is linked with a personal knowledge of Christ.

3. Believers share in the divine nature.

4. The letter makes a negative verdict on the perishable world and looks for its replacement by a new heaven and a new earth.

5. Second Peter attaches great importance to holding fast to the apostolic tradition and to the correct understanding of it.

# 27

# Diversity and Unity in the New Testament

The purpose of this book is to present the theology in the New Testament in a manner that does justice both to the distinctiveness and to the unity of the documents and their authors. Our book-by-book presentation has shown something of the distinctiveness of the different parts of the New Testament. At the same time in the course of the exposition we have made some comparisons of the various areas of the New Testament with one another, to see whether they share the same general understanding.

We began by looking at the way in which the Synoptic Gospels present Jesus' mission and message. We showed that Matthew and Luke present essentially the same picture as Mark, yet with greater detail and with some changes in emphases, which do not significantly alter the general impression. Further, we stated that there is every reason to believe that the substance of this presentation faithfully reflects the earliest traditions about Jesus, which in turn reflect what Jesus did and said.

We then brought the account of the early church in Acts into the discussion. The presentation there fits within the general framework provided by the Gospels (and specifically by Luke) and offers a picture of the early Christians' beliefs and theology that appears credible as the development of Jesus' message in the light of Christian experience of Jesus' resurrection, the outpouring of the Spirit, and the ongoing mission of the church. There is essentially a harmonious development from the theology of Jesus, as presented by the Evangelists, to the theology of the early church, as presented in Acts.

The next stage was to examine the letters in the Pauline corpus in something like their chronological order and then to offer a synthesis of Paul's theology. Within the limited scope of this volume, we were not able to discuss questions about developments in Paul's thought and about the possible share of his colleagues and successors in composing the letters. A comparison between the theology of the early church in Acts and the theology of Paul showed that there is a clear identity in basic matters, yet the Pauline letters offer a much fuller picture both in terms of the range of material covered and in the depth of the treatment.

The third major area is the Johannine literature. The theology of the Johannine letters is closely related to that of the Gospel of John in the manner of expression and the content. The theology of the Gospel is expressed in a quite distinctive fashion, including its use of a dualistic framework, which makes it stand out by comparison with the Synoptic Gospels. The Johannine way of putting things does differ in many ways from what we find elsewhere in the New Testament; nevertheless, the same basic concerns can be identified, and the central core of the theology is fundamentally the same. The general character and theology of Revelation make it stand rather apart from the other Johannine writings, but it shows similarities to some of the teachings in the Synoptic Gospels and Paul.

Finally, we brought the remaining New Testament books into the discussion and looked at each in turn. The letter to the Hebrews produces its own remarkable angle on the person and work of Christ and on the nature of the Christian life; its purpose is to deal with a specific danger of Christian fatigue and the threat of apostatizing. But once again, the fundamental understanding of the faith is the same as elsewhere. James is unusual in its concentration on Christian behavior, but there is more theology in it than is often noticed, and it reveals an author in close touch with the tradition of Jesus' teaching and in critical contact with some misunderstanding of Pauline theology. The first letter of Peter is a gem in its extraordinarily dense and deep expression of theology in a brief space, and its similarities to Pauline theology (though not so close as to make us assign it to a close follower of Paul) show how closely it belongs to the mainstream of New Testament theology. Jude and 2 Peter are often neglected in accounts of New Testament theology, but we discovered that they both demonstrate an underlying theology akin to that found elsewhere, together with a particular use of apocalyptic traditions to understand and evaluate the false teaching that they feel obliged to oppose. In short, there is considerable variety in this broad area of the New Testament, but the individual writings can without difficulty be included in the map of New Testament theology rather than being relegated outside its boundaries.

Thus our analysis suggests that there is a significant core of broad agreement and identity within the theologies of the individual constituents of the New Testament. We now try to offer a brief synthesis of what we have discovered.

## THE MAIN THEME

Throughout the New Testament we are presented with a religion of redemption. Four stages can be traced that are common to all the writers:

1. A situation of human need, understood as sin, places sinners under divine judgment.

2. A saving act by God is accomplished through Jesus Christ, who is the Son of God manifested as a human being and whose death and resurrection constitute the saving act that must be proclaimed to the world, both to Jews and to Gentiles.

3. A new life is provided for those who show faith in God and Jesus Christ, and this new life, mediated by the Holy Spirit, is experienced both individually and as members of the community of believers.

4. God will bring his redemptive action to its consummation with the advent of Christ, the final judgment and destruction of evil, and the

establishment of the new world, in which his people enjoy his presence forevermore.

## THE FRAMEWORK OF THOUGHT

All our theologians work within the same Jewish framework of understanding the world as God's creation and history as the narrative of God's ongoing relation with the people whom he has chosen out of the nations, initially the Jews, but then the people, both Jewish and Gentile, who have a spiritual relationship with him. They tend to accept the apocalyptic understanding of history, and some writings make use of a cosmic and ethical dualism between God and the sinful world. These writers accept the Jewish Scriptures (the Old Testament) as the divinely authorized and inspired account of God's dealings with his people and as the record of his communications with them through his prophets, who foretold what God would do in the future. In bringing out the continuity between the old and new covenants, several authors use the original account of the exodus, together with "new exodus" terminology, particularly in Isaiah 40—55.

## DEVELOPING THE THEME

*The context of mission: God the Father.* God is understood as the sovereign Creator and ruler of the universe, holy and righteous, loving, compassionate and faithful. He is both the judge of human sin and the Savior of sinners. In the New Testament he is characteristically the Father of Jesus Christ and of believers. God is the author of salvation. The concept of his fatherhood is marginally present in the Old Testament, is developed by Jesus, and is taken for granted by the New Testament writers. There is thus a fuller and deeper understanding of God as entering into personal relationships with individual believers.

*The context of mission: The story of God and humanity.* The New Testament writers assume the biblical story of the creation of human beings, who were expected to love and obey God; the fall of humanity into rebellion and sin; God's calling and appointment of the patriarchs and their descendants to be his people, with whom he made a covenant; and the subsequent checkered history of the covenant people, a cyclical story of rebellion, judgment, repentance and redemption repeated over and over. They pick up God's promises to make a new start with his people, and their story tells of this new covenant being established. There is thus a profound continuity between the acts of God in both Testaments.

*The center of mission: Jesus Christ.* All our theologians understand Jesus to be the (only significant) mediator between the world and God. They are all agreed that Jesus is a human being, and yet they assign to him a status that also puts him alongside God the Father. At the very least he is the appointed agent of God, with authority and insight that make him the supreme prophet. The concept of Messiah or Christ expresses this role. The Jewish hope of an agent of God who would rule over his people, inaugurating or revivifying the rule (kingdom) of God, was believed to be fulfilled in Jesus; there is good evidence that Jesus saw himself as acting out this role, although he radically transformed it in doing so. To some extent *Christ* became a "name" for Jesus that carried less meaning for Gentile Christians, but the significance conveyed by it was not lost and was expressed in other ways. Jesus himself was conscious of a relationship with God as his Father, in what was at least an unusual and probably indeed a unique manner. In the light of Jesus' resurrection, understood as exaltation to be with God, he is understood more and more by early Christians to be God's principal agent; is accorded the title *Lord*, which was also the Old Testament title for God; and is recognized as the *Son of God* (other related expressions include *Wisdom* and *Word*). This status is understood to be something that, for want of a better word, we might call an "ontological" relationship placing him within the identity of God, and occasionally the term "God" is used of Jesus Christ. Accordingly, Christ is understood as a being who was with God before he became incarnate as a human being.

*The center of mission: The saving event.* The death of Jesus and his resurrection are highly significant. All sorts of ways are explored to develop the significance of these events, with varying emphases. The basic idea of a death on behalf of other people appears throughout the New Testament. The fact that the death delivers people from sins and their consequences and reconciles them to God is again common to all. Different sets of images encapsulate different facets of the saving act. Common to them all is that Christ died for or on behalf of human beings and that his death deals with the sin(s) that separate them from God, enslave them in evildoing, and place them under divine judgment, which is active both now and in a final rejection of those who reject the gospel. Jesus' death is understood in categories taken from the Old Testament understanding of sacrifice to remove the barrier that sin caused between humanity and God. *Forgiveness, justification, redemption* and *reconciliation* are the key categories of interpretation.

Likewise the fact that God raised Jesus from the dead and exalted him to a heavenly position alongside himself (a glorification) is common, basic Christian belief. The death and resurrection of Jesus are seen as one, single saving event, with the action of God in raising Christ rather than Christ raising himself. Through this action the forces of evil are defeated, and death is overcome for God's people.

The saving event is made known through the proclamation of the gospel, which lies at the heart of the mission that Christ entrusted to his followers. Whether people can be saved without having heard the gospel is not a question that is discussed in the New Testament; what is emphasized is the divine command to the church for believers to go and make disciples. This mission is itself an integral part of the saving event.

*The community of mission: The renewed Israel.* God originally chose the nation of Israel/Judah to be his people, and membership within it was on the basis of birth, ratified by (male) circumcision, and expressed in obedience to the law. The New Testament authors also knew that many Jews were in many ways not fulfilling their side of the covenant. Jesus came as the Messiah, and the Messiah's role, in at least some Jewish minds, was both to rid Israel of its enemies and to free the people from their oppression; yet he was also to purge Israel itself so that the people might be holy (*Ps. Sol.* 17). Jesus accordingly had a mission to Israel. On the assumption that he believed himself to be fulfilling the role of the Messiah, it is not surprising that he called people to respond to him. His followers saw him as the Messiah and pled with the Jews to accept him as the Messiah and Lord. There thus developed a new people, standing in continuity with the faithful Israel of the past, who were the continuing people of God. Those who rejected Jesus as Messiah were excluded from this people (just as the case in Old Testament times for those who rebelled against the law and went after idols). The racial qualification was dropped as believers became more and more aware that Jesus' mission was not confined to racial Jews, and that God was not the God of the Jews only but also of the Gentiles. The tree (olive or a vine) thus gained engrafted branches.

There are only intimations of this in the first three Gospels, and for the most part it appears that Jesus' mission is confined to Jews. Yet the three Evangelists are aware of the implications. The gospel is to be preached to all nations. Gentiles will come into the kingdom of God. Luke especially develops the theme in Acts. The fullest thematic treatment is in Paul, who knows himself as the apostle to the Gentiles. John also knows that the flock will be increased by other sheep not belonging to the original pen, and that Jesus' appeal will be to all people and not just to the Jews. There is thus not so much a supersession of the ancient promises to the Jews that they will be God's people as rather a spiritual renewal of those promises in the new covenant. Thereby the spiritual element of faith and love toward God (which was always fundamental to the maintenance of the old covenant) is now given fresh expression in the revelation of God's Messiah, Jesus, and the extension of the covenant people to include all who are spiritually descendants of Abraham through their faith in the Messiah.

The theologian who travels furthest on his own in this theme is Paul, who in his churches has to face the problem of how the Jewish law applies to Gentiles, and who recognizes that the law has become something in which people place their confidence rather than in Christ. Although certain groups in the church insist that Gentiles should keep the Jewish law (especially circumcision), none of the New Testament writers adopt this position. This leads Paul into a profound discussion of the law's place in God's purpose, which is one of his major individual contributions to New Testament theology. Paul shows the deepest understanding of sin as it affects and takes control of humanity from Adam onward.

*The community of mission: The response of faith.* Basic also is the understanding that because of what Jesus has done, people can be delivered from sin and put right with God. The gospel is about a divine initiative, a divine offer that leaves no room for any human actions as a means of being saved. Nevertheless, it is crucial that for salvation to be truly received, there must be human response. Such a response is not something that human beings do to make themselves acceptable but rather is acceptance of what God has done for them through Jesus, an acceptance that requires a total, ongoing commitment from them, expressed in steadfastness and perseverance. Such faith is an acceptance of what God has done and is doing to save his people, without any reliance on whatever human beings might try to do to gain acceptance. Hence *faith* is a defining characteristic of Christianity in a way that distinguishes it from other ancient religions.

In some contexts even faith can be considered as a gift of God in that it is aroused and made possible through the Spirit-empowered proclamation of the gospel. This has led some scholars to argue that behind the New Testament writings generally lies a concept of God's purpose to save only specific individuals out of humanity in general, put into effect by sending Christ to die specifically and only for them (although his death is sufficient for all humanity); God calls these foreordained individuals through the preaching of the gospel, creating faith in them and giving them the gift of perseverance so that God's purpose for them will not fail but be brought to completion. Although some texts may appear to support such a position, it does not do justice to the passages indicating that Christ died for all and that the gospel is truly offered to all people who hear it. We must avoid the danger of forcing the New Testament teaching into a tight, logical system that does not sufficiently recognize the mysteries and paradoxes that run through it.

Even less likely is the proposal claiming the New Testament as teaching that God plans for all people ultimately and inevitably to be saved. However congenial such a thought may be to people today, there is no clear evidence that God will act to achieve this, and the overwhelming trend of the New Testament writers is to warn against the danger of judgment and call people to faith here and now. To recognize this, however, is not the same as asserting that only people who have consciously heard and responded to the gospel can be finally saved; on this point the New Testament is reticent, and Christians have always recognized that there are special cases, such as infants and mentally disabled people.

*The community of mission: The Holy Spirit.* Although in the Synoptics Jesus has little to say about the Spirit, it is recognized that his own work is done in the power of the Spirit. The Synoptic Gospels do not say very much about the life of disciples after Jesus has left them, beyond warning of the difficulties and tribulations that lie ahead and calling for watch-fulness and steadfastness. Only Matthew preserves the promise of Jesus' presence with his assembled disciples. Thus for the most part, the Spirit and the presence of the risen Jesus lie outside the horizon of the Synoptic Gospels. Nevertheless, the work of Luke culminates in the book of Acts, which does refer to the Spirit's power in the disciples and to their experi-ences of the risen Lord. Luke, therefore, sees no problem in the contrast between the Gospel's limited coverage of experiencing the Spirit and the new experiences of the Spirit that dominate Christian consciousness after Pentecost.

The place of the Spirit in the life of individual believers and in the congregations is developed most fully in the Pauline corpus and in John and 1 John. Paul sees the Spirit as the agent that transforms believers to be holy and loving and empowers them for their struggle with evil. Yet the power of the Spirit is not such that it cannot be resisted and thwarted. The paradox of the relationship between human willing and divine transfor-mation is not lightly resolved. The Spirit bestows gifts on believers, to be used in the community for upbuilding one another as well as themselves. John sees the Spirit's role especially as the Counselor, to take the place of Jesus after his resurrection, bearing witness to him and conveying eternal life to them.

*The community of mission: The church.* The goal and result of Jesus' work are the redemption of individuals and their formation into a community. These two aims belong closely together, since the purpose of redemption is not simply to deliver individuals from the consequences of their sinful-ness but also to create a new life characterized by righteousness and love; but since righteousness and love cannot be practiced in a vacuum but only in a community, it inevitably follows that redemption should result in a new community characterized by the mutual exercise of love and right-eousness. Thus God's purpose of creating a people who will honor him is brought about.

There is little about the followers of Jesus forming what we might call an organized community in the Synoptic Gospels. During the lifetime of Jesus, there was no need for organization (beyond John's report that the traveling group had a "purse" held by Judas, and Luke's report that various women with material resources helped to support them). Matthew does have some instructions applicable to a more formal group. Luke was not organization-minded, and Acts deals rather casually with the organization of the congregations. The Pauline letters reveal the development of various forms of ministry and types of activity within the groups of disciples, with a mix of formal and less-formal assignments of tasks within the congregations. Here the congregations meet together, and the meeting is the characteristic Christian activity. Contrast the Gospels, where there is no telling whether, let us say, the disciples of Jesus in Capernaum have any common gatherings or activities when Jesus is not there. We have a picture of disciples gathered round Jesus to be taught and perhaps to pray, but that is all; in any case, at this point, they presumably still go to the synagogues for the normal religious activities expected of Jews. In John, the picture resembles that in the Synoptic Gospels, and there is no anticipation of the life of Christian congregations.

Entry into salvation and into the community of believers is symbolically expressed in baptism, a rite that is eloquent of being cleansed from sin, sharing in the death and resurrection of Jesus, and receiving the Holy Spirit. The continuing relationship of believers to Christ is also symbolically expressed in the Lord's Supper, which is eloquent of the sacrificial death of Jesus, spiritual nourishment, and the bond of unity and love between those who share in the one loaf and cup. The common life of believers further includes the manifestation of the Spirit's gifts, intended to build up believers in their faith, especially through teaching, practical love and care for one another, and worship, thanksgiving and prayer to God.

*The community of mission: The love commandment.* The clearest common motif in many of the sources, especially in Jesus and Paul and John, is undoubtedly the love command. Its centrality in the behavior of disciples and believers is obvious in all three cases. It appears in its most radical form in the Sermon of Jesus, where love of enemies is enjoined. But this motif is also present in Paul (Rom 12). In John, the emphasis is more on love within the Christian community (Jn 13:34-35). John is thinking of *mutual* love as the mark that distinguishes the Christian community; loving care for the poor outside the community is not his focus, although concern for the poor brother and sister is emphasized in 1 John. John too is more aware of the enmity of the outside world toward the believers. Granting these differences regarding the scope of love, there is still no denying the centrality of the motif as lying at the heart of Christian behavior.

Of a piece with the love commandment is the concept of leadership as humble service and not as the self-serving exercise of power and authority. The Son of Man came to serve, and he commended humility to his followers; true greatness lies in serving, not in being served. John presents the example of the Lord and Master washing the feet of the disciples. The motif may not be so obvious in Paul, but it is there also. The church certainly has leadership, and there is authority attached to it, but the authority is exercised for the benefit of the others and not for self-aggrandizement, and this transforms its character.

*The consummation of mission: The fullness of salvation.* Finally, in all our sources, we are conscious of the imminent end of the present age and its overlap with the dawn of the new age to come. It is notorious that in the Synoptic Gospels the kingdom of God is presented both as a quite near future entity and also as something already exercising its power in the here and now. The kingdom is both now and not yet. Equally, the Messiah is here now and yet not fully recognized. His power is seen in mighty works, but he can be arrested and put to death. The resurrection undoes the opposition and leads into the era preceding the second advent, when the Son of Man will reign and judge. Salvation is both here to be experienced and not yet consummated. This broad picture can be accepted despite disagreements on the finer points. It is also the picture in Paul, who can speak of salvation in the future tense and also speak of the present realities of Christian experience, such as justification and reconciliation. Ephesians 2:8 accurately sums up a theology insisting that believers have been saved and can therefore look forward with confidence to being saved from divine wrath at the final judgment. The belief in the imminence of the End is also there in the Pauline hope of Christ's second advent and the resurrection of the dead; there should be no controversy over the affirmation that for Paul the End was certainly something that could come in the near future, whether or not he committed himself to saying that it must do so. As for John, we have seen that he is particularly concerned with the believers' present experience of eternal life, yet without forgetting the resurrection of the dead; John 11 in particular depicts the tensions between eternal life now and the continuing experience of death until the time comes when the dead are resurrected, and between the present coming of Jesus to his people and his future advent.

None of our sources makes the error of thinking that believers are already living in the fullness of the new world. They insist on the preliminary, incomplete mode of Christian experience amid suffering, temptation, and physical weakness and death; yet they equally insist that this experience is a genuine anticipation of the consummation. Consequently, there is a tension between strength and weakness, so that in the midst of utter human weakness, God's power may be manifested to believers. Tensions of this kind are to be found throughout the New Testament, although naturally they are more apparent in some writings than in others.

## CONCLUSION

On the basis of this analysis, we can claim that our witnesses do bear testimony to what is palpably the same complex reality. There is a common, basic theology that can be traced in all our witnesses, but it is developed by each in their own distinctive ways.

# BIBLIOGRAPHY

**Introductory matters** concerning the composition and circumstances of the various books of the New Testament are treated in the following:

Walton, S., and D. Wenham. *Exploring the New Testament.* Vol. 1, *The Gospels and Acts.* London: SPCK; Downers Grove, Ill.: InterVarsity Press, 2001.

Marshall, I. H., S. Travis and I. Paul. *Exploring the New Testament.* Vol. 2, *The Letters and Revelation.* London: SPCK; Downers Grove, Ill.: InterVarsity Press, 2002.

**Shorter and simpler accounts** of New Testament theology can be found in the following:

Bruce, F. F. *The Message of the New Testament.* 1972. Reprint, Carlisle, U.K.: Paternoster Press, 2004.

Hunter, A. M. *Introducing New Testament Theology.* 1957. 2nd ed., 1963. Reprint of 2nd ed., Carlisle, U.K.: Paternoster Press, 1997.

Morris, L. *New Testament Theology.* Grand Rapids: Zondervan, 1986.

Schweizer, E. *A Theological Introduction to the New Testament.* London: SPCK, 1992.

Zuck, R. B., ed. *A Biblical Theology of the New Testament.* Chicago: Moody Press, 1994.

**More advanced works** include the following:

Caird, G. B. *New Testament Theology*. Edited by L. D. Hurst. Oxford: Clarendon Press, 1994.

Guthrie, D. *New Testament Theology*. Leicester, U.K.: Inter-Varsity Press, 1981.

Kümmel, W. G. *The Theology of the New Testament According to Its Major Witnesses*. Nashville: Abingdon, 1973; London: SCM Press, 1974.

Ladd, G. E. *A Theology of the New Testament*. Grand Rapids: Eerdmans, 1974. 2nd edition, edited by D. A. Hagner, 1993.

Marshall, I. H. *New Testament Theology: Many Witnesses, One Gospel*. Downers Grove, Ill.: InterVarsity Press, 2004.

Matera, F. J. *New Testament Theology: Exploring Diversity and Unity*. Louisville and London: Westminster John Knox Press, 2007.

Schreiner, Thomas R. *New Testament Theology: Magnifying God in Christ*. Grand Rapids, Mich.: Baker Academic, 2008.

Stauffer, E. *New Testament Theology*. London: SCM Press, 1955.

Strecker, G. *Theology of the New Testament*. Berlin and New York: de Gruyter; Louisville: Westminster John Knox Press, 2000.

Thielman, F. *Theology of the New Testament: A Canonical and Synthetic Approach*. Grand Rapids: Zondervan, 2005.


**Reference works** treating the individual biblical books and theological topics include the following:

Alexander, T. D., and B. S. Rosner, ed. *New Dictionary of Biblical Theology*. Leicester, U.K.: Inter-Varsity Press, 2000.

Elwell, W., ed. *Evangelical Dictionary of Biblical Theology*. Grand Rapids: Baker, 1996.

# Name and Subject Index

# Scripture Index